To Ashley & Darrell,
    Love, Mom

 IMAGINING POSTCOMMUNISM

EUGENIA AND HUGH M. STEWART '26 SERIES ON EASTERN EUROPE

IMAGINING POSTCOMMUNISM

VISUAL NARRATIVES OF HUNGARY'S 1956 REVOLUTION

BEVERLY A. JAMES

TEXAS A&M UNIVERSITY PRESS, COLLEGE STATION

Library of Congress Cataloging-in-Publication Data

James, Beverly A. (Beverly Ann), 1947–
    Imagining postcommunism : visual narratives of Hungary's 1956
Revolution / Beverly A. James.—1st ed.
        p.   cm.—(Eugenia and Hugh M. Stewart '26 series on Eastern Europe)
    Includes bibliographical references and index.
    ISBN 1-58544-405-7 (cloth : alk. paper)
    1. Hungary—History—Revolution, 1956.   2. Post-communism—
Hungary.   I. Title.   II. Series.

DB957 .J36 2005
943.905'2—dc22
                                                                        2004020633

FOR PAT, ASHLEY, AND MATTHEW

CONTENTS

ILLUSTRATIONS

ACKNOWLEDGMENTS

THIS BOOK COULD NOT HAVE BEEN WRITTEN without the help of a number of people. Two research facilities in Budapest, the Open Society Archives and the 1956 Institute, proved indispensable. Among the attentive staff at the two institutions, László Győri and Judith Gyenes, librarians at the 1956 Institute, deserve special thanks for their kind assistance. For their help in securing reproductions of art held by the Hungarian National Gallery, I would like to thank László Szabó and Eszter Orbán. Katalin Jalsovszky assisted me with photos at the Hungarian National Museum, as did Réka Sárközi at the 1956 Institute. Zsolt Bátori took most of the new photographs, working with Gábor Domján to process them. I am deeply grateful to Zsolt and Gábor for their splendid work.

I would also like to thank those cultural creators who consented to be interviewed about the process of representing the past. Chapter 5, in particular, could not have been written without the generous cooperation of Gergely Pongrátz, owner of the 1956 Museum, and Györgyi Kalavszky Bánffyné, curator at Hungary's Military History Museum.

Ildikó Kováts and János Tölgyesi provided me with a home away from home in Budapest. Ildikó fed me tripe, blood sausage, and other "real Hungarian dishes," all the while warning me not to be seduced by the nationalism of people who dwell on the 1956 revolution. She also set up appointments, helped me with fieldwork, and tied up loose ends when I had to return to the United States. Zsuzsa Nun, my chief political correspondent, accompanied me on a bike trip through Hungary in the summer of 2000 to photograph monuments to the 1956 revolution. Younger than I, Zsuzsa wound up with half of my camping gear on the back of her bike. I thank her for her political insights, good cheer, and unfailing sense of direction. Other people who helped with the arrangements or research in Hungary include Michael Donnelly, Gary Kish, László Komlósi, Margit Mundruczó, and Zita Török. Marsha Siefert was a constant source of inspiration and understanding. Here in New Hampshire, Györgyi Fekete gave up countless lunch breaks to help transcribe the tapes of celebratory speeches, and so much more.

Hanno Hardt first introduced me to East Central Europe and then encouraged me to write about the shifting visual culture when the dreams of a "Third Way" faded. His steadfast interest in my work means a great deal to me. Joe Arpad, Zsolt Bátori, Krisztina Domján, Dina Iordanova, and Larry Prelli provided useful critiques to drafts of individual chapters. The anonymous reviewers for Texas A&M University Press understood what I was trying to accomplish better than I did. Their suggestions for revision truly helped me turn the manuscript into a book.

A National Endowment for the Humanities Summer Stipend supported the writing of chapter 5, while a Leslie Z. and Marie J. Kish Grant supported the writing of chapter 6 and gave me much-needed release time to complete the entire manuscript. Fees for the reproduction and use of photographs by Hungarian museums were paid for by a grant from the University of New Hampshire College of Liberal Arts Alumni Annual Gifts Fund. Trips to Hungary were funded by the University of New Hampshire's Faculty Development Fund, the Center for International Education, the Institute for Policy and Social Science Research, and the Center for the Humanities. Sage Publication Ltd. kindly granted permission to reprint portions of my article, "Fencing in the Past: Budapest's Statue Park Museum," which was published in *Media, Culture, and Society* 21, no. 3 (1999). My departmental colleagues and dean, Marilyn Hoskin, have been unfailingly supportive of this project. I thank them for providing an atmosphere conducive to thoughtful scholarship.

 IMAGINING POSTCOMMUNISM

VISUAL RECOVERY OF A REPRESSED PAST

THE LATEST POLITICAL-CULTURAL SPECTACLE in Budapest is a museum that commemorates the victims of tyranny. The House of Terror is located on Andrássy Street, one of the city's most beautiful boulevards, in an elegant neo-renaissance building that served as the headquarters of the Hungarian fascists from 1937 until the end of the Second World War. It was then occupied until 1956 by the dreaded ÁVO, the communist secret police.[1] Opened in February 2002 by Prime Minister Viktor Orbán, the museum honors the victims of both murderous regimes through chilling exhibits of dank prison cells, torture chambers, and the black limousine used by Nikita Khrushchev when he visited Budapest. Orbán stated in his opening address that the purpose of the museum was to show young Hungarians how their ancestors had suffered to achieve freedom, peace, and prosperity.

At the time of the museum's opening, Orbán's party, the conservative FIDESZ-Hungarian Civic Party, was in the midst of a tight election campaign. The chief contenders were the Socialists, a group that rose from the ashes of the former Communist Party when the one-party state imploded in 1989. Critics charged that the $10 million museum project was politically motivated, designed to provide visual evidence linking the Stalinist terror of the 1950s with contemporary Socialists. Beyond the timing of the museum's inauguration—six weeks before the election—they claimed that a disproportionate representation of the fascist and communist eras confirmed their contention that the museum was designed to discredit the Socialists. The fascist Arrow Cross Party was complicit in the deportation of hundreds of thousands of Jews to the Nazi death camps. When the cattle cars were full, the fascists simply shot their victims along the banks of the Danube and tossed their bodies, whether dead or alive, into the icy waters. Despite this barbarity, the museum's

Prison cell in the House of Terror Museum. Photograph by Zsolt Bátori. Courtesy House of Terror Museum, Budapest

critics charged, only a couple of rooms out of some two dozen focused on the story of fascist atrocities, the rest being devoted to communism. The Socialists pledged to change the institution's name to the House of Reconciliation if elected. But, following their razor-thin victory, they dropped the idea when Orbán threatened to mobilize millions of demonstrators in response to any interference with the museum.

In his pathbreaking work on collective memory, Maurice Halbwachs (1992) argues that the past is recalled through language and social interaction. Following Roland Barthes's extension of linguistic models of signification to a much broader set of cultural practices (1972, 1977), the House of Terror can be thought of as a *language*, a system of representations that uses objects arranged into displays to produce and convey meaning about national identity. This book is about how a nation collectively reconstructs its past through such visual media. Using the post-communist commemoration of Hungary's 1956 revolution as a case study, it focuses on what Stuart Hall refers to as the "signifying practices"—the production of meaning through representation—surrounding heroes and martyrs, museums and monuments, and ceremonies and rituals (1997b, 28). To adopt Benedict Anderson's influential conception of the nation as an imagined community (1991, 6), these phenomena can be understood as cultural sites where the nation is discursively constructed. With enormous instructional, inspirational, and evocative capacities, these constellations of national symbols are profoundly rhetorical and thus amenable to a textual analysis adapting the approaches that one might apply to studying a Shakespearean sonnet or a presidential address.

Officially branded a *counter*-revolution from the time of its suppression until the end of the communist era, the 1956 revolution against totalitarianism is now celebrated as the initial salvo in a long, ultimately successful struggle for national sovereignty and political pluralism. To put it another way, "1956" has taken on the status of a foundational myth,

Khrushchev's limousine on display in the House of Terror Museum. Photograph by Zsolt Bátori. Courtesy House of Terror Museum, Budapest

according to which the bloody events of that fall led inexorably to the ceremonial reburial of the martyred revolutionary prime minister Imre Nagy on June 16, 1989; free elections in the spring of 1990; and the withdrawal of the last Soviet soldiers on June 19, 1991. Since the fall of communism, the 1956 revolution has been commemorated and celebrated through a dazzling array of visual representations, including state ceremonies, parades, exhibits, statuary, shrines, and so forth. Such symbolic production of the nation through reference to 1956 is the subject of this book. The controversy surrounding the House of Terror illustrates several major themes.

First, the transformations set in motion by the 1989 collapse of communist rule in East Central Europe extended far beyond technical, strategic questions of economic and political decision making. As Katherine Verdery argues (1999, 35), "the postsocialist change is much bigger" than the creation of markets or the writing of democratic constitutions: "It means a reordering of people's entire meaningful worlds." Western observers have tended to conceive of the historic end of communism in narrow terms. As a result, they have given scant attention to the cultural transformations, particularly the formation of new national identities. Michael Kennedy puts it well when he writes (1994, 6), "The rhetoric of markets and democracy needs entrepreneurs, consumers, and citizens but nothing more complicated." As the establishment of the House of Terror shows, the postcommunist reconfiguration of national identities took place through the production of new narratives, stories about the nation's past that run counter to the official communist versions. In Richard Esbenshade's words (1995, 73), the communist empire's master narrative of history as an international class struggle destined to culminate in the triumph of the Soviet Union gave way throughout the region to national narratives that reclaimed and reinvented each nation's past.

Yet as the House of Terror contretemps shows, the postcommunist production of national memory is a contentious process. Vladimir Tismaneanu writes that once the certainties of the communist era vanished, "long repressed (but not suppressed) passions, sentiments, and resentments" resurfaced throughout Eastern Europe (1994, 104). In Hungary the partisan conflicts over the museum reflect a longstanding ideological schism between populist-nationalism and urbanist-cosmopolitanism. Writing about the formation of oppositional politics in the mid-1980s, Timothy Garton Ash describes these conflicting worldviews: "The 'populists' have traditionally celebrated the folk virtues of Hungarian village life, *la terre et les morts, Kultur* rather than *Zivilisation.* The 'urbanists' were (and are) more cosmopolitan and often Jewish. . . . Traditionally to be found on the left bank of the Danube, in the cafes of Pest rather than the hills of Buda, they have looked outward to Vienna and the West rather than inward to the Transylvanian strongholds of agrarian Hungarianness. They have been drawn to sociology rather than to ethnography, and to socialism rather than to nationalism" (1985, 6).

The opposition movements that took shape in the 1980s kept these ideological differences in check as the groups faced off against their common adversary, the entrenched Communist Party but splintered along the old fault line once they had achieved multiparty democracy. The two most important parties to emerge in that transitional period were the Hungarian Democratic Forum and the Alliance of Free Democrats, heirs, respectively, to populism and urbanism. A decade later these parties had lost considerable power, but FIDESZ had taken up the ideological concerns of the populists—above all the fate of Hungarians living outside the nation's borders—while the Socialist Party fashioned itself as the Hungarian representative of European social democracy. Unlike the communists' master narrative, then, with its smug, false, seamless unity, the stories that discursively produced the postcommunist Hungarian nation are multiple, belligerent, and polemical, reflecting this polarized political landscape.

In the years since the transition to parliamentary democracy, the old antagonisms have been overlaid by tensions stemming from people's actions and experiences during the years of authoritarianism. As communist power was consolidated through terror in the late 1940s and early 1950s, the regime's police investigated approximately 1 million of Hungary's 9.3 million citizens. Thousands of people were convicted and served time in the notorious prisons and labor camps that constituted Hungary's gulag. The political opposition was liquidated as show trials modeled after those in the Soviet Union resulted in several hundred death sentences. In addition, thousands of "class enemies"—nobles, statesmen, army officers, and wealthy capitalists—were resettled in the countryside, where they were forced to work as agricultural laborers. Their villas were confiscated and assigned to high-ranking party functionaries, the new elite (Romsics 1999, 272–73; Schöpflin 1993, 96–97, 101–2). Another wave of terror swept the country after the 1956 revolution. Some 16,000 people were convicted of participating in the uprising, while many more were harassed and lost their jobs. An estimated

350 Hungarians were executed (Kis 1989, 28; Litván 1996, 144). As the fray over the House of Terror demonstrates, positions regarding questions of culpability, accountability, and retribution tend to line up on either side of the populist/urbanist divide. While the Right demands the extraction of justice and the settling of old scores, the Left counsels restraint, arguing that the past should be put to rest in the interests of social harmony.

These divisive tendencies of the communist past, however, exist in tension with its capacity to unify the nation. On a mythic level the communist era represents a common experience, one that unites the nation through the collective memory of suffering and humiliation at the hands of an external enemy. By deflecting attention from their own actions to those of the conquerors from the East, Hungarians adopt the morally superior position of victim. István Rév writes (1995b, 33), "According to post-Communist revisionism, Communism in Hungary was the tragic result of a conspiracy organized from abroad; it was the work of outsiders in the service of foreign powers, and as such, was no part of Hungarian history."

In a parallel fashion, memories of the 1956 revolution are marked by contradictory impulses of division and unification. The uprising was crushed within days, which meant that competing conceptions of a post-totalitarian Hungarian state were never aired, much less resolved. When it finally became possible to assess the causes, events, and goals of the revolt, the search for answers quickly degenerated into a corrosive rivalry between the aging street fighters who fought the revolution and the intellectuals who instigated it (Litván 1992, 13). Yet at the same time, 1956 is remembered longingly as the only time the nation was ever really united. Historian György Litván refers to this as "the myth of unparalleled national unity." Central to public consciousness about the revolution, this myth holds that the Hungarian people—with the exception of high-ranking party officials and ÁVOs—were more closely bound together in 1956 through their desire for freedom from Soviet authority and communist dictatorship than at any other time in the nation's history (Litván 2000, 208).

HUNGARY'S LONG REVOLUTION

The frustrations, tensions, and humiliations that gave rise to the revolution go back to the late 1940s. Most of the hard-line communists who came to power after the war, including party secretary Mátyás Rákosi, had been exiles in the Soviet Union. Using their famous salami tactics to slice away the opposition, these Soviet-backed communists gained decisive control of the government and all major institutions by 1948. The main weapon used in the consolidation of the Communist Party's control was the ÁVO. This police force grew out of an organization established in 1945 to hunt down war criminals. But from early on, its operatives were charged with discrediting opponents to the regime such as Cardinal József Mindszenty, who was arrested in 1948, or potential political rivals such as the dedicated communist László Rajk, who was sentenced to death in a show trial and executed in 1949. More broadly, the ÁVO was the most potent symbol of the mass terror that marked the period, responsible for subjecting countless people to surveillance, arrest, torture, secret trial, imprisonment, and in several hundred cases, execution.

Following the Soviet model, the communists launched a nationwide program aimed at bringing all sectors of the economy under state control and transforming Hungary into a land of iron and steel. The mines had been nationalized right after the war; factories, banks, and other businesses were then added to the list, with no compensation given to their former owners. A staggering percentage of the national income was allocated toward the expansion of heavy industry, a goal that made little sense in a traditionally agrarian country. Even more disruptive from a cultural standpoint was the forced collectivization of agriculture. Implemented through violence and terror, this policy was aimed at destroying private ownership of the land and forcing all peasants to join cooperative farms. Altogether, the reckless application of the Stalinist economic model in Hungary lowered the average standard of living precipitously and led to massive shortages in consumer products as well as food. Indeed, by 1951 food rationing had to be reintroduced.

Following the death of Stalin in 1953, the Hungarian party leadership was summoned to Moscow and called to account for its ruinous economic policies, particularly the destruction of agriculture. While Rákosi was allowed to retain the chairmanship of the party, Imre Nagy was elevated to the head of the government. Nagy had entered public life after returning to Hungary from wartime exile in the Soviet Union and was appointed minister of agriculture. In that capacity he had overseen the dismantling of the large estates and the redistribution of land to the peasantry. A dedicated communist and an expert in agrarian economics, Nagy supported the principle of collective ownership and management of the land. Still, he had been appalled to see the peasants stripped of their prop-

erty just a few short years after acquiring it. Now, with Moscow's bless-
ing, he set about revitalizing the nation's stagnant economic, political,
and social life. Peasants were allowed to leave the cooperative farms if
they chose, the prices of consumer goods were lowered, and the wages of
industrial workers were raised. The climate of oppression softened as the
government closed internment camps and released political prisoners.

In the background, however, Rákosi plotted against his archrival, and
in less than two years, he convinced a now more hard-line Soviet leadership that Nagy had gone too far in his liberalization. In the spring of 1955,
Nagy was stripped of his positions as well as his membership in the Communist Party. But the changes he had instigated could not be reversed.
In the absence of press or radio coverage, the earlier reign of terror had
been shrouded in mystery and rumor. But with the closure of the deten-
tion camps, former prisoners came home, and information about the
suspected brutalities was confirmed. Former high-ranking communists,
old warriors in the underground struggle against fascism, reappeared after years of absence and began to speak about the beatings and torture
they had endured in the ÁVO headquarters on Andrássy Street. A grow-
ing circle of people who shared Nagy's commitment to a more humane
form of communism broke ranks with the party leadership. They were no
longer willing to tolerate the abuse of their ideals, nor were they willing
to remain silent any longer.

The main channel through which criticism spread from communist
intellectuals to ordinary men and women in the months leading up to the
revolution was the Petőfi Circle. Established as a debating club within
the DISZ, the Alliance of Working Youth, the Petőfi Circle was initially
sanctioned by authorities as a safety valve for the controlled expression
of dissent. But a series of public meetings in the spring of 1956 attracted
ever-growing audiences as such contentious topics as the falsification of
history, the failure of the five-year economic plans, and Hungarian-
Yugoslav relations were openly debated. According to Litván (1996, 40),
the only topics off-limits were Hungary's subordinate relationship to
the Soviet Union and the one-party system. The series culminated in a
June 27 meeting on the press and public information. There a crowd estimated at seven thousand heard the popular Hungarian writer Tibor Déry
appeal to the heritage of Hungary's 1848 War of Independence against
the Austrian Hapsburgs in calling the nation's youth to action: "I ask
the young people, the Hungarian youth, don't forget your ancestors, the
March youth. We call them the youth of 1848. It is my desire, comrades,

that there be a youth of 1956 that will help the nation conquer the future" (quoted in Berecz 1986, 50). Two days later, news of the Poznan riots in Poland provided Rákosi with an excuse to suspend the debates (Váli 1961, 231). Before the year was out, however, Hungary would have her youth of 1956.

Perhaps the most dramatic moment in the Petőfi Circle debates occurred when László Rajk's widow took the floor to demand that her husband be rehabilitated and his murderers punished. Arrested with her husband, Júlia Rajk had recently been released after spending five years in prison. She told the audience of some two thousand about her imprisonment: "I was nursing my four-month-old baby when they took me and my husband away. My child was 5½ years-old when I saw him again. During all that time, I didn't get any information, visits, clothing, or provisions. There I was starving in prison, while the comrades were lying about how we were spies, conspirators, and traitors" (Rajk 2001, 247).[2] Called the "partisan debate," the purpose of this particular assembly was to allow those communists who had remained in Hungary and fought in the illegal underground movements during the fascist years to express their views about the nation's situation (Pető 2001, 133). Rajk called for an alliance between the old underground communists and the young intellectuals, one that would wrest power from the Muscovites headed by Rákosi: "When I got out of prison, I didn't find a single old comrade left in his position. Instead, they were all working as shoe salesmen or book salesmen. . . . The dictatorial regime was set in motion in 1949 by the Rajk trial, and so I ask the comrades to help place the memory of my husband before the young intellectuals, showing that his was the life of a pure, fighting communist" (Rajk 2001, 249–50).

As the reform movement within the Communist Party gathered strength, Hungary's leaders had no choice but to accede to Rajk's demands for her husband's full rehabilitation and ceremonial reburial. On October 6, a day of remembrance for thirteen Hungarian generals executed by the Habsburgs in 1849, some two hundred thousand people, including Nagy, attended the solemn ceremony honoring László Rajk and several comrades. By that time, Rákosi had been forced to resign and take refuge in the Soviet Union; his successor, Ernő Gerő, was visiting Moscow at the time of the funeral. The speeches "glowed with bitterness" as representatives of the Communist Party, the Spanish Brigade, and Rajk's friends denounced Rákosi, Stalinism, and the cult of personality (Ignotus 1972, 235). Rajk's reburial was the first major public demonstration for reform and a prelude to the revolutionary events that were to erupt a few weeks later. At universities throughout Hungary, students began drafting sets of demands that included reciprocal relations with the Soviet Union and the withdrawal of Russian troops; freedom of expression, the press, and religion; and the formation of an interim government, under the leadership of Nagy, followed by free elections and multiparty democracy.

The revolution began on October 23 when Budapest students held a march as a gesture of solidarity with the Polish reform movement. Over the course of the day, hundreds of thousands of sympathizers spontaneously took to the streets. The actual shooting began that evening, when a group of students converged on the central radio headquarters and insisted that their demands for reform be broadcast. Guards fired into the crowd, instigating the armed uprising as the young demonstrators secured weapons from soldiers sent to restore order. The following day Nagy was appointed prime minister. He declared martial law and appealed for the restoration of order. But his words went unheeded. Using classic urban guerilla tactics, a force of several thousand insurgents, mainly young workers, clashed with the Soviet army during the coming days (Romsics 1999, 306).

For a time Soviet leaders seemed amenable to Hungary's demands for neutrality. By October 30 they began to withdraw troops from Budapest and other parts of the country. Meanwhile, Nagy announced the end of the one-party system and the formation of a coalition government pending national elections. But at the very time that some Soviet forces were leaving Budapest, others were spotted crossing the eastern border into Hungary. In desperation Nagy announced Hungary's withdrawal from the Warsaw Pact and called on the United Nations to ensure the nation's neutrality. Hopes were raised on November 3, when a contingent of Soviets showed up at Parliament and initiated discussions about the withdrawal of their troops. Talks began immediately, with the Hungarian delegation headed by Defense Minister Pál Maléter. That night, as the discussions continued at the Soviet military headquarters at Tököl, Maléter and the other Hungarians were arrested by the KGB. With the military leaders of the revolution out of the way, the Russians launched a decisive attack at dawn. Imre Nagy issued a terse radio announcement just after 5:00 A.M., stating that Soviet forces had attacked the capital with the obvious intention of overthrowing the legal, democratic government of Hungary. He then took refuge in the Yugoslav embassy. János Kádár, who had replaced Gerő as head of the party during the uprising, was selected by the Soviets to form a new "Revolutionary Workers' and Peasants' Government."

While the revolt lasted only a couple of weeks, the suppression of continued resistance in the form of strikes, reform movements within the party, workers' councils, and other democratic initiatives involved months of purges and terror, including police surveillance, mass arrests, show trials, and executions. During this post-revolutionary period, a rhetorical shift took place as well. Initially the Kádár government spoke of the October events as a spontaneous uprising. Within weeks they began to call it a conspiracy or an assault on the system covertly organized by the West. By December the government had upgraded it to an unqualified counter-revolution aimed at restoring power to the capitalists (Litván 1996, 116). In keeping with these official reconstructions of the events, Nagy was cast as a traitor and executed on June 16, 1958.

Kádár first articulated his formula for stabilizing the nation at a party congress in 1957, where he declared, "the working masses are not interested in the general problems of politics, but in the correct solution of the economic and cultural questions affecting their everyday lives" (quoted in Kis 1989, 69–70). In other words, if the masses were offered comfortable, secure lives, they would stop meddling in politics. To a traumatized, exhausted public, further resistance made little sense. In 1961 the bargain was sealed when Kádár issued his famous statement, "He who is not against us is with us." As András Bozóki explains (1994, 123), the leadership abandoned the communist ideals of a permanently mobilized, politicized society and pushed the public into a "depoliticized world of individual progress." For the next twenty years, the public was willing to suffer what psychologist Ferenc Mérei has called "collective amnesia," the repression of the memory of the humiliating defeat in 1956 and the brutal terror that followed.[3]

As a result of this tacit agreement, Kádár's betrayal was blotted out of the nation's official memory, and Hungary became the "happiest barracks" in the Soviet camp. The standard of living steadily increased through economic policies that emphasized consumption over production. The state permitted the development of a second economy and implemented monetary policies that cushioned the effects of cyclical downturns. Party control over the cultural sphere loosened as well, with the gradual lifting of restrictions on travel and on Western books, periodicals, and films. In exchange for economic prosperity, a docile, obedient public withdrew into private life (Urbán 1989, 109–110). György Konrád and

Iván Szelényi describe what life was like in the high Kádár period: "Politics is a vanishing topic of conversation; after one or two jokes or anecdotes about the latest corruption scandal the talk turns to more important subjects, like one's summer house, vacation travel plans, matters of personal and domestic fashion, last night's TV movie, and marital problems" (Konrád and Szelényi 1979, 200).

This tranquility lasted until the late 1970s, by which time systemic problems in the economy—still fundamentally socialist—had exhausted its potential for expansion. By the mid-1980s the situation reached crisis proportions. The debt to Western creditors spiraled out of control, and these lenders demanded structural changes in the Hungarian economy as conditions for further extensions of credit. An aging Kádár refused to concede, and he was ousted from power in May 1988. His replacement, Károly Grósz, advocated reforms to the rapidly imploding economy, but he firmly opposed any fundamental alterations to the political structure. Before the year was out, he was replaced by Miklós Németh, an economist whose administration would oversee the transformation of Hungary into a democratic republic in 1989.

DISCOURSE, NARRATIVE, AND MYTH

The reprisals that followed the 1956 revolution effectively crushed all opposition, and from that point on, the uprising became taboo as a topic of public debate. Yet its memory was never obliterated. Thus, the postcommunist process of rescuing the past was fundamentally communicative in the sense of making manifest that which was hidden or latent. Visual media are well suited to this process of historical recovery as evidenced by the metaphoric association of *showing* with rhetorical proof: the past is *illuminated*; the suppressed is *brought to light*; the public's *eyes are opened*; the meaning of events is *clarified* or *elucidated*; the truth is *revealed* at last. But there is a limit to how far this model of communication can take us. As a mimetic or reflective approach to representation, it assumes that the truth was there all along, hiding in the shadows and waiting to be brought to light. Certainly, with the unsealing of archives and the accessibility of documentation that was once off limits, the post-1989 historiography regarding the uprising *is* a far more accurate reflection of the actual events. But from a social constructionist standpoint, representations of 1956, whether they take the form of historical treatises, documentary films, photography exhibits, or monuments to fallen martyrs, are always *constitutive* of the past. In turn, those readings of the nation's past experiences are implicated in the formation of contemporary notions of self, community, nation, democracy, and statehood. My examination of these creative dimensions of postcommunist identity formation will be informed by the concepts of discourse, narrative, and myth.

As formulated by Michel Foucault, *discourse* captures the relationships between language, thought, knowledge, and power. Discourse, the social production of knowledge and expression in a particular domain of thought, is central to Foucault's analyses of the techniques through which power is exerted in his histories of insanity, criminality, medicine, and sexuality (Foucault 1980, 115–17). At the heart of his notion of discourse is its ability to regulate and channel thought. Stuart Hall explains (1992, 291): "When statements about a topic are made within a particular discourse, the discourse makes it possible to construct the topic in a certain way. It also limits the other ways in which the topic can be constructed." Thus, discourse is centrally concerned with the production of knowledge and, ultimately, power. To quote Hall once again (1997a, 6): "[Discourse] examines not only how language and representation produce meaning, but how the knowledge which a particular discourse produces connects with power, regulates conduct, makes up or constructs identities and subjectivities, and defines the way certain things are represented, thought about, practised and studied."

Two aspects of this concept make it especially useful for this project. First, with its central concern over power relations, discourse helps draw out and theorize the *contested* aspect of memory work. As noted above, the recovery of memory surrounding the revolution is marked by its competing tendencies to divide and to unify the nation. Insofar as visual representations of that event act as fuel for the culture wars, they are amenable to discursive analysis. Second, a discursive approach emphasizes the production of knowledge through language as historically situated *practice*. As applied to the visual phenomena discussed herein, discourse focuses our attention on the performance of political action as carried out through the commissioning, creation, exhibition, reception, and interpretation of visual artifacts and practices in a given time and place. This is not a neutral process. It takes place within contested frameworks of knowledge, and one of the aims of this book is to explore the interests behind these ways of seeing.

Throughout his writings, Raymond Williams offers a view of human nature that is characterized by the drive to create and express meaning through the media that are available in a given culture—theater, dance, painting, film, music, puppetry, poetry, and such. In a chapter titled "The Creative Mind" in *The Long Revolution*, he argues that the artistic impulse is a manifestation of the deeper human need to communicate, which, he emphasizes, is an essentially *productive* activity: "It is, in the first instance, to every man, a matter of urgent personal importance to 'describe' his experience, because this is literally a remaking of himself, a creative change in his personal organization, to include and control the experience" (1961, 26). I share Williams's faith in the creative imagination, and from this perspective, discourse is limited by its displacement of the subject from a privileged position in the production of meaning, knowledge, and history. For Foucault, discourse produces the subject: He is passively positioned by discourse as "the questioning subject," "the listening subject," "the seeing subject," and "the observing subject" (Foucault 1972, 52). Walter Fisher (1997, 311) challenges the postmodern contention that "all public discourse is infected with power" and that the democratic, emancipatory ideals of community, consensus, and communication as conceived by John Dewey and Jürgen Habermas are obsolete. A communication scholar, Fisher develops a model of decision making and action that restores human reason to the equation, locating it within *narrative.*

Arguing that people are essentially storytellers, Fisher (1997, 313) uses the term "narrative" to refer to "the 'stories' we tell each other— whether such 'stories' are in the form of argumentation, narration, exposition, or esthetic writings and performance." Narratives are rhetorical, he writes, in that the stuff of stories is "good reasons," warrants that are designed to appeal to the hearts and minds of reasoning listeners and to influence their beliefs, values, attitudes, and actions. In this sense narrative is implicated in power struggles, as public life is negotiated through debate and deliberation over competing stories. But for Fisher this process is a positive one. He argues that the stories we tell "give order to life by inducing others to dwell in them to establish ways of living in common, in intellectual and spiritual communities in which there is confirmation for the story that constitutes one's life" (314).

Narrative thus provides a way of theorizing the *unifying* dimension of postcommunist memory work. It is also advantageous in that it recenters the human subject in the form of storytellers and circles of listeners. As Lewis Hinchman and Sandra Hinchman put it (1997, xvi), "In narrative, there has to be a teller of the story and an audience to hear it."

In the case studies that follow, the concept of narrative will not only draw our attention to the "plot" that is semiotically encoded in a monument or the sequential structure of a holiday address but also prod us to explore the metanarratives of the "storytellers" as they describe the social and political ideals that inspired their creative activities. The contributions of their "listeners" are less visible, but reader-response theories of narrative will remind us to pay heed to their productive work in the co-construction of meaning (Martin 1986, 152–72).

Robert Fulford observes that when we take raw events and fashion them into narratives, we are often struggling to come to terms with the most enigmatic and difficult aspects of existence. "Large parts of life, sometimes the most crucial parts, depend on random happenings, contingency," he writes. "Storytelling is an attempt to deal with and at least partly *contain* the terrifyingly haphazard quality of life" (1999, 14). The political, economic, and social transformations of 1989 were enormously disruptive. Katherine Verdery describes the sense of disorientation felt by many Eastern Europeans as the old assumptions, expectations, and "rules of the game" dissolved: "They could no longer be sure what to say in what contexts, how to conduct politics with more than one political party, how to make a living in the absence of socialist subsidies and against spiraling inflation, and so on. . . . Moreover, their accustomed relations with other people became suddenly tense. Quarrels over property, for example, severed long-amicable bonds between siblings and neighbors; . . . increasing numbers of parents saw their plans for security and retirement evaporate as more of their children headed abroad. In these circumstances, people of all kinds could no longer count on their previous grasp of how the world works" (1999, 35).

The creation of narratives provides a way of giving order to, and exercising control over, seemingly random events. It is thus a means of stabilizing the new social order. By naming the unknown and locating it within the safe parameters of a parable, a saga, or a morality tale, storytellers simplify the complicated, domesticate the foreign, and make familiar the strange. *Myth*, a particular kind of narrative, is especially well suited to these tasks. William G. Doty explains what it is about mythic narratives that sets them apart (2000, 15): "They are not little but big stories, touching not just the everyday, but sacred or specially marked topics that concern much more than any immediate situation." At their core are the archetypal mysteries, problems, and concerns that define the human condition.

The political discourse of East Central Europe is freighted with myths of victimhood, martyrdom, treason, and racial superiority. According to Tismaneanu, the prevalence of conservative conspiratorial mythology in the former communist countries has to do with the weakness of liberal democratic traditions and the need to explain the dramatic changes people have experienced. "Political myths," he writes, "have the power to satisfy this thirst for immediate understanding; causalities are simplified or invented, images are presented in a vivid, metaphorical way, and the individual can discover sources for reassurance and psychological security" (1998, 12). As we will see, the reconstitution of memory about 1956 draws upon some of the archetypal myths of East Central Europe— those of territory as sacred space, of suffering and redemption, of unjust treatment, and of military valor (Schöpflin 1997, 28–32).[4]

SITES OF MEMORY

Pierre Nora argues that the disappearance of peasant life and the advent of mass culture have all but eradicated the conditions for collective, embodied memory. History, a secular, prosaic, analytic production, threatens to overwhelm memory, the realm of the sacred and the magic (1989, 8–9). Yet the memorial consciousness survives, and the more that internal memory is lost, the more it is maintained by the exterior scaffolding that Nora refers to as *lieux de mémoire*, sites of memory, that preserve the illusion of eternity: monuments, museums, anniversaries, archives, festivals, and fraternal orders (12). The forced forgetting imposed by the Kádár regime resulted in a similar impulse to mark the memory sites connected to the uprising when it became possible to do so. The following chapters examine a series of sites that, as *lieux de mémoire*, are designed "to stop time, to block the work of forgetting, to establish a state of things, to immortalize death, to materialize the immaterial" (19).

An open-air museum was established on the outskirts of Budapest in 1993 as a repository for the city's monuments to communism. Chapter one examines the Statue Park Museum as an arena for the formation of collective memories about Hungary's forty years of communism, with the 1956 uprising standing as a key moment. Based on an analysis of the museum as symbolic space, I argue that it contributes to an emerging postcommunist discourse of history and society that spans partisan politics and provides a site for coming to terms with the past from diverse points of view.

On the night that the 1956 revolution erupted, a jubilant crowd of demonstrators toppled a massive bronze statue of Stalin in Budapest's City Park. As communism disintegrated in the late 1980s, the destruction of the Stalin monument became a key episode in narratives about the uprising. Chapter two examines this iconoclastic act and its subsequent commemoration. I argue that they are best understood as epideictic moments where participants, spectators, and the general public experience a sense of visceral, anarchic joy in the presence of this symbolic resistance to tyranny.

One of the monuments that now stands in the Statue Park Museum was commissioned by the communists to honor the martyrs of the 1956 "counter-revolution." It stood in Republic Square, where insurgents besieged the Budapest Communist Party Headquarters. During the fighting, a number of the building's occupants were shot, hanged, or beaten to death by the rebels. Party officials used this episode to construct a narrative of 1956 as a counter-revolution carried out by "hooligans," "thugs," and "prostitutes." Chapter three examines the communists' commemoration of the events in Republic Square as the backdrop against which postcommunist accounts must be developed.

Ilona Tóth was a medical student involved in the resistance following the Soviet attack on November 4, 1956, which essentially ended the uprising. In the most public of the retaliatory show trials, Tóth confessed to murdering a man she believed to be a secret-police infiltrator. Later known as "Hungary's Jeanne d'Arc," she was hanged in 1957. Long convinced of Tóth's innocence, former classmates and other supporters sought to have her rehabilitated after the fall of communism. On October 23, 2000, a national holiday commemorating the outbreak of the revolution, a bust of Tóth was unveiled in the garden of a private folklore museum; at the time, legislation clearing her name was working its way through Parliament. Chapter four analyzes the ceremony as a ritual through which participants enacted a conservative cultural identity.

The only museum devoted solely to the 1956 revolution is a private operation owned by an aging freedom fighter. Housed in a former rural school far from the capital, the collection constitutes a modern cabinet of curiosities. Chapter five compares the inception, arrangement, and presentation of this collection with the Military History Museum's exhibit on the revolution in an effort to tease out the rhetorical intentions of the designers. The analysis reveals two distinctly different modes of objectifying the past, which are aimed at stabilizing divergent national identities.

Convicted of treason, Imre Nagy was executed in 1958, and his body was dumped in an unmarked grave. Following his ceremonial reburial in 1989, Nagy seemed poised to enter the pantheon of national heroes alongside Lajos Kossuth, the hero of the 1848 revolution, and Saint Stephen, the founder of the nation. That has not happened. Chapter six examines the intertextual discourse surrounding a monument to Nagy as a way of exploring the competing stories that construct him as a historical figure. This analysis suggests that the failure to elevate Nagy to the status of an unqualified national hero reflects a negative attitude toward politics that is characteristic of postcommunist thought.

In relating a story about the mysterious circumstances under which one of Imre Nagy's revolutionary comrades died in prison, Hungarian writer György Konrád remarks parenthetically, "In this country there are commonly several versions of historical fact" (1984, 157). The suspension of communist censorship has only marginally (if at all) tempered the validity of his understatement. Beyond the near impossibility of separating out fact and fiction, my disciplinary training and background are such that my concern is not for the validity of truth claims. My aim is to understand the stories about all of these people, places, and events on their own terms and to analyze their significance for the construction of postcommunist identities and ideologies. I leave it to the historians to ferret out the truth.

CHAPTER ONE

BUDAPEST'S STATUE PARK MUSEUM

THE POLITICAL, ECONOMIC, AND MILITARY consolidation of East Central Europe by the Soviet Union in the late 1940s was cemented by an aggressive ideological campaign. Its most visible aspect was the massive public display of revolutionary symbols: Buildings, bridges, and towers were crowned with the Red Star of communism. Factory and classroom walls were decorated with posters of Marx-Engels-Lenin-Stalin gazing into a utopian future. Flags and national coats-of-arms were redesigned to feature the hammer and sickle, symbolic of the common interests of industrial workers and peasants in the international class struggle. Monuments to the Soviet Army—expressions of gratitude for liberation from fascism—were erected in parks and squares, themselves newly named to commemorate revolutionary leaders or events.

Such works were "relentlessly didactic," to use Miklós Haraszti's phrase (1987, 116), constant reminders of the utopian project and of solidarity with the Soviet Union. Yet as cultural signifiers, socialist realist art and artifacts were highly unstable. There was always a great disjuncture between their inscribed meaning and the significance attached to them by those whose class standing placed them in opposition to communism. Moreover, the meanings ascribed to them in the immediate post-revolutionary period by supporters of progressive change shifted dramatically over a relatively short span of time as disenchantment with the class struggle set in (Condee 1995, xviii). Originally intended to galvanize and inspire the masses, socialist iconography soon became symbolic of unwanted external control. In Hungary, "Russian street names that twisted the Magyar tongue and Soviet emblems that broke the Magyar heart" were among the most visible manifestations of the "Russification" of Hungarian culture (Ignotus 1972, 209). Several of the demands issued by students in the days leading up to the 1956 revolution were purely symbolic and thus indicative of the deep desire for national sovereignty. Their terms included replacing the 1949 communist emblem with the Kossuth arms, with its red, white, and green tricolor and Apostolic Cross; restoring March 15 as a national holiday marking the 1848 revolution; and discarding Soviet-style army uniforms in favor of Hungarian designs.

The 1989 fall of communism in Eastern Europe has taken on mythic qualities. Accordingly, the story is commonly told through reference to spectacular, disruptive moments that marked the end of the old regime: the opening of the Berlin Wall on November 9 or the overthrow of Romanian dictator Nicolae Ceausescu on December 22. Indeed, scenes of crowds scaling the wall or toppling statues of Lenin became dominant tropes in international news reports about the unfolding events. In contrast to most of her neighbors, Hungary underwent what Antal Örkény and György Csepeli call a "silent revolution" (1994, 260). Notwithstanding such dramatic events as the June 16 reburial of Imre Nagy and other martyrs of the 1956 revolution, the communist regime in Hungary "melted like butter in late summer sunshine" (Rév 1995b, 23). Nevertheless, there was plenty of ideological rubble to be swept away. In Budapest over three hundred streets, squares, and parks were renamed. Designations such as Tractor Street, Red Army Road, and November 7th Square were dropped, often in favor of their presocialist names honoring monarchs or saints: Hungarian-Soviet Friendship Park became Old Hill Park; Socialist Brigade Park became New Hill Park. Place names commemorating communist heroes were reinscribed with allusions to the 1956 revolution: Zoltán Schönherz Road became October 23 Road, and Elek Bolgár Square became Imre Nagy Square.[1]

One of Raymond Williams's main contributions to Marxist cultural theory was his correction of reductionist notions of art and literature as "mere ideology." He argued that consciousness and its products are in fact material social processes through which groups of people create specific ways of life. "Thinking" and "imagining," he writes, are social processes that only become accessible in undeniably material and physical ways: "in voices, in sounds made by instruments, in penned or printed writing, in arranged pigments on canvas or plaster, in worked marble or stone" (Williams 1977, 62). If the design, execution, and display of a poster, statue, or building ornament are culturally constitutive, their *re*design and displacement or destruction are arguably even more significant as highly charged political acts.

This chapter focuses on an open-air museum established on the outskirts of Budapest in 1993 as a repository for the city's monuments to

The former Elek Bolgár Square, renamed to honor Imre Nagy. The marble plaque identifies the building as the site where Nagy was condemned to death.

socialism. Following Williams's emphasis on the importance of studying the material processes through which culture is constructed, this discussion analyzes the Statue Park Museum as an arena for the formation of collective memories about Hungarians' forty-year experiences with communism.

MUSEUMS, MONUMENTS, AND MEMORIES

National cohesion requires groups of people to develop a sense of commonality. As David Morley and Kevin Robins explain (1995, 3), this involves the formation of a collective cultural identity that is sustained over time through the formation of a common history, outlook, and vision of the future. Questions of identity, memory, and heritage are continuously being worked out in various cultural, educational, and informational arenas, including museums. In Ivan Karp's words (1992, 6), museums are one of a number of settings where civil society is constituted, where various communities and institutions assert, contest, and negotiate social interests and ideals.

While this process is always contentious, at certain historical intersections such as East Central Europe in 1989, the established bases of collective identity are shaken. Coherence and continuity are threatened by fragmentation and chaos (Morley and Robins 1995, 72). The reassertion of stability through the development of a reconfigured common cultural identity is critical. Along these lines, John Jackson (1980, 92) notes that every new revolutionary social order is anxious to establish its image and acquire public support. To do so, it produces a wealth of commemorative monuments, public symbols, and national celebrations to teach the public what to believe and how to act. Mikhail Yampolsky (1995, 100) draws our attention to the double semiotics of iconoclasm in revolutionary periods when he writes that the act of destroying a monument and replacing it with a new one is a twofold symbol of victory. The new monument not only represents the ideals of the victors but also stands as a vestige of what is now absent.

All constructions of the past contain an element of myth. History inscribes the past, giving a coherent shape to what William James has called "the blooming and buzzing confusion" of unmediated reality. Still, as Barry Schwartz points out (1982, 374), we do not fully understand how collective interpretations of the past emerge. As a sociologist, Schwartz is interested in the relationship between social structure and collective memory. Through an analysis of the iconography of the U.S. Capitol, he demonstrates how the past is constructed in accordance with contemporary social-political needs. But as Schwartz himself notes, the historical backdrop to his analysis of the American case is relatively stable. The Hungarian case allows us to study how commemoration works in a more dynamic historical setting.

One way to look at the process of commemoration is to consider a memorial's function in the context of major social transformations in Western industrialized societies. Traditional monuments celebrate heroic men, their deeds (waging wars, winning battles), or their virtues (heroism, bravery, courage) and exhort the visitor to imitate the latter (Lowenthal 1985, 322; Prost 1997, 329). Modernist monuments such as the bombed-out cathedral in the middle of Berlin or the museum at Buchenwald speak a rhetoric of admonition, warning the public not to let history repeat itself (Farmer 1995; Wood 1991). Postmodern monuments—the Vietnam Veterans Memorial in Washington and the memorial at Kent State University in Ohio—demand engagement but offer multiple, often conflicting, meanings that defy resolution (Blair, Jeppeson, and Pucci 1991; Foss 1986; Gregory and Lewis 1988). Carole Blair, Martha Jeppeson, and Enrico Pucci write (1991, 278): "the Vietnam Veterans Memorial provokes engagement; it is not easily consumed or immediately intelligible. Its rhetoric does not sanction a touristic, consumptive response; it invites an engaged and thoughtful reading."

In some respects Budapest's Statue Park Museum is postmodern. Its holdings—inherently symbolic objects whose ideological significance has never been stable—had yet another layer of meaning slapped on them when they were uprooted from their familiar locations and repositioned in the fabricated terrain of an open-air park. Here David Lowenthal's comments about relics are relevant to monuments as well when he writes that their value and meaning largely derive from their surroundings (1985, 282); they are profoundly altered when they are moved away from their place of origin and robbed of their context. The relocation of the communist monuments radically destabilized whatever meanings they had come to embody to the various publics that encountered them in their original settings.

The museum is postmodern too in that it juxtaposes pieces that embody seemingly incongruous versions of communism. A description of the museum and some of its contents will illustrate this eclecticism. The museum's entrance is a large, symmetric colonnade capped with a pediment. It is made of red brick, "an ancient, noble material" according to the museum's designer, Ákos Eleőd (1993, 61). Matching rounded arches, built into walls extending from the entrance, frame the founding fathers of communism—a bronze Lenin (by Pál Pátzay, 1965) and a granite statue of Marx and Engels (by György Segesdi, 1971). Altogether, the museum houses about forty artifacts arranged into three sections. The first set of monuments are highly stylized representations of generic Soviet heroes, designed to commemorate the liberation of Hungary from Nazi Germany and the enduring friendship of Hungary and the Soviet Union. Typical is Zsigmond Kisfaludi Strobl's 1956 bronze statue of an authoritative uni-

Entrance to the Statue Park Museum. Photograph by Zsolt Bátori. Courtesy
http://www.szoborpark.hu

formed Russian soldier shaking hands with a grateful Hungarian worker.
The second section contains statues, plaques, busts, and reliefs commemorating specific individuals, almost all Hungarians, who were active
in working-class movements. Most striking is Imre Varga's 1986 memorial to Béla Kun, leader of the 1919 Hungarian Soviet Republic. Sculpted
of bronze, steel, and copper, its shimmering surfaces and complex angles
convey the sharp, feverish excitement of pre-Stalinist revolutionaries.
The museum's third section houses monuments to various working-class
episodes or ideals. Examples include a plaque identifying the site of an illegal antifascist press in the 1920s and a monument to the twelve hundred Hungarians who fought in the International Brigade during the
Spanish Civil War.

In addition to this pastiche of holdings, the museum is postmodern in
that it is a polysemic collage/montage, where bits and pieces of the communist past provide the raw material for countless possible narratives.
Eleőd explains that he deliberately minimized his own creative authority in order to respect the diverse memories and experiences of visitors:

"I had to realize that if I used more direct, more drastic, more timely devices for constructing the park—as many people expected—that is, if I had built a counter-propaganda park out of these propaganda statues, then I would be following the prescribed ways of thinking we inherited from the dictatorship" (in Váradi 1994, 24).

While the museum does embody certain postmodernist elements, it is more accurately understood as reflective of a postcommunist social order whose sense of the past and of politics is quite different from that of postmodernism, where any sense of historical continuity or vision of a better future has been abandoned (Meštrovič 1994). In trying to make sense of the process of commemoration in contemporary East Central Europe, István Rév's notion of "remembering otherwise" is helpful. Writing about historical recollections surrounding 1989, Rév uses the term to emphasize that reconstructions of the past involve new narratives whose authentication necessarily means the de-authentication of other existing or

Zsigmond Kisfaludi Strobl's *Memorial to Hungarian-Soviet Friendship* (1956). Now located in the Statue Park Museum, the memorial stood in Kőbánya's Pataki (now Saint László) Square. Photograph by Zsolt Bátori. Courtesy http://www.szoborpark.hu

Imre Varga's memorial to Béla Kun (1986). This memorial stood briefly in
Vérmező near Budapest's Southern Railroad Station before being transferred to
the Statue Park Museum. Photograph by Zsolt Bátori. Courtesy http://www
.szoborpark.hu

possible narratives: "In order to compose a new story, elements of the old
one are restructured, rearranged, refigured, left out, put aside, overlooked,
disremembered—forgotten. . . . Forgetting is constitutive, an essential element of 'remembering otherwise,' of rewriting history, of reconstituting
identity" (1995a, 9). He sees 1989 as a liberating moment in the sense
that the past as it had been experienced and recorded no longer made
sense. Old definitions of the past had to be at least repressed, and new
narratives had to be written.

Richard Esbenshade reveals the complexity of this process in his ex-
ploration of the role of memory in the construction of national narratives
in postwar East Central Europe. He analyzes conceptions of oppositional
remembering in the writings of dissidents György Konrád and Milan
Kundera and shows how the individual counter-narratives that developed
in reaction to the state's official collective memories of the past were
themselves problematic. While memory-as-resistance was assumed to be

a disinterested, univocal, pristine antidote to state-imposed forgetting, the counter-narratives were psychologically self-serving and overlooked the existence of still other counter-memorial positions (Esbenshade 1995, 75–77). Esbenshade insists, "The celebration of counter-memory or counter-history begs the question of *who* is doing the remembering and the rewriting of history" (77). Reinscribing the past, then, is a highly contentious, hegemonic process that raises questions about who has the authority to do the rewriting and on what grounds. Furthermore, it raises questions about the interests behind the dominant narratives as well as their relationship to other social or political forces. In order to explore these questions as they relate to the Statue Park Museum, we need to look into its founding.

THE DECISION TO ESTABLISH A MUSEUM

Literary historian László Szörényi (1989) first proposed the establishment of a "Lenin Garden" on Csepel Island, the traditional center of Budapest's industrial working-class movements, in the summer of 1989.[2] He suggested, tongue in cheek, that foreign tourists would pay hard currency to visit a park of communist monuments. The following spring a conference on "Monuments in Hungary" was held in Debrecen to consider the question. The meeting centered around presentations by historians and art historians, with sculptors, delegates from political parties, and representatives of other organizations also participating.

The upshot of the Debrecen conference was a public statement imploring the nation not to destroy the monuments erected during the forty years of Communist rule but to preserve them as documents of an era and to make them accessible to the public. The group further recommended that the removal of public statuary and memorials be handled by local governing bodies and with the participation of committees of independent experts (Sz. Kürti 1995; Szűcs 1994a, 103; 1994b, 159). Parliament thus adopted legislation in 1991 giving local governments, in concert with experts, the right to make decisions about the removal, transfer, and demolition of public monuments. In Budapest the central municipal government was required to get the approval of the relevant district before removing or destroying a statue or monument ("A Helyi Önkormányzatok" 1991). As a result the city and district councils considered the fate of the monuments and plaques in their jurisdictions one by one.[3]

The decision to establish a museum that would hold the removed monuments was made in December, 1991, by the General Assembly of Budapest, a body predominantly controlled by the Alliance of Free Democrats. The origins of the Free Democrats as a political party go back to the 1980s, when an opposition group of Budapest-based intellectuals coalesced around the samizdat journal *Beszélő*. Their orientation was liberal and cosmopolitan. The party enjoyed both political and financial support from the West and had a history of close cooperation with human-rights activists in Czechoslovakia and Poland (Tőkés 1996, 312). Free Democrats had won the second-largest number of seats in Parliament in the first free elections in 1990 and constituted the major opposition party to the ruling Hungarian Democratic Forum.

Like the Free Democrats, the Democratic Forum emerged during the 1980s as an opposition movement. Its founders were a group of populist writers and other intellectuals and professionals whose main concern was with the treatment of Hungarian ethnic minorities in Romania and Slovakia (Garton Ash 1985, 6). After the 1990 elections, the Democratic Forum and the Free Democrats had no choice but to work together and craft a new government. But antagonism between the two parties ran deep as a result of their fundamental ideological differences. During and after the elections, some members of the Democratic Forum accused the Free Democrats of Marxist or Maoist sympathies, and Free Democrats labeled members of the Democratic Forum anti-Semites, communist fellow-travelers, and right-wing extremists (Tőkés 1996, 380, 389).

This brittle political atmosphere was the context in which the decision was made to establish the Statue Park. The removal of communist monuments from their accustomed locations among the trees and parks of the city was essentially a political compromise that allowed various factions to maintain their identities as bearers of an authentic national memory of resistance. Thus, the Statue Park monuments maintain a complicated existence as exiles that silently, stonily mark their own absence from the city and the delegitimization of the political movements they once embodied. Collectively they represent a cultural form whose discourse is constitutive of postcommunism.

THE MUSEUM AND POSTCOMMUNISM

György Schöpflin argues that the term "postcommunism" is more than a temporal description, having authentic content that applies more or less evenly to the individual postcommunist nations. In a series of writings and interviews, he outlines its features (Bíró 1995; Schöpflin 1994, 1995). The essence of postcommunism "is that it now constitutes a *sui generis* system which is marked by some democratic practices, with stronger or weaker commitments to pluralism, so that both political and economic competition have become a reality. At the same time, anti-democratic ideas and practices are also current" (Schöpflin 1995, 63). He describes postcommunism as democratic in form but nationalistic in practice. Its fundamental weaknesses are a lack of trust in institutions and a lack of respect for the rule of law, factors that impede the development of civil society. Paradoxically, citizens both worship and detest the state. They expect it to satisfy their every need, yet at the same time they use every means at their disposal to outwit authorities (Bíró 1995, 3).

As Schöpflin and others describe postcommunism, its characteristics are partly a result of the legacy of communism itself. But the appearance of communism in East Central Europe has a certain historical logic. Philip Longworth (1994, 6–7) argues that a number of distinctive traits and tendencies existed in Eastern Europe long before Yalta, setting the region apart from the West and giving it a certain coherence that still endures. Utopianism, mysticism, idealism, and romanticism are deeply rooted tendencies, evidenced in the strength of nationalistic feeling, in the passion for poetry, in the popularity of the heroic image, and in the Christ-like suffering of martyrs to independence during centuries of domination by the Austrian, Russian, and Ottoman empires. Such traits made the ground fertile for communism, and they remain significant features of the landscape. Longworth writes (1994, 7), "If one regards Soviet Communism as a disease, then it seems that Eastern Europe may have had a pre-disposition to the infection."

Several closely intertwined features of postcommunism are relevant to this analysis of the Statue Park Museum. These elements include a strong sense of national identity, a desire to adopt Western institutions, and a deep respect for the past. Let us consider some of the ways in which the museum invites the public to engage with these dimensions of postcommunism in the collective reconstruction of Hungarian identity.

Peter Berger (1994, 294–95) notes that nationalist sentiments and movements were a powerful form of resistance to the forced internationalism of the Soviet empire. The loss of political sovereignty, the presence of Soviet soldiers, and the compulsory Russian-language classes all intensified nationalism, though nationalist impulses were largely kept under control by the strong central-party apparatus. But the primary source of

nationalistic outbursts since 1989 was the ill-conceived peace settle-
ments following the First World War. As Eric Hobsbawm puts it (1990,
164), "The eggs of Versailles and Brest Litowsk are still hatching." Writing about the Treaty of Trianon, which stripped Hungary of two-thirds
of its territory, Sabrina Ramet argues that Britain and France ignored the
preferences of local populations and imposed a territorial configuration
that reflected their own insatiable hunger for vengeance: "Far from being
an 'ancient' problem, the ethnic hatreds that plague Eastern Europe are a
relatively recent 'gift' from the Great Powers" (1996, 100).

Partly as a result of such injustices, then, postcommunism is characterized by a heightened sense of national identity that emphasizes the di-
visions between who belongs to the nation and who does not. This establishment of boundaries that exclude the "Other" is central to Morley
and Robins's conception of how cultural identity is formed. Following
the foundational work of such scholars as Geoffrey Barraclough and Edward Said, they argue that (Western) European identity is constructed and
maintained in opposition to—and often hostility toward—non-Euro-
peans. "European culture," they write, is "constituted precisely through
its distinctions from and oppositions to American culture, Asian culture,
Islamic culture, etc." (Morley and Robins 1995, 45).

The Statue Park Museum discursively establishes borders that separate postcommunist Hungary from the forty-year experience of communism. Monuments that once embodied ideals of international solidarity
and implored Hungarian men and women to emulate the courage and
selflessness of party leaders and martyrs to the cause were banished from
their places of honor in Budapest. In Hungary, as in other highly central-
ized European countries such as France, the capital city is both materially and symbolically the center of activity. To remove monuments from
the city to the suburbs, to situate them among such banal objects as bill-
boards, power lines, and highways, is to emasculate them of their rhetorical power to instill awe, respect, terror, or other strong emotions. In addition, brick walls and wire fences define the Statue Park's boundaries.
One is tempted to say that these devices "imprison" the collection, but a
prison metaphor is just one of many possible readings; "quarantine" is an
alternative for those who see the recuperation of tarnished ideals as a pos-
sibility. In any case, it is safe to say that the walls and fences symbolically
segregate communism from the flow of everyday life.

Related to the distancing of present-day Hungary from communism,
the museum activates a reading of Hungarian identity that is markedly
independent of Russian influence. The inclusion of some ten memorials

to Hungarian-Soviet friendship, to Soviet heroes, and to the Soviet liberation of Hungary underscores the autonomy of the Hungarian nation from Russia under the new geopolitical order. Recall too that the museum's entrance is dominated not only by the towering figures of Marx and Engels but also by Pátzay's imposing statue of Lenin, who embodied a double persona as leader of the world proletariat and chief architect of Russian communism (Coquin 1989, 236).

Structurally, this turning away from the East orients postcommunism toward the West. In 1999, Hungary became a member of NATO, and it is slated to join the European Union in 2004. The Statue Park Museum symbolically underscores the legitimacy of the nation's efforts to join these and other Western institutions and to adopt Western practices and values through its repudiation of their former Eastern counterparts. Thus, the museum implicitly endorses political pluralism when it rejects the monopolistic authority of the Communist Party; it endorses a reconfiguration of military alliances when it rejects the hegemony of the Russian Army; it endorses a new Western-style pragmatism when it rejects utopianism. Finally, the excommunication of monuments that embody the ideals of central planning and the equal distribution of wealth affirms the value of a market economy. This economic reorientation is underscored by the financial structure of the museum. While it is owned by the state, it is franchised to operate on a self-sustaining basis through entry fees and the sale of souvenirs—postcards, reproductions of Lenin and Stalin statues, model Trabant cars, "McLenin" T-shirts, and "Best of Communism" CDs produced by the museum's entrepreneurial director, Ákos Réthly.

The "Other" against whom the political identity of Hungarians is being constituted through the museum's rhetoric is their own earlier subordinate selves. That is, "who we are now" is being constructed in opposition to "who we were." Soviet communist hegemony was just the latest example; earlier episodes of subjugation remain equally vivid in the national memory. An April, 2003, referendum on joining the European Union passed by 84 percent, but most voters simply stayed home, apparently sympathetic to opponents' pleas for national independence and neutrality. One anti-EU spokesman compared the anti-democratic and bureaucratic structures of the EU to the Warsaw Pact and COMECON, the former Soviet bloc's Council of Mutual Economic Assistance (Drábik 2003, 132). Thus, almost all of the individuals memorialized in the Statue Park are Hungarian, and a good share of the social or political struggles that are commemorated were local movements. Yet the museum must accommodate the wide range of stances taken toward communism and the myriad experiences of Hungarians during the forty years of communist rule. With the exception of those who were jailed, forced into exile, or executed for their allegedly subversive activities, everyone found ways of adapting to the system. As Schöpflin puts it (1995, 68), "Anyone living under communism—except those under the age of, say, 30 in 1989—had to have made some compromise with it."

The Statue Park's designer was particularly sensitive to the vulnerability of socialist realist sculptors or architects to charges of political-aesthetic prostitution because of the public nature and the dimensions of their art. Unlike the sculptor, Eleőd has stated, "the poet, who perhaps wrote some very illustrious Stalin cantatas, can put his works to rest secretly under his pillow now" (Váradi 1994, 19). Thus, the intention of the museum is not to pass judgment on either the statues themselves or the artists who created them. Eleőd explains, "There were some sculptors who staked their whole career on their belief in the autocratic quality of the previous political system, but there were also statues which were born under duress, made 'under order' or rather 'under directions issued by the party,' or given as a 'payment' for a commission for another work that was important for the sculptor" (Váradi 1994, 19).

The museum invites reconciliation between those who might have been complicit in the maintenance of a one-party system and those who were compelled to submit to its authority by adopting a nondirective, polysemic discourse. One form this discourse takes is the absence of evaluative or explanatory labels on the monuments. Other than their original inscriptions, they bear only numbers that correspond to entries in a guidebook sold at the ticket window. As a result of this absence, even the most literal of the works carries a sense of enigma and evokes a contemplative reading that resolves the past without explaining it. The guidebook itself is descriptive and dispassionate in tone. In addition to some background information about the museum, it contains entries on each of the artifacts, correcting some historical inaccuracies, though in a restrained manner. For example, the Statue Park contains a plaque inscribed as follows: "Kató Hámán, an eminent figure in the workers' movement who was murdered in a fascist prison of Horthy, lived in this house from 1919 to 1931." The plaque's entry in the guidebook repeats the inscription, with its statement that Hámán was murdered in prison ("a Horthy-fasizmus börtönében gyilkolták meg"). Without commenting on the discrepancy, the entry's biographical sketch of Hámán states that she died as a result of an illness she contracted in prison ("ott szerzett betegség következtében halt meg"). Through such discursive strategies, the museum enables Hungarians to insert communism into a common heritage. Regardless of individual memories, the Statue Park is a reminder that "we lived through those years together." Once again, this narrative was carefully and deliberately crafted by Eleőd. In his original proposal for the commission, he states, "There is pleasure in participating in the *absence* of book burning" (Eleőd 1993, 60).

Paul Connerton (1989, 14–15) writes that the mental enslavement of the subjects of totalitarian regimes begins when their memories are taken away from them. Historians and others who keep the past alive are fired from their jobs and forced into silence. What is most horrifying is the fear that no one will be left who can bear witness to the past. Certainly this Orwellian specter contributed to the decision to establish a museum that would safeguard the memories of an unpleasant epoch. Eleőd has said that one reason for preserving the statues and the repressive atmosphere that they embody is so that if a future regime decides to start expressing itself with 31-foot-tall, 11-ton statues, it would be possible to warn, "Look out!" (Váradi 1994, 21). Beyond the admonitory function of history, a deep respect for the past is characteristic of postcommunist cultures, where the present sense of Self is fundamentally bound to mythic, medieval origins of the people and the nation. The present is an organic outgrowth of the past, with all its suffering and martyrdom. In a twisted way, the more brutal the past, the better: if the people can survive through unspeakable hardships, they can endure anything. Thus, the past—*especially* the communist period—must be remembered and, in a sense, celebrated.

Still, the past must be rendered safe psychologically. Personal indignities and tragedies, as well as a sense of profound collective loss over the forty years of economic stagnation and infrastructural neglect, have left their mark. Barry Schwartz's aforementioned work on commemoration is useful for thinking about how the Statue Park Museum might assist the public in confronting the recent, painful past. His analysis shows that in periods of American history where the integrity of the Union was questionable or where significant social-political cleavages existed, "safe" events or episodes that could be consensually celebrated were commemorated. Later, when national unity was no longer an issue, regional or other forms of diversity could be safely cultivated.

In the politics of transformation, narratives about the past can easily be constructed in such a way that they discredit political rivals and enhance one's own claims to represent the nation's "legitimate" ideals and interests. Given Hungary's political fragility in the early 1990s, the establishment of a museum that puts to pasture various incarnations of socialism makes sense. In other words, the juxtaposition of monuments to antifascism, social democracy, labor unionism, and Soviet-dominated totalitarianism is not as strange as it first seems. Schwartz's work further suggests that with the passage of time, the urgency to fence off an undifferentiated past will lessen, and socialism may be publicly thought about and commemorated in more nuanced ways. For now, however, Hungarians who fought against Franco's armies in Spain must stand side by side with Stalin's soldiers.

PUTTING THE PAST TO REST

The political and economic transformation of Hungary in 1989 was widely understood by the public as the final outcome of a revolution initiated in 1956 and put on hold for over thirty years. While the "long revolution of '56" was ignited by the masses, its resolution in the late 1980s was left to the technocrats, mainly economic experts. The major symbolic act during the earlier "hot" phase of the revolution was when a crowd of demonstrators destroyed a huge statue of Stalin near Heroes' Square in Budapest's City Park (discussed in chapter two). By the time of the mopping-up phase in 1989, iconoclasm or other violent acts would have been senseless. The damnatio memoriae—"obliteration of the memory"—of Stalinist communism had long been accomplished. Life had been quite bearable under Kádárism, but the masses suffered no illusions about the price they were paying.

The depoliticization of the Hungarian public accomplished by Kádár meant that the economic transformations of the postcommunist period were much more consequential and worrisome than liberalized politics. Many people have suffered enormously from the loss of socialist egalitarianism, and all but the new entrepreneurial class have experienced hardships associated with privatization. Given these economic burdens, the public widely regarded the removal of communist monuments as an unnecessary expenditure of scarce public funds (Esbenshade 1995, 72).[4] Many people would have been just as pleased with some new official canonization of how these statues were to be interpreted, inasmuch as they had lost any pretense to their official, originally intended meanings years ago.

Beyond economic objections to the Statue Park, people have criticized its establishment on political, aesthetic, and historical grounds. Politically, the decision to build the museum can be seen as a matter of partisan politics, as various factions sought to appropriate the memory of 1956 and establish their anticommunist credentials. Aesthetically, the public objected to the government's failure to distinguish between communist kitsch and genuine works of art in organizing the collection. While few people objected to the removal of red stars or mass-produced busts of Lenin, many of the statues that were relegated to the museum are the works of internationally acclaimed Hungarian sculptors.[5] By virtue of an aesthetic dimension beyond politics, many of the monuments deserved to remain in the parks or squares they had graced for years. Finally, many people believe the pieces should have been left in Budapest because they are authentic markers of a particular historical period. A parallel is often drawn to Hungary's Turkish mosques, minarets, and baths. While no one thinks the subjugation of large parts of Hungary by the Ottomans was a positive episode, the architectural remnants are appreciated simply because they are part of the nation's rich history.

The Statue Park Museum is not a burning issue for most Hungarians. In a sense, the monuments preserved there were insignificant and their relocation was inconsequential. But in a deeper sense, these works were important anchors that helped constitute a familiar, secure, and comprehensible landscape. Their removal has thus meant the loss of a discourse through which the people of Budapest experienced their daily lives as inhabitants of the city. A friend who grew up in Budapest described this loss through the example of the statue "Fegyverbe!" (To Arms!), István Kiss's massive bronze tribute to the 1919 Hungarian Soviet Republic: "The statue was close to my parents' apartment; I could see it from my window. Its common name was 'Futóbolond' (Running Fool), and it was an important meeting point or orientation place. But now, 'Kettőkor a Futóbolondnál!' ('See you at two at the Running Fool!') no longer means anything." As he explained, the loss goes beyond nostalgia to an awareness of the always present absence of an ironic discourse through which life under communism was interpreted.

A photo essay in the *New York Times Magazine* dismisses the Statue Park as a "graveyard for fallen idols" (Plachy 1993). At first glance this epithet seems to tell more about the politics of its author than about the museum. But perhaps the metaphor of a cemetery is useful for conceptualizing how the museum might enable Hungarians to come to terms with

István Kiss's monument to the 1919 Hungarian Soviet Republic. Erected in 1969 on the site of the Regnum Marianum Church, it now towers above all the other artifacts in the Statue Park Museum. Photograph by Zsolt Bátori. Courtesy http://www.szoborpark.hu

the past. Wilbur Zelinsky describes the functions of a graveyard (1975, 173): "The cemetery may be classified either as a this-worldly park, a place of solace and comfort intended primarily for the bereaved, or as a metaphor or working model of the afterlife, a sort of vestibule into the land of the departed and a point of attachment between the here and the there, or as both simultaneously."

Like a burial ground, the Statue Park Museum is a space where the past can be mourned and where loss can be assimilated, regardless of one's relationship with the deceased. The site has an air of finality about it, the source of which is hard to pinpoint. It may be the weight and durability of the red brick or the design's suggestion of classical ruins. It may be the wide, open space of the suburban landscape. Whatever it is, the Statue Park conveys the sense that the past has not been erased, but it has been put to rest.

CHAPTER TWO

THE DESTRUCTION OF THE STALIN MONUMENT

AMONG THE DEMANDS drawn up by Budapest students in the days leading to the 1956 revolution was the removal of a massive statue of
Stalin that stood on the edge of City Park. As events spun out of control
on the evening of October 23, a crowd estimated at one hundred thousand
converged at the monument. Their impatience soon gave way to performance, and the bronze effigy came crashing to the ground. The spontaneous destruction of the Stalin monument by an emboldened, jubilant
crowd is central to the postcommunist mythology surrounding the 1956
revolution.

This chapter is concerned with the rhetorical power of that absent
symbol. Mikhail Yampolsky argues that the pageantry associated with
the destruction of a monument and the visual retelling of such an iconoclastic moment through film and other media elevate what might otherwise be an unremarkable dot on the urban landscape to the status of a su-
per symbol. He writes, "The moment of explosion is, from the point of
view of spectacle, undoubtedly the most significant in the whole biography of the monument" (Yampolsky 1995, 101). The mythic power of the
now-absent likeness of Stalin is indeed largely a function of the visceral,
anarchic joy experienced, for the city was purged of its presence. The
scene of its destruction bears a carnivalesque atmosphere as the roles of
master and subject were reversed and retributive justice was symbolically
served (Bakhtin 1984, 10–15; Stites 1985, 3).

The medieval carnival involved a break in the cycle of time, a suspension of hierarchy, privileges, and prohibitions on designated feast, fair, or
market days. Similarly, the destruction of a monument, because of its intended durability, is a powerful intervention into the flow of time. Cast
in bronze or carved of marble, the memorial is designed to cheat history
through the eternal commemoration of an individual, event, or concept.

As a result, images of ruins or scenes with fragments of broken, abandoned statuary take on a special poignancy. It is the hubris of the King of Kings in Shelley's "Ozymandias" that makes the image of his "colossal wreck," half-buried in the desert sand and long forgotten, so powerful (Berger 1969, 75). Peter Blume's surrealistic take on Italian fascism, "The Eternal City," likewise draws its strength from the ideals of democracy that lie broken in the form of shattered sculpture as a jack-in-the-box head of Mussolini leers over their remnants (Aradi 1974, 226; Trapp 1987, 57).

Beyond its original ideological intentions—and the emotional force of exorcizing them—the Stalin monument's "phantom existence" (Yamplosky 1995, 101) is further infused with meaning as a result of the repression of memories of that glorious moment throughout the thirty-one years of the Kádár regime. The public reconstitution of these memories in the postcommunist period is best understood as epideictic commemoration along the lines suggested by Lawrence Rosenfield. Epideictic, he writes, "suggests an exhibiting or making apparent (in the sense of showing or highlighting) what might otherwise remain unnoticed or invisible" (Rosenfield 1980, 135). It is concerned with the luminosity or radiance that emanates from noble acts or thoughts and beckons us to join with our community in recognizing and celebrating what is—grace, goodness, and courage: "Such thoughtful beholding in commemoration constitutes memorializing" (133). Rosenfield's reference to the act of *beholding* is intriguing. As applied to the relationship between the Hungarian public and the monument to Stalin, it takes on a number of layers. For instance, the power of monumental art as visual rhetoric in the first place is bound up with its ability to captivate observers, a point well understood by Lenin (see Tolstoy, Bibikova, and Cooke 1990; Lodder 1993).

In order to establish how the destruction of the monument has carried so much rhetorical weight over the decades, we need to explore the act of beholding in its various dimensions. The statue was conceived during the aesthetic and political era of High Stalinism, when socialist realist art served as the cornerstone of official doctrine (Milosz 1960, 10) and when Hungary's leader, Mátyás Rákosi, reigned as "Stalin's best pupil." It was toppled shortly after Krushchev's denunciation of the cult of personality at the Twentieth Party Congress in 1956, which ushered in a period when "rigid adherence to the 'monolithic' Marxist theory of the arts was no longer obligatory" (Fischer 1963, 108). The memory of the statue was actively resurrected in the present period of multiparty democracy and liberal economics, where public art is generated through an uneasy alliance between state and private interests and where commemorative activities are often a flashpoint for competing political agendas. In other words, the codes that governed (or were intended to govern) the collective consciousness of Hungarians were radically revised several times over the course of the monument's life and afterlife.

HAPPY BIRTHDAY, DEAR STALIN

On August 20, 1949, a holiday honoring Saint Stephen, the founder of the nation, Hungary adopted a new constitution. Modeled along the lines of the Soviet Union's 1936 constitution, it declared the nation a "People's Republic" aimed at building a socialist popular democracy with the support of the Soviet Union. Four months later, on December 21, Stalin's seventieth birthday was marked by a feverish display of loyalty to the Soviet ruler, led by the fawning Rákosi, whose adulation was practically boundless. Stalin had long cultivated the image of the firm but compassionate father of the Soviet people. With the extension of his patriarchal role to embrace the nations of Central and Eastern Europe, his birthday offered an opportunity for his adopted children to display their loyalty (Brooks 2000, 69–70, 219–23). No one was more enthusiastic in taking on the role of loyal son than Rákosi. In conveying his greetings at the birthday celebration in Moscow's Bolshoi Theater, he gushed that "the Hungarian workers and peasants recognize Comrade Stalin as our dear father" (quoted in Murányi 1999). The tens of thousands of gifts offered by Hungarians to their "dear father" ranged from fine art (Zsigmond Kisfaludi Strobl's "Family Statue") to folk art (the homespun creations of peasant women) to kitsch (a Kremlin-shaped floor lamp with a clock that chimed Radio Moscow's break signal every half-hour) (Murányi 1999). But the main offering was a pledge to create a monument to Stalin worthy of the generalissimo in its artistic quality and size.

In research conducted during the twilight of communism, historian János Pótó traced the maneuvering behind the scenes as plans were worked out for the design and placement of the monument. In brief, the Secretariat of the Hungarian Workers' Party made all of the important decisions, but they were often fronted by either ad hoc committees such as the Selection Committee, formed to decide among entries, or existing bodies such as the Budapest City Council. The Ministry of Culture and the Budapest Mayor's Office jointly announced a competition for the commission, inviting twenty-five artists to take part. The sculptors were instructed to submit ¹/₁₀ scale plaster models of works that would ultimately stand between sixteen and twenty feet and be rendered of either bronze or marble. The guidelines also spelled out the ideological aura that the monument was to radiate: "The submission must express on behalf of us all the beloved, great Stalin as the leader of the world's socialists and peace-loving people, the commander of the glorious Soviet Army that liberated Hungary, and the protective father of the People's Democracies" (quoted in Pótó 1989, 76).

The results were appalling. The designs were submitted to Kálmán Pongrácz, chairman of the Budapest City Council's executive committee. While the press reported only that a second round of competition would be held, Pótó has found a terse press release regarding Pongrácz's report to the council. The chairman is quoted as saying that the entries "are atrociously bad. . . . They are figures that are so deformed that investigations of their creators should be immediately launched" (quoted in Pótó 1989, 77). Art historian László Prohászka maintains that Chairman Pongrácz was not overstating the case. "We can imagine that some of them weren't thrilled with the assignment," he writes, "but nobody would hardly have thought to caricature the figure of Stalin intentionally" (Prohászka 1994, 162, 164). The majority of the artists, Prohászka believes, were simply afraid. One of the competitors, Károly Antal, recalled years later how state-security agents launched a search for perpetrators of "sabotage" after the nose on a plaster cast of Stalin's face used in some ceremony was damaged. Prohászka relates this story to underscore his point: The artists had reason to be nervous, and "it's not possible to create great works of art with trembling hands" (164).

REVOLUTIONARY ART IN HUNGARY

The power to force conformity to an ill-defined socialist realist aesthetic was in the hands of József Révai, Hungary's minister of culture from 1949 to 1953. As Tamás Aczél and Tibor Méray (1959, 82–83) describe him, Révai was an erudite man and an outstanding writer whose essays on Hungarian literature and history are national treasures. Yet this "haughty despot" was driven by the single-minded goal of advancing a cultural revolution guided by principles of vigilance and ideological struggle inherited from the Soviet Union. Under his watchful eye, the shelves of Budapest's antiquarian book stores and libraries were purged of the great works of literature: in November, 1950, alone, 120,000 volumes were reduced to pulp (Urbán 1993, 11–12). Thus, while Révai himself was feasting on each new edition of Thomas Mann, not a single book by Mann was published in Hungary while Révai was minister of culture (Aczél and Méray 1959, 86).

In a lengthy speech delivered at the Second Congress of the Hungarian Workers' Party early in 1951, Révai took on the thorny issue of the relationship between Soviet and Hungarian culture. He bluntly identified Russia as the source of inspiration in his country's cultural revolution. "The model, the school master of our new socialist culture: Soviet culture" (Révai 1951, 32). He then proceeded to deflect criticism from the charge that Hungary was mechanically reproducing Soviet culture: "They babble on about how we're 'Russianizing' Hungarian culture. It's not worth spending many words arguing against this stupid slander. They dare to say this, those people whose cultural life of chewing gum, Coca Cola, and American detective movies is eroding the national character" (33).

Despite such disclaimers, Soviet cultural forms and aesthetic principles were imposed monolithically in all of the new people's democracies. Eastern Europeans resented this because it was alien, because it was felt to be "not ours" (Schöpflin 1993, 84). Hungary had its own indigenous avant-garde movements, dating from the *fin de siècle* and culminating in the politically charged art of the Hungarian Soviet Republic in 1919. The central theme of this earlier generation of socialist artists and writers was the nation's semifeudal status, and they looked to the West in their search for progressive politics and modes of expression (see Frigyesi 1998; Hanák 1998; Lukacs 1988). Peter Hanák emphasizes the pull of Western Europe in their aesthetics: "Here, where Asia was the product of the soil and of dreams, the time had come when they were catching up with Europe. Europe was there in the subject matter, the way they perceived things, in their depth of thinking—in short, in the society's way of responding to the challenges and problems of becoming bourgeois" (1998, 81).

A period of white terror followed the collapse of the 1919 Hungarian Soviet Republic, and many of the nation's most creative artists and intellectuals—Béla Bartók, László Moholy-Nagy, Béla Balázs, and György Lukács—were forced into exile. Those who remained were subject to the repressive cultural dictates of Miklós Horthy, whose conservative regime would last almost until the end of World War II, when he was forced to concede power to the extreme right. The war took a heavy toll on Hungary's cultural, intellectual, and scientific life. "Yet destructive as the devastation was," Ignác Romsics writes, "it also resulted in the release of new forces, fresh energies; the brake was suddenly taken off the impetus for democratic reform, which had been given so little scope before and during the war" (1999, 254). While the Left consolidated its political power, diverse literary and artistic styles found expression, for novelists, poets, musicians, painters, and graphic designers built upon the residual cultural formations of early twentieth-century modernism in Hungary, enriched by trends introduced by returning exiles. But with the establishment of the Communist Party's hegemony in the late 1940s, innovation and experimentation were suspended in favor of the clichéd iconography and rhetoric of socialist realism as formulated in the Soviet Union of the 1930s.

THE HAPPIEST SCULPTOR

Following the unsatisfactory outcome of the first competition, the city council invited the top four contenders to submit new designs. They selected that of Sándor Mikus, leading the press to dub him "the happiest Hungarian sculptor" (G. J. 1950). Mikus was a well-established artist, talented by any measure. He had exhibited pieces in the Venice Biennele in 1930 and had won a gold prize in the Paris World Exhibit in 1937. The bronze female figure was his favored mode of expression, rendered in his early work in small-scale sculptures but later in full scale. Reminiscent of Degas's ballerinas, Mikus's figures radiate a simplicity and sensitivity that transcend politics. As an artist who successfully underwent the transition from market- to state-sponsored culture, Mikus's personal history is worth glancing at. In many ways his story presents a *tableau vivant* of the positive hero favored in socialist realist literature, the modest man of humble origins whose upward path toward a full, creative life exemplifies the inevitable march of history toward a utopian future.

Sándor Mikus was born in 1903 as one of five children in the family of a forest guardsman and came of age in the economic mire of postwar Hungary.[1] Advanced education was out of the question, so in 1924 he went to work as a mechanic in a lighting factory. Mikus began to draw in his spare time. His talents came to the attention of the factory's chief engineer, who provided him with a five-year scholarship out of his own pocket. Through this support, he traveled to Rome and was given workspace in the studio of Hungarian sculptor Pál Pátzay, who was also there on a scholarship. Mikus returned home in 1930 with the keys to Pátzay's Budapest studio. His first major exhibit was held in 1932, and from then on his work was shown often and received well both in Hungary and abroad. During this early period, he created small pieces—medallions, busts, and figurines (Székely 1980, 237–38; Szíj 1977, 1–5).

Mikus was directly caught up in the nationalization of the culture industries after the Second World War. Apparently the transition was smooth. One of his official biographers writes that after the Liberation (the going term of art), Mikus "accepted the era's aesthetic requirements" (Székely 1980, 237). In 1949 he was appointed to the Sculpture Department of Hungary's Fine Arts Academy, and that same year he became one of the founding members of the Hungarian Union of Fine and Applied Artists (Szíj 1977, 4). His small pieces were now supplemented with state commissions for works of monumental proportions, culminating in the Stalin statue. Judging from the official biographies of Mikus written during the Kádár years, the ultimate fate of this monument had little effect on his standing or reputation. Both the piece and the circumstances surrounding its destruction have been treated as interesting but minor footnotes in his career (see Székely 1980, 237; Szíj 1977, 8). Long after the dust had settled, Mikus continued to work (see B. R. 1978).

BRINGING STALIN TO LIFE

Early in 1951, Mikus went to work in a studio specially built to hold the gargantua. The source of the bronze used in casting the monument is of interest. The Budapest City Memorial Authority had at its disposal some twenty-three tons of bronze in the form of statuary that had been damaged during the war or dismantled afterward for political reasons. The figures represented included János Hunyadi, who led the struggle against the Ottoman Turks in the fifteenth century; Artúr Görgey, an army officer who chased imperial forces out of Hungary during the 1848 revolution; Ignác Darányi, a cabinet minister in the Wekerle government of 1906–10; and Counts Gyula Andrássy and István Tisza. Some of the damaged monuments were to be repaired and returned to their original sites, but the Hunyadi statue was the only one ever restored. The rest, János Pótó writes (1989, 76), "disappeared before our eyes forever; probably these counts and 'traitors' were 'amalgamated' into the bronze figure of Stalin." While Pótó is correct that these old statutes were never seen again, the story of the provenance of the bronze used for the Stalin monument is part of the lore that surrounds it. Observers of the Stalin monument "saw" reflected in its patina the heavy hand of the state, with its clumsy attempt to recast history. Thus, in his recent account of the events of October 23, 1956, Ignác Romsics writes (1999, 305), "Quite apart from the fact that Stalin, along with Rákosi, was the prime symbol of everything bad, people held a grudge that the bronze for this eight-metre monstrosity, on its ten-metre-high podium, had been obtained by melting down the statues of a host of still widely respected Hungarian figures, such as István Tisza, Gyula Andrássy and Artúr Görgey."

As work on the statue proceeded, party leaders decided to locate it at the axis of Gorkij (now Városligeti) Avenue and Dózsa Road, a major thoroughfare that fronts City Park. Here they would construct Procession Square, with the figure's base serving as a reviewing stand for party and state dignitaries on May Day and other obligatory mass spectacles. The monument—a statue of Stalin standing rigidly with his right arm outstretched—was unveiled before a crowd of eighty thousand on the morning of December 16, 1951. Révai gave the inaugural address, hailing Stalin as "the leader of the people of the Soviet Union, the teacher of the whole world's working class, the flag bearer of the entire progressive humanity, whom all people, big and small, hold dear to their hearts." He proceeded to extend the gratitude of the Hungarian people to the Russian leader for all that he had done for them: "We thank Stalin that the soil of our homeland was not ravaged by civil war after the Liberation. We thank Stalin that the tree of reactionary conspirators did not grow to the sky, that the alliance of the Hungarian working class and peasantry victoriously fought the struggle with the internal reactionaries to inaugurate the peaceful building of socialism." Then, to the hushed tones of the Soviet national anthem, a gigantic sheet covering the statue fell to the ground.[2]

Reflecting the proportional excesses of Stalinism—what György Schöpflin refers to as the "romance of size" (1993, 86)—the most remarkable feature of the monument was its dimensions. The statue itself was twenty-six feet tall, approximately five times the Man of Steel's actual height, and weighed 6.5 tons. It stood on a thirteen-foot-high limestone pedestal, which was supported by the twenty-foot-high tribune. Altogether, the monument reached fifty-nine feet, or about six stories, high.

Sándor Mikus's monument to Stalin, Procession Square, Budapest, May Day, 1953. Courtesy Hungarian National Museum

Even official paeans to the creation could not contain the awe observers experienced at the sheer size of the thing. In the lead article of *Irodalmi Újság*, Iván Boldizsár (1951), head of the Writers' Union, stammered: "How huge it is: This is our first thought. Then immediately after that: How good it is."[3]

Documentary clips of the inaugural ceremony reveal the complex relationships between observers and observed that were established through the proportions and configuration of the monument. The dignitaries on the tribune, including Rákosi, the Soviet ambassador, and members of the Politburo, stand high above the crowds. Literally and figura-

Military dress assembly at Procession Square, Liberation Day, 1953. Courtesy 1956 Institute and Hungarian National Museum

tively backed up by the force of the towering Stalin, they survey the scene with satisfaction. The cheering masses crowded into the square lift their faces as they pay homage to the iconic Stalin and the living Rákosi from street level. The soldiers in the military parade are similarly dwarfed by the monument. They march past in lock step with their gazes fixed straight ahead, displaying their unwavering obedience to authority. And the enormous bronze Stalin dominates the entire scene, eclipsing not only the crowds but also his own functionaries with his imposing shadow. But before examining the iconography of the statue more closely, we first must consider the question of how Mikus and other artists absorbed the undeniably crude approach of socialist realism during the Stalinist period.

IMITATIVE ART

As formulated by the Soviet communist Andrei Zhdanov in 1934, socialist realist art was to be ideologically instructive, to transmit the party's point of view, in ways that would be readily understandable to the masses. But how were these principles actually transferred to Hungary?

Aczél and Méray provide a horrifying but fascinating account of a constant flow of Soviet artists and cultural functionaries to Hungary in the late 1940s and early 1950s (1959, 119–43). The mission of these visitors was to instruct Hungarian writers and artists in the fundamentals of socialist realism through exhibits, performances, lectures, and workshops. In other words, the yokels were to assimilate the principles of socialist art through the close observation of exemplars, interpreted by those who had already mastered the formula. Most of these missionaries were second-rate artists at best, a fact that apparently bothered them little, for they undertook their assignments with complete self-assurance. Aczél and Méray write: "Had, let us say, Shostakovich come to Hungary and given good advice or explained his method of composing, this might have been useful. But at that time Shostakovich was in disfavor. . . . Hungary did, however, receive a visit from the Secretary of the Soviet Composers' Association, a composer of cheap popular music and accordionist by the name of Hrennikov. This Hrennikov criticized Bartók tactfully and praised Kodály—with reservations, of course" (131).[4]

Beyond these "inspirational" visits, the cream of Hungarian artists were invited to the Soviet Union to witness first hand the fruits of socialist realism in Russian museums, art galleries, schools, and architecture. Of the sculptors who competed for the Stalin commission, only Mikus had been privileged to go on one of these trips. Pótó (1989, 79) speculates that this direct observation may have given Mikus a slight edge. The photographs of entries that are included in Pótó's book strongly suggest that the Hungarian sculptors were drawing upon a common stock of familiar Stalin images produced in the Soviet Union. For instance, in a couple of entries (those of Dezső Bokros Biermann and Sándor Ék), Stalin's hand is slipped into his jacket in a Napoleonic gesture reminiscent of Iraklii Toidze's 1943 poster, "Stalin Is Leading Us to Victory," and Naum Karpovskii's "Labor with Martial Perseverance So Your Kolkhoz Becomes Part of the Vanguard!" (reproduced in Bonnell 1997, 272, 276).

Mikus himself describes the process of visual imagination and the importance of Russian films as a source of inspiration in an interview published right after he was awarded the commission: "Since the announcement of the competition for the monument, I've concerned myself with nothing but this theme night and day. Often, during the night, I turned on the lights and drew figures of Stalin, as if, with closed eyes, I saw him in front of me. The lines of his face, the movements of his hand, the way he held his body, rooted themselves into me. In a film about the life of Lenin, Stalin is visible for several minutes. I looked at this film numerous times.

. . . I watched the films, The Battle of Stalingrad, and The Fall of Berlin, in which actors bring the figure of Stalin to life" (G. J. 1950).

THE STALIN MONUMENT AS VISUAL DISCOURSE

Despite Mikus's gifted touch, the Stalin monument could only be considered remarkable from the twisted aesthetics of socialist realism. Swedish art historian Anders Aman calls it "a figure with no artistic authority" (1992, 194). Similarly Prohászka writes that it was "essentially vacant of meaning" (1994, 164). Still, Mikus was awarded the Kossuth Prize, Hungary's highest artistic honor. His contemporaries applauded him for capturing simultaneously the two faces of Stalin: the modest, avuncular mortal who patted small children on the head, and the "mysterious, omniscient, all-powerful" being who "needed only one quality to become God—immortality" (Tertz 1960, 92). Later picked up by other commentators, this reading was initially crafted by Révai when he stated in his inaugural address that Mikus had depicted Stalin as "great in his simplicity and simple in his greatness."

According to Christina Lodder (1993, 17), socialist realist sculpture is marked by "an essential descriptiveness which is reliant for its impact on a stark monumentality combined with a degree of simplification of the figure, and an idealisation of its facial and physical features in accordance with the 'heroic' qualities of socialist man." Stalin's humanity was conveyed by the simplicity of Mikus's composition. The statue is immediately recognizable as a visual descriptor of Stalin, an iconic sign in the Peircean sense. The figure is standing still; the only suggestion of motion is the right arm, which is extended from the elbow. Similarly, the facial expression appears insignificant, devoid of signs that might complicate its claim to referential candor. The modesty and familiarity of the figure's clothing—Stalin's simple trademark military tunic, buttoned up to the chin—further enhance the wise father's humanity. Victoria Bonnell (1997, 252) notes that by the end of the Second World War, Stalin had cast off his plain military tunic in favor of the tailored uniform of an officer, complete with epaulets and insignia. In bronze, however, the only symbol of military rank or decoration is a single medal on the left side of the figure's chest, the Hero's Gold Star of the Soviet Union. The Soviet leader is a vision of serene modesty.

But when we look again, we see the other Stalin, "the infallible leader who stood above other men by virtue of his superhuman powers, iron willpower, and contagious magic" (Bonnell 1997, 254). This is best portrayed by the hands and the head, "the most naturally expressive parts of the human body" (Berger 1969, 141).

STALIN'S HAND: CREATING A DREAM WORLD

The extension of the right hand takes on meaning when we notice the similarity of the gesture to Christian iconography of the Savior. In countless biblical scenes such as Giotto's fresco *Christ Entering Jerusalem* or Rembrandt's etching *Christ Preaching*, Christ is shown with one or both arms extended or lifted as he greets his disciples, instructs the faithful, or entreats the skeptics. In the Rembrandt piece, the Jews of Amsterdam huddle around Christ. Wolfgang Holz uses the term "dream theater" to refer to this device for integrating the viewer into a work of art and notes that it was frequently used in socialist realist painting. In such scenes a central character is surrounded by observers. Viewers of the painting identify with these "doubles" and experience the same emotions they display in the painting: pride, wonder, acclamation, or awe: "Aesthetically manipulated, the viewer thus becomes physically and psychologically part of the 'ideological dream reality'" (Holz 1993, 77).

A number of sculptors who competed for the Stalin commission created such dream theaters by surrounding the central figure with secondary characters—honor guards bearing flags, young people presenting wreaths or flowers, or soldiers marching with rifles and peasants with scythes. In some cases they are free standing, but in others they are carved into friezes on the base or on separate walls. The most intrusive of these secondary characters appears in András Beck's submission. A boy is standing alongside the figure of Stalin. Both are facing forward, slightly turned toward one another, and Stalin's hand appears to be on the boy's shoulder. The leader looks off into the distance while the boy gazes up at his face, reaching toward it in a gesture that suggests he is presenting Stalin to observers as an object of wonder. Beck was not invited to the second round of competitions; evidently, he overshot the mark by placing the secondary figure on the same level and scale as Stalin. Mikus's composition includes sixty-two larger-than-life figures carved in high relief in a limestone pedestal. Completed only after Stalin's death in 1953, the frieze circles the base of the monument and depicts the story of the Soviet army liberating Hungary and the building of socialism.

STALIN'S FACE: MYTH AND MAGIC

Just as the figures on the base draw the observer into the Mikus monument, the absence of inscribed meaning on Stalin's face compels the viewer to fill in the blanks. Prohászka describes the face as sphinxlike. A quick glance reveals nothing, he writes, but if a person looks at it for a long time, he can read anything in the expression (Prohászka 1994, 164). Roland Barthes would argue that the interpretive process is never so free. The bronze face is a metonym for the man, a signifier *designed* to propagate the myth of a Stalinist utopia. According to Barthes, myth hides itself behind the literalness of the sign. Even as it interpellates the listener, mythic speech "suspends itself, turns away and assumes the look of a generality: it stiffens, it makes itself look neutral and innocent" (Barthes 1972, 125). Yet socialist realism refuses this coy stance, brashly proclaiming its ideological work. While the mythology of the Right is "well-fed, sleek, expansive, [and] garrulous," the mythology of the Left is barren: "Whatever it does, there remains about it something stiff and literal, a suggestion of something done to order. . . . In fact, what can be more meagre than the Stalin myth? No inventiveness here, and only a clumsy appropriation: the signifier of the myth . . . is not varied in the least: it is reduced to a litany" (148).

Although the monument was blatant propaganda, it still had the power to convey Stalin's "contagious magic." Its rhetorical force was a product of the "privileging of the eye in the task of political education" that dated back to the Bolshevik revolution: "Visual methods for persuasion and indoctrination appealed to Bolshevik leaders because of the low level of literacy in the country and the strong visual traditions of the Russian people" (Bonnell 1997, 3). This emphasis on the visual in Russian culture grew out of the Eastern Orthodox tradition, where the icon was not simply a representation of a sacred person or object but rather the incarnation of holiness. In other words, both communist ideology and Eastern Orthodox thinking were articulated through symbolic systems in which distinctions between the sign and the referent are absent or at least obscure (Aulich and Sylvestrová 1999, 7–8). Regardless of its cultural fit, the exaggerated attention to visual communication persisted as the Zhdanovian model of revolutionary art was applied in the various people's republics. The formula issued from the Kremlin was ill suited indeed to postwar Hungary, where the literacy rate was over 90 percent, where Roman Catholicism and Reform Protestantism were the dominant religions, and where poetry had long held pride of place in the cultural pantheon.

In any case, likenesses of Stalin were designed to do more than represent the authority commanded by the leader of the Soviet Communist Party. They were to function as totems, to be experienced not analytically but directly as the instantiation of obedience and submission. Katalin Sinkó (1992, 81) writes, "Stalin statues were not 'statues' in the Western, secularized and artistic sense of the term; instead they were cultic objects which served to introduce the great man's mystical presence." In 1952, before disillusion led communist writers to split with the party, Tamás Aczél offered a "proper" reading of the monument: "Until now, Stalin *was* with us. From now on, he *is* with us. With his eyes, he watches our work; with his smile, he lights our path. . . . Up until now we have consulted his writings for advice; now we will go to him and personally 'discuss' what we must do; we'll tell him about our difficulties and our joys. And it is certain that the father and protector of our peace will never deny us his counsel" (1952).

Cast in bronze, this relationship was projected into an infinite future. But Berger raises an interesting point when he argues that, precisely because of their enduring nature, statues—as opposed to, say, posters or flyers—are inherently unsuited for propaganda purposes: "Works which are intended to have a long-term effect need to be far more complex and to embrace contradictions. It is the existence of these contradictions which may enable them to survive" (Berger 1969, 55).

With little subtlety to recommend it, the Stalin statue soon became the primary symbol of an alien ideology. The monument lost any pretense to inspirational or seductive power as the Stalin era came to an end. Indeed, to a disillusioned public, it embodied the nation's humiliating surrender of cultural and political sovereignty to a foreign power. Following Khrushchev's criticism of the cult of personality in early 1956, Hungarian authorities began to discuss the removal of all symbolic references to Stalin, including the monument. But before this could happen, history took its own course as the events of October unfolded.

THE LEGEND OF THE MONUMENT

Some two hundred thousand Hungarians left the country after the suppression of the 1956 uprising. Over the years, exiled writers and historians produced scores of monographs about the events of that revolt, peppered with descriptions of the dramatic scene surrounding the destruction of the Stalin monument (see, e.g., Méray 1969, 238–40; Molnár 1968, 128; Váli 1961, 268). In Hungary itself, totalitarian practices of concealing political developments through complete silence or the use of absurd Orwellian inversions softened after order was restored. But certain topics—chief among them the 1956 uprising—could still be broached only with great circumspection, following the party line. For example, a history of the Hungarian workers' movement that appeared in a series of historical picture books describes Imre Nagy as a traitor and, in both photographs and text, emphasizes the shameful behavior of the "counter-revolutionaries"—the burning of books as well as the seizure of the Budapest Communist Party Headquarters and the lynching of its guards (Blaskovits 1978, 123–25). Such publications, designed for popular audiences, are silent on the matter of the Stalin statue, but references to it do appear in more specialized texts. Rezső Szíj's 1977 study of Mikus, for example, includes a page about the competition and Mikus's creation, although it is telling that Szíj has little to say about the mediocre artistic quality of the statue itself, concentrating instead on the reliefs. About the destruction of the monument, he writes only: "The Stalin statue was toppled in the fall of 1956. Some people say it was the only good statue of Stalin" (Szíj 1977, 8).

Still, visible traces of the absent Stalin endured for many years. The iron-reinforced concrete base was left intact and continued to serve as a reviewing stand. The ghostly presence of the demolished monument was a constant reminder of the euphoric act of iconoclasm, pure in its bloodlessness, majestic in its audacity. The base was finally dismantled in 1990. By that time the "counter-revolution" had been redesignated first as a popular uprising, then, according to the 1990 Law on the Memory of the Revolution, as a revolution and freedom struggle. The story of the Stalin statue is prominent in the discursive revisions that have ensued, as the following examples show.

In 1989 Miklós Ómolnár published a collection of documents related to the revolution and descriptions of events by those who witnessed or participated in them. Several of these personal stories include references to the toppling of the Stalin statue. Aurel Molnár, a retired Magyar Radio reporter, remembers hearing about the destruction of the monument from his children when he returned home the night of the twenty-third: "Jaj, if only I'd known, I would have gone over there! Because when Comrade Révai unveiled it, I gave the introductory speech! So beautifully, according to a lot of people, that tears came to their eyes. . . . Of course, I would gladly have watched how they toppled to dust the colossus that I helped inaugurate" (Ómolnár 1989, 79). Writer Tamás Aczél mentions the statue in his 1994 account of the reestablishment in exile of *Irodalmi Újság*: "At the time of my escape, it turned out that I'd brought with me in my little suitcase not only some worn shirts, underwear, and socks, but the Stalin statue's *nose*, which I then sold to an American millionaire for thousands of dollars. I lived high off the hog in Vienna with that money" (Aczél 1994, 79).

Népszabadság, Hungary's leading newspaper, ran a piece on the fortieth anniversary of the revolution. It consisted of recollections distilled from oral histories collected by the 1956 Institute, including several eyewitness accounts of the scene at Procession Square. From Ferdinand Szabó, a civil servant in 1956: "An incredible crowd was at the Stalin statue. I was standing on the steps of the builders' headquarters [across the street]. The crowd yelled, 'Let's take it down, let's topple it!' Twenty-five or thirty trucks showed up, and they attached winch cables to Stalin's neck. A signal was given and they took off, but they didn't take into account that this was a massive statue, so that every one of the trucks' back ends were lifted up. Then somebody shouted, 'Let's do it!' In minutes, forty or fifty people had climbed up on cars. It was impossible to pull them down. They brought a blowtorch from somewhere. They cut around the two legs under the knees. It fell to the railing, from there it spun around once, and then plunged to the ground. Everybody who could get close to it spat on it and kicked it." From Gábor Karátson, a law student: "It took a long time to topple the Stalin statue. It was really hard to bring it down. The people were really funny. It had a great impact on me when they shouted, 'Hang in there, Joey!' This was absolutely not a Stalinist shout, but a kind of folksy sport, that no matter how big he was, he was alone, while there were a lot of us to make sure he kept up the effort. Meanwhile, the star from the Trade Union building was also torn off. When the statue came crashing down, we sang, 'The villain has died, the ugly feud is over.'[5] The crowd sang this very quickly, it had an interesting operatic effect." And from Tamás Mikes, a student: "This was the story of Gulliver and the Lilliputians. They tugged at that carcass up there with every possible kind of tool, and it still wouldn't move, until somebody realized it would have to be cut off at the boots with a blowtorch. This was beautiful. It had already gotten a little bit dark, and the sparks flew all the way to the edge of the boots. The large numbers of little people finally brought the big piece of garbage to the ground. This was the moment

The toppled monument to Stalin surrounded by curious onlookers, 1956. Courtesy 1956 Institute and Hungarian National Museum

when—it's a terrible phrase and I never want to say it again, but really—I felt the majesty of the people" (in Hegedűs and Kőrösi 1996).

As these examples show, narratives about the statue's fall are laced with irony: the radio announcer who laments missing the spectacular destruction of the idol he himself had extolled; the gifted writer who once gave his soul to communism and then sold the nose of its personification for U.S. dollars. The scene is recounted through language that is highly metaphoric, with its references to Gulliver and the Lilliputians, and highly visual, with its images of fiery sparks flying against the clear, black October night. Such recollections are reinforced by the discourse of black-and-white photographs that have been brought out of hiding and are now widely reproduced and circulated as dominant forms of post-communist iconography (see, e.g., Jobbágyi 1998; Bayer 2000). Images that have achieved iconic status include antlike figures scaling the statue on ladders made of matchsticks; the massive, severed head lying ignominiously in the street; the gigantic boots, all that remained of the statue, with twisted reinforcing steel jutting awkwardly out of their tops.

The images of the empty boots are particularly evocative. As Nóra Aradi explains (1974, 60–61), the boot was a motif frequently used in socialist iconography to represent the brutal repression of a people by force, either internal or external. While it was associated throughout Europe with militarism, particularly the goosestep of fascists, in Hungary it also resonated with feudal images of the barefoot peasant who lived at the mercy of the boot-wearing landlord. The intensity of the symbol is demonstrated in Gyula Derkovits's 1930 painting, *For Bread* (*Kenyérért*). This graphic indictment of the white terror that followed the suppression of the 1919 Hungarian Soviet Republic depicts the upper torso and head of a slain worker lying in a snow-covered street. Next to the head is a pair of boots and the butt of a rifle, unmistakable signifiers of authoritarian violence.

The rhetorical force of the Stalin statue's boots was further exaggerated by a piece of lore that still circulates. Regnum Marianum, a Roman Catholic church, was built in Budapest's City Park in 1931 as an expression of the Horthy regime's gratitude for the crushing of the Hungarian Soviet Republic. One of the most beautiful churches in the city, Regnum Marianum stood on the site selected for Procession Square and was unceremoniously leveled in August, 1951. Popular belief claims that Stalin's bronze boots stood on the very spot where the alter had been. (Pótó reports that the statue was actually erected some 150–200 yards from the church site, but the story is still spun today.) In 1992 the fathers of Reg-

The Stalin monument's head, with the twisted cables that pulled it down still visible around the neck. Courtesy 1956 Institute and Hungarian National Museum

Protesters chip away at the Stalin monument's empty boots. Courtesy 1956 Institute and Hungarian National Museum

num Marianum marked the site with a simple crucifix and sign on which was written, "Here stood the Regnum Marianum Church. Mátyás Rákosi destroyed it in 1951."[6]

What is most striking about the narratives is how the visual imagery illuminates the courage and will to freedom that motivated the destruction of the monument. The memory of that episode takes on an epideictic quality as the spectator-story tellers position themselves among the crowd and bear witness to the collective experience of jubilation and autonomous action. Rosenfield insists that "epideictic" is concerned with the *acknowledgment* of goodness, not its assessment or evaluation. Appealing to Pericles, he writes that "no one could award the Athenians an 'A' for courage; rather, their courage would make a claim on men's respect for all time" (Rosenfield 1980, 135). The intoxicating moment when the monument was brought crashing to the ground would make such a claim in the mind's eye during the dark days of terror and the monotonous years that followed. It would be resurrected openly and joyously when the old regime crumbled, enveloping the public in memories of resistance to tyranny.

The ultimate fate of the Stalin statue and its place in the history of Hungarian national mythology is captured in a story László Prohászka tells (1994, 167). Actor Sándor Pécsi, an art collector, was able to secure the right hand of the fallen idol and take it home with the help of an entrepreneurial taxi driver. When the Soviets crushed the revolution, he buried the historic bronze object in his garden, where it lay hidden for thirty-five years. In 1991 his widow sold it to the Contemporary History Museum for forty thousand forints (roughly five hundred dollars). In the panoptics of power, the relationship between viewer and viewed was

Gyula Derkovits, *For Bread* (1930). Courtesy Hungarian National Gallery

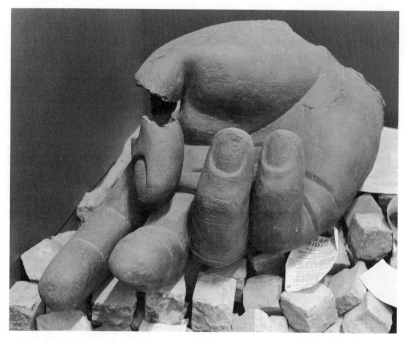

The Stalin monument's hand, buried for decades, is now on display in the Hungarian National Museum. Photograph by Zsolt Bátori

finally turned on its head, as fragments of the iconographic stand-in for an all-knowing, all-seeing dictator became objects of morbid curiosity for the citizens who were once his target. But then, the story of the Stalin monument has been one of multidirectional gazes.

Of the students' lists of demands that sparked the revolution, other symbolic points would be quietly addressed during the years of Kádárian appeasement. The communist star on the coat-of-arms would be shrunk; the calendar of holidays would be revised. But the most potent symbol of the regime had been destroyed at the hands of the people, an event that endures in Hungary's collective memory. If socialist realism loomed large in its physical scale and in its ability to inspire terror, the destruction of its epitome by a people armed only with the tools of their trade is a powerful narrative indeed. The humiliation and physical suffering inflicted on Hungarians during the period of reprisals was (bitter)sweetened by the memory of this mythic event. And when the end of the long revolution finally came, the memories would come out of hiding as objects to behold, just like Pécsi's Stalin hand.

CHAPTER THREE

MEMORIAL TO THE MARTYRS OF THE COUNTER-REVOLUTION

IN KEEPING WITH the Kádár regime's efforts to suppress memories of the 1956 uprising, relatively few monuments to the "counter-revolution" were erected during the communist years. The main exception is Viktor Kalló's *Memorial to the Martyrs of the Counter-Revolution* (also known as the Martyrs Monument).[1] Reflecting the dimensions and rhetorical overstatement of socialist realism, it is a colossal bronze statue of a mortally wounded worker reaching for the sky in a final gesture of victory as he falls to the ground. Banished to the Statue Park Museum after the collapse of communism, the monument stood for more than thirty years in Republic Square (Köztársaság tér) in Budapest's Eighth District, a major area of resistance in 1956.

Today Republic Square is a quiet park known mainly as the site of the Erkel Theater. But more-disturbing associations dating back to the revolution cast their shadows. On October 30, 1956, armed insurgents besieged the headquarters of the Communist Party's municipal branch, located across the street from the theater. The building had been defended by state-security police—the hated ÁVO—and rumor had it that prisoners had been languishing for years in secret underground prison cells. During the course of the fighting, a number of the building's occupants were shot in cold blood or beaten to death as they attempted to surrender or escape. Several police and military personnel were hanged on the spot, and their bodies were mutilated. Following the siege, excavators were brought in and the square was dug up, but no trace of an underground prison was uncovered. Republic Square was the scene of the revolutionaries' most reprehensible actions in the thirteen days of the uprising.

But by the mid-1970s, the episode had faded from public discourse. The foreword to a book published in 1974 on the siege of the party building and the violence that ensued notes that the events had been largely

Viktor Kalló's *Memorial to the Martyrs of the Counter-Revolution* (1960). Photograph by Zsolt Bátori. Courtesy http://www.szoborpark.hu

forgotten, their memory preserved only through the iconographic work of Kalló's monument: "If we were to stand today in Republic Square and go into the party building, we wouldn't encounter a single trace of what happened here on October 30, 1956. Looking out the window of the Party headquarters, we're met with the familiar image of the wooded square's peaceful atmosphere. The only reminder of what happened on that late October day is the statue that stands in front of the party building, the figure of a fatally wounded worker, collapsing but raising his powerful fist in a final show of strength" (Katona 1974, 7–8).

As virtually the only public memento of October 30, 1956, *Memorial to the Martyrs of the Counter-Revolution* shouldered a heavy rhetorical responsibility. But what was the nature of this responsibility if the party's aim was the obliteration of the memory of 1956? The Martyrs Monument embodied a narrative that was generated in various public discursive spaces long before the bronze was cast. This discourse was replete with images and metaphors of the body, which were then amalgamated into the work. There they exercised a disciplinary function in the Foucauldian sense. With the suspension of the terror that had been enacted in the form of imprisonments, show trials, and executions, the state could now exercise social control through the microphysics of power. And Kalló's monument would blend into the landscape as one more barely noticed apparatus of control.

Now enjoying retirement in the Statue Park, the Martyrs Monument amuses foreign visitors who have no idea what prompted its histrionic pose. But remnants of its earlier life can still be seen in Republic Square in the form of a rectangular platform about sixty feet long and twenty feet wide. Spray-painted with graffiti, it appears to be the foundation of a razed building. On closer inspection, however, one finds that the sides of this curious structure are faced with marble, now chipped off in places. A small inscription framed with stars appears on one end: "In memory of the martyrs who fell for the freedom of the Hungarian working people" (A magyar dolgozó nép szabadságáért elesett mártírok emlékére). This is the pedestal of Kalló's monument, left behind and forgotten when the "counter-revolution" was renamed and the monument to its communist victims was removed.

The purity of the revolution was a point of pride during the uprising itself, and it has taken on the character of a central myth in the post-

A postcard sold at the Statue Park Museum takes a playful spin on Kalló's martyr. Courtesy http://www.szoborpark.hu

The empty pedestal in Budapest's Republic Square where the Martyrs Monument stood for thirty years. The building behind it is the former headquarters of the Budapest Communist Party. Photograph by Zsolt Bátori

communist rehabilitation of 1956 (Litván 2000, 208). With national sovereignty as a rallying point, Hungarians experienced a deep sense of solidarity and national honor during the thirteen days of the uprising. A small country with limited resources had faced off against a superpower bent on world domination, and they had pursued this cause with a standard of honor and integrity seldom experienced in peacetime. Vignettes in the revolutionary press already attested to the honor of citizen and insurgent alike, laying the foundations for the myth: Large boxes with signs appealing for donations to help the families of victims appeared on city streets. Filled with cash, they stood unguarded and untouched. Jewelry, watches, and other valuables lay there for the taking in shattered shop windows, but no one touched them. And at night, hungry freedom fighters foraged food from grocery stores, leaving lists of what they had taken along with the payment they figured was due. These scenes have been described in countless retellings, and photographs of the cash boxes with their handmade signs are frequently exhibited as visual evidence of the uprising's nobility.

The massacres in Republic Square were immediately denounced by the various revolutionary groups at the time. Indeed, later accounts of the events emphasize the dismay felt not only by bystanders but also by armed insurgents themselves as they witnessed a scene of fighting gone out of control. Evidently, there were numerous efforts to restrain the frenzied mobs, some successful and some not. Gergely Pongrátz, commander of one of the rebel groups, writes about trying in vain to dissuade a group that was "out for blood" from lining up security police against a wall and shooting them. He intervened, "not because I was protecting the ÁVOs, but rather, the revolution, so that they not be allowed to sully it with these executions" (1982, 136).

Despite such protests, Republic Square is the black eye of the uprising. The events were central to the communists' master narrative of the "counter-revolution" propagated in its aftermath and were used to support their contention that the revolt was the work of "hooligans" and "prostitutes" cheered on by the West. Moreover, the mob violence was waved about as evidence that the situation in Hungary had gotten out of control and that responsible authorities had had no choice but to appeal

The inscription on the empty pedestal in Republic Square is still visible. It reads, "In memory of the martyrs who fell for the freedom of the Hungarian working people." Photograph by Zsolt Bátori

to the Soviet Union for help. Finally, the atrocities were used to justify the brutal reprisals exercised against "common criminals" and "white terrorists" that followed the "restoration of order."

Postcommunist accounts of the revolution are burdened by the weight of the communist master narrative, which unfolds along a trajectory that moves swiftly from heated demands that the killings never be forgotten to near silence. Hungarian Radio ran a series of broadcasts early in 1957 called "What Happened in Hungary between October 23 and November 4, 1956?" that included an installment describing the "merciless bloodbath" at Republic Square (Hungarian Radio 1957). *Népszabadság* printed stories about the exhumation and identification of the bodies of hastily buried secret police who had been killed in the siege, with grim descriptions of family members recognizing the remnants of a familiar article of clothing (B. T. 1957). But as György Litván writes, "This smear campaign . . . lasted for only a short period, then gave way to the tactic of concealment that continued for decades" (1996, 161). Following the path from the initial decision to build a monument to its unveiling three years later, one sees the rhetoric surrounding Republic Square turn stone cold. Scholars have argued about the extent of the "collective amnesia" experienced after 1956, and an analysis provides some evidence about the early stages of state-directed forgetting.

MARCH 29, 1957

In the spring of 1957, as the government began to crank out the death sentences, György Marosán, a member of the Hungarian Politburo and a strong advocate of reprisals, signaled the party's intention to erect a monument in Republic Square. The occasion was a public assembly at the site on March 29, 1957, that drew some fifty thousand people. This gathering was the largest of four held simultaneously in various locations throughout the city.

The purpose behind these meetings stemmed from Hungary's major national holiday, March 15, the anniversary of the outbreak of the 1848 revolution. As Martha Lampland points out (1990, 189), the 1956 revolutionaries drew heavily from the stock of national imagery associated with that earlier struggle for national sovereignty, pinning the red, white, and green cockades of 1848 on their jackets; painting the Kossuth crest on their military equipment; and drawing inspiration from the fiery poetry of Sándor Petőfi. The demands that sparked the 1956 uprising were explicitly modeled on a twelve-point manifesto issued March 15, 1848. And Hungarians had not forgotten that this earlier revolution was crushed only when the Russian tsar intervened on behalf of the Austrians.

In addition, a movement to revive the revolution had been afoot under the slogan MUK (Márciusban újra kezdjük!), "In March We Start Again!" According to Litván (1996, 114), the slogan was a last sign of resistance but not backed by any real threat or serious organization. Nevertheless, authorities were fearful about what might happen on March 15 and took special precautions to control activities, ordering that any mass demonstrations not officially sanctioned be considered oppositional provocation and "be liquidated with an iron hand" (Pozsonyi 1998).

When the date passed without incident, the assemblies were organized to demonstrate that the Communist Party now had the sole authority to mobilize the masses.[2] At Republic Square, Marosán conveyed the party's message, leaving no doubt about who had the power to determine the meanings associated with the site. In doing so, he employed language that was redolent with images of the body: "We organized today's assembly in this place because we want to engrave this square, this building, these trees, in everybody's mind. Look at the walls! They cry tears of blood. The true people's youngsters and elders, the real Hungarians and communists, were murdered among these trees. Look at the trees! Never forget that the mercenaries of the cultured, free West hung the loyal people and the communists by their legs in the name of freedom" (Geréb and Hajdú 1986, 217).

Then, addressing the city council, Marosán directed them to see to it that a monument proclaiming the memory of the communist heroes be erected in the square. Two days later the council and the Ministry of Culture announced a competition for a memorial that would, in the incendiary language of the newspaper article, "eternalize the memories of the heroic communist martyrs murdered by the counter-revolutionaries" (MTI 1957). Thus began the work of distilling memories of the bloody scene, with its grotesque images of bodies swinging from trees, into the form of a monument.

VIKTOR KALLÓ

The competition drew thirty-two entries, and the jury selected the model submitted by Viktor Kalló. In interviews the sculptor has said that his emotional response to the events in Republic Square grew out of his social background ("Én is" 1959; Lóska 1980; Ujvári 1978). As was the case with Sándor Mikus, Kalló grew up poor. He was born in 1931 at Babócsa, a tiny village near the Yugoslav border. Abandoned by his parents, he was raised by his grandmother, described in his official biography as a caring and literate woman, "from whom he first heard of Lenin" as she read to him as a child (Ujvári 1978, 6). Upon completion of elementary school, Kalló was forced to quit school and go to work. He held a series of jobs as an unskilled laborer, eventually becoming apprenticed to an ironsmith in Pécs, where he discovered his artistic interests and talent while working with metals. Kalló enrolled in evening art classes, and in 1950 his drawings, part of an exhibit of students' work, caught the attention of talent scouts. Through their encouragement, he applied and was accepted to the Fine Arts Academy in Budapest, where he studied from 1950 to 1956.

By virtue of his social background and temperament, Kalló accommodated official expectations about the relationship between art and politics with little difficulty (Andrási et al. 1999, 147–48). The educational policies of the early 1950s dictated that people from peasant and working-class backgrounds would be given preference in admissions. Thus, like the majority of his classmates, Kalló had had virtually no exposure to the world of art and high culture prior to enrolling in the academy: "I had to start completely from zero. We were nurtured and taught along the lines of socialist realism, and we believed all of it" (Lóska 1980, 24). He emphasizes that his sense of aesthetic responsibility grew out of his class position and genuine commitment to socialist ideals: "I belong to the people, politically, professionally, I got everything from them. . . . I'd like to express thanks through my work that I'm not making windows for stables. I'd like to return that trust with which they lifted me up, nourished me, taught me" (27).

In September, 1956, Kalló was drafted into the army. He was stationed in southern Hungary at the time of the uprising and had little direct contact with the events. But in interviews he has described how his experiences compelled him to express his anguish in the language of sculpture:

When the armed disturbances erupted, I was a soldier in Nagyatád. I didn't know much about anything, but I did know I had this system to thank for everything. Like others, we were in favor of a reckoning of the mistakes [committed during the Stalinist years], but we were also very much afraid that the whole thing was going to be lost.

In November of '56, I was assigned the duty of transporting a load of fish to Budapest. I came up on the 1st, I was here on the 2nd, and

I went back on the 3rd. While I was here, I went over to Republic Square and I saw terrible things. The dead were no longer there, but everything had been ravaged. The spectacle was so disturbing that immediately after my discharge I started to sculpt. (Lóska 1980, 24)

Kalló's monument would be erected in the fall of 1960. In the meantime a marble plaque was unveiled on the wall of the party headquarters on October 30, 1957, the first anniversary of the siege. This occasion established a pattern for annual wreath-laying ceremonies commemorating those who had lost their lives "defending the proletarian dictatorship" in 1956. The selection of Republic Square as the site for these rituals and October 30 as the date affirmed the communists' contention that the aim of the uprising was to savagely destroy all that the nation had accomplished since World War II and to engulf the people's democracy in a wave of white terror. In subsequent years this annual rite would become increasingly subdued, but in 1957 it was the occasion for a major assembly that well illustrates the active, intense phase of cultural management and directed public remembering following the revolution.

OCTOBER 30, 1957

The Republic Square ceremony on October 30, 1957, followed the usual contours of the closely scripted, carefully rehearsed mass spectacle that marked the celebration of all major public holidays in communist societies. Not unlike bringing up the stage lights to signal the beginning of a play, floodlights illuminating the square were turned on at 5:00 P.M. According to the press report, a quarter of a million workers from factories, offices, and institutions—old hands at demonstrating revolutionary zeal—streamed in from throughout the city. As loudspeakers carried the sounds of workers' movement songs to the far reaches of the plaza, crowds formed "impromptu" recitation choruses, chanting revolutionary slogans. The leading cast of party and state leaders assembled on the decorated platform, backed by a large sign reading "Strengthen the Party, Protect the Workers' Power."

They were joined by some of the surviving defenders of the building and by the widows and widower of the higher-ranking military and party officials who died in the siege. By now the public was well acquainted with the victims' names and the dreadful stories of their deaths: Imre Mező, veteran of the Spanish Civil War and the French Resistance and sympathizer of Imre Nagy's revolutionary government, shot after he exited the party headquarters waving a white flag; army colonel János Asztalos, the "nameless officer" whose remains were difficult to identify because, when his body was exhumed, it had no face; army colonel József Papp, shot in the head, hung by his feet from a lamppost, doused with gasoline, and set afire; Éva Kállai, mother of three, who died in April, 1957, from injuries sustained when she tried to escape the insurgents by jumping out of a third-story window (Hollós and Lajtai 1974, 178, 321; Hungarian Radio 1957). A marble plaque, inscribed in gold letters with the names of the fallen, was unveiled by Mrs. József Csikesz, a Budapest Party Committee secretary.

But the main event was an address delivered by Marosán, in which he described the events of October 30, and condemned the "counter-revolutionaries" in the strongest possible terms. Organized fighting had ended within days of the Soviet invasion on November 4, but resistance continued for a couple of months, mainly in the form of strikes organized by workers' councils formed during the uprising. In response the government issued decrees in January, 1957, invoking the death penalty for refusal to work and for virtually all other forms of critical expression (Litván 1996, 113). By the spring of 1957, the prisons were choked with people charged with participating in the revolt. Resistance had thus crumbled by the time of Marosán's speech, but he nevertheless emphasized national unity and left no doubt about the fate of dissenters: "We have gathered together not to mourn, but to strengthen our resolve, not to celebrate the anniversary, but to commemorate the anniversary. We have come together as one to make a pledge: *If necessary, with fire and iron, if necessary, with the spilling of blood, we will prevent the shame of October 23rd and the treachery of October 30th from ever again being repeated. This we swear!*" ("Begyógyítjuk" 1957). He described the events of October 30 as a premeditated conspiracy masterminded by Imre Nagy: "*For days before the attack*, the counter-revolutionaries' packs of fascist hounds and gangs of riff-raff prowled around the building. It had become common knowledge before October 30th that *the cease-fire announced by Imre Nagy was designed to advance the interests of the counter-revolutionaries*, because the counter-revolutionaries did not comply with the cease-fire" ("Begyógyítjuk" 1957).

By this point Kádár had evidently cut a deal with the Kremlin. Rákosi and his Stalinist clique, who represented the greatest threats to Kádár's shaky political footing, would remain "guests" of the Soviet Union. In return Kádár would show no mercy in dealing with Nagy, thus demonstrating to all Soviet allies that any breach in the unity and discipline of the socialist camp was intolerable (Dornbach 1994, 164, 172). Nagy was now held in solitary confinement in Budapest's Gyorskocsi Prison; less than three months later he would be indicted for initiating and leading a conspiracy aimed at subverting the state and for treason. While the public would only learn about the fate of Nagy and his colleagues with the announcement of their executions in the summer of 1958, the Communist Party's propaganda apparatus was already positioning the men as scapegoats. Marosán assailed them as traitors who had known in advance of plans to attack the party headquarters but had made no attempts to avert the assault. Instead, they first had placed weapons in the hands of the "underworld deposits of scum" and then had left the heroic defenders of the building in the lurch, doomed to die ("Begyógyítjuk" 1957).

Marosán hammered relentlessly at the themes of remembrance and retribution, furiously rejecting calls for clemency: *"we will never forget what happened a year ago here in this square, in the streets of this city, in the country.* We will not forget, and for this reason we are seized with anger when here at home and in the cultured West the instigators, direct supporters, and counter-revolutionary agents provocateur insolently dare to demand amnesty for the murderers and gangs. We've said it before and we'll say it again emphatically: . . . *those whose hands are bloody and those who inspired the counter-revolution belong on the bench of the accused. The force of the law will thunder down on them in proportion to their crimes"* ("Begyógyítjuk" 1957).

Judging from the newspaper accounts, the October 30 ceremonies in Republic Square in both 1958 and 1959 were much more modest affairs. A short article in 1958, titled "Budapest Workers Recall with Devotion the Martyrs of the 1956 Counter-Revolutionary Attack" and accompanied by a photograph of people laying wreaths beneath the marble plaque, states that hundreds of workers as well as representatives of the Communist Youth Alliance and the Young Pioneers gathered at party headquarters to commemorate the martyrs. Meanwhile, Marosán and other Communist Party leaders marked the occasion in a less public spot, laying wreaths at Imre Mező's grave in Budapest's Kerepesi Cemetery. A similar news item appeared in 1959. This time, though, the story was not illustrated, indicating a further diminishment of public attention placed on the "counter-revolution" ("Budapest Dolgozói" 1959; MTI 1958).

The period of mass retaliation lasted from April, 1957, when police arrested a great number of people, until the spring of 1959, when a partial amnesty was announced (Rainer 1999b, 251). During these years, Kádár gradually consolidated his power, and the more secure he felt, the less repressive his regime became. Only a handful of people condemned to death in political trials for their role in the uprising were executed after 1959 (Szakolczai 1994). A general amnesty in 1963 freed most of those who had been imprisoned, including those with life sentences. Thus, by the time the monument was unveiled in October, 1960, the reign of terror had subsided significantly. This shifting climate had important consequences for how the *Memorial to the Martyrs of the Counter-Revolution* would be inscribed and how it would be presented to the Hungarian public.

INSCRIBING THE MONUMENT

The reading of visual displays is reigned in and channeled through the text that accompanies them—the captions of photographs, the explanatory panels of museum displays, the titles of paintings, and the inscriptions on monuments. Given the didactic function of socialist art, the matter of text was not to be taken lightly,[3] and the inscription for the Martyrs Monument was an unsettled question up to the last minute. As originally conceived, the memorial was to be tied exclusively to the "counterrevolution." Evidently, Communist Party officials began to rethink its referential scope as the thunderous commands to remember quieted down to an occasional distant rumble. Gyula Kállai, a member of the Politburo, suggested at a meeting of that body on July 29, 1958, that the Republic Square monument should commemorate comrades who fell in 1919, in the period between the world wars, in the Second World War, and in the 1956 counter-revolution (Boros 1997, 11).

Even more revealing is a letter dated August 24, 1960, from József Moharos, the head of the Cultural Department of the Budapest City Council, to János Hantos, leader of the Cultural and Education Department of the Communist Party's Budapest Committee. Written just a couple of months before the monument's scheduled unveiling, the purpose of the letter was to prod the party committee to come to a decision about the inscription. In doing so, Moharos reveals how official opinions had shifted over time: "The original conception for the establishment of a monument in Republic Square was that it would eternalize the memories of the heroic martyrs who fell during the siege of the party building. Later, in different periods, different opinions could be heard, suggesting that the monument in Republic Square should perpetuate not just the memory of our 1956 martyrs, but more generally, the memories of the heroes and martyrs who fell in the struggles against counter-revolution in the working-class movement. We have not gotten information about how this issue was settled through either a party decision or other directive" (Moharos 1960). He then offered six possible inscriptions. Three of his suggestions were broadly worded, with no references to any particular historical episodes, along the lines of "Honor to the heroes who sacrificed their lives for the freedom of the Hungarian people and for the cause of peace and socialism." The other three referred to "1956"—"the heroes who sacrificed their lives in 1956," "the heroes who died a martyr's death in 1956," "the heroic martyrs who fell in 1956"—but in no case was the "counter-revolution" explicitly named.

The Communist Party's delay in reaching a decision about the inscription prompted a similar letter from Lajos Skoda, the architect who actually constructed the monument. He offered three proposals. His first suggestion was for the words "In memory of the communists who fell for the liberation and freedom of the Hungarian working people" to be inscribed on the front wall of the pedestal. His second built upon the first, adding the names of those killed in smaller letters on the sides of the pedestal. Skoda's third option was to use a couple of appropriate lines from some communist poet (Skoda n.d.).

The inscription ultimately chosen—"In memory of the martyrs who fell for the freedom of the Hungarian working people"—was terser than any of the lines suggested by Moharos or Skoda. It most closely resembles the architect's first suggestion, but with two important differences: the reference to Hungary's *liberation,* saturated with connotations of the Soviet army's intervention in both 1945 and 1956, was excised, and the reference to "communists" was changed to the much less ideologically charged term "martyrs." Thus, not only was no mention made of "1956," itself a euphemistic metonym for the "counter-revolution," but even the words "liberation" and "communists" were rejected. Furthermore, the names of those killed in the siege were not listed, another indication that authorities wanted to avoid direct reminders of the uprising.[4]

While these delays and the indecision about the inscription might be chalked up to bureaucratic inertia, they provide one more piece of evidence about the shift toward repressing memories of the uprising. A monument originally proposed, to use the fiery words of the headline announcing the competition in 1957, to "eternalize the memories of those murdered by the counter-revolutionaries" had become something far more muted.

UNVEILING THE MONUMENT

The *Memorial to the Martyrs of the Counter-Revolution* was unveiled on October 30, 1960, the fourth anniversary of the siege. The annual commemorative ritual that had made front-page news when the marble plaque was dedicated three years earlier was now given much shorter coverage on the inside pages. A *Népszabadság* article described the event with the innocuous headline "Monument of Heroes Who Fell for Hungarian Freedom Inaugurated in Republic Square." Readers learned that participants in the ceremony included representatives of the party, the government, the armed forces, and various social and workplace organizations. The main address was given by Sándor Gáspár, a deputy member of the Hungarian Politburo and the first secretary of the Budapest Party Committee. At least as reflected in the press account, the speech was noteworthy only in the absence of any references to 1956. "The chronicle of the history of the Hungarian workers' movement records many victims and much bereavement," Gáspár said. Referring to the repressive years when the Communist Party was illegal and its members were persecuted, he continued: "Over the course of a long period of time, our working class could only mourn but not bury its own dead. Now, in our free homeland, this monument proclaims the glory of those who sacrificed their lives for national honor, for workers' power, and for the independence of our homeland" ("A Magyar Szabadságért" 1960).

When the sheet covering the monument was dropped, it revealed—in the words of *Népszabadság*—a figure that faithfully expresses the message that the monument is intended to convey: *"they can kill the fighter but his ideas are victorious."* The newspaper was merely advancing the party line in its semiotic assessment of the monument as a vision of proletarian victory rising from the blood of the martyr (as discussed below). But what is most remarkable about the press account is that it contains only one reference to the "counter-revolution," which is buried at the end of the story. The context is a lengthy list of the names of people who laid wreaths and the organizations they represented, running the gamut from the Central Committee of the Communist Party to the Partisan League to the Communist Youth Alliance. The sole mention of 1956 appears at the end of the list of sixteen names: "Then, on behalf of the families of the victims of the 1956 counter-revolution, Mrs. Imre Mező and Miklós Szántó [widower of Éva Kállai] placed wreaths, and representatives of the city's factories, institutions, and citizens placed flowers on the monument" ("A Magyar Szabadságért" 1960).

With a generic inscription and inauguration, what had become of the monument's responsibility to express anger and indignation? What were its rhetorical responsibilities, and how was it expected to perform them? The answers are found by examining the monument itself.

SOCIALIST REALISM AND THE BODY

The political thaw that followed the death of Stalin in 1953 was mirrored in the arts, and by the time Viktor Kalló completed his training in 1956, painters and sculptors were experimenting with new (or recovered) modes of expression (Andrási et al. 1999, 140; Ujvári 1978, 5). Yet the stiff, iconographic political monument was still dominant, and Kalló was aware that he was departing from official expectations as he began work on the statue. He claims that he was warned that the design would never be selected but that he ignored the advice, working instinctively and giving free rein to his own creative impulses (Lóska 1980, 24–25).

The result was a monument that is undeniably more subjective, expressive, and dynamic than Sándor Mikus's Stalin. While the only hint of movement in the Stalin statue was the extended right arm, the martyr is all motion, with his head thrown back, his knees buckling, his left arm stretched overhead, and his right arm extended from the shoulder. A deep, oblique fold in the figure's clothing stretches from his left arm to his right thigh, suggesting that he has been thrown off balance and is falling to the left. And while Stalin's face confronted his worshipers directly, demanding their awe, wonder, and terror, the angle of the martyr's head makes his facial expression resistant to reading. The effect is that the figure appears more distant to the viewer, less approachable, ironically, than the steely autocrat with his magnetic, enigmatic gaze. Finally, the martyr's clothing—unlike Stalin's instantly recognizable military uniform—is indistinct, suggestive perhaps of a worker's tunic.

Nevertheless, Kalló's figure still adheres to the features of socialist realist statuary in the "classic" sense. Thematically it represents the struggle against the reactionary enemies of the socialist project, and sty-

With his head thrown back and his knees buckling, Viktor Kalló's martyr is captured motion. Photograph by Zsolt Bátori. Courtesy http://www.szoborpark.hu

listically it meets Christina Lodder's specifications: "an essential descriptiveness which is reliant for its impact on a stark monumentality" (1993, 17). Kalló notes that he originally planned to make the statue nearly nine feet tall, but the authorities, "who still felt great sorrow for what had taken place," wanted it to be as big as possible. They proposed a thirty-foot statue but finally agreed to a sixteen-foot version (Lóska 1980, 25). A further hallmark of socialist realist sculpture, according to Lodder (1993, 17), is a simplified figure whose facial and physical qualities are idealized in accordance with the heroic qualities of the new socialist man. One of the most striking aspects of the Martyrs Monument is the extent to which its expressive power is a function of the figure's *physical* qualities. Drawing from the semiotics of difference, it is neither the face nor the head that convey meaning, but the physique. The figure's muscularity and bulk are exaggerated almost to the point of caricature. With bare feet and only a hint of clothing, he is pure body.

What is this emphasis on the body all about? Tibor Wehner's work on socialist realist sculpture helps us make sense of it. He writes that most of the statues commissioned in Hungary during the 1950s and 1960s depicted the generic worker or peasant engaged in productive activity. In keeping with the didactic function of Zhdanovian art, such representations almost always featured a tool so that the public could easily read the figure's occupation and understand the role he or she played in the building of socialist society—the miner was armed with his lamp, the welder with his torch, the engineer with his compass, the soldier with his rifle, the peasant with her scythe, and the student with her book. In the final moment of his life, though, Kalló's figure is no longer defined by the clichéd tools of socialist production. He has now become the archetypal martyr, and his "tool" is the body he sacrifices in performing this role.

The image of the martyr is bound up in myths of suffering and redemption, products in large part of the Christian legacy. Following the example of Christ's suffering and bodily sacrifice, early Christians sought to transcend the body and all of its physical needs, desires, and pleasures in order to move closer to God (Sennett 1994, 124). But unlike the martyr of Christianity, whose virtues of fatalism and passivity evoke a sense of pathos, the martyr of communism—following Marx's admonition to make *man* the agent of history—is resolute, determined, and self-controlled. The result, iconographically, is that the robust, heroic body of the communist displaces the sickly, weak, pale body of the Christian martyr (Aradi 1974, 140).

Representations of the communist martyr's physical body reflect the broader trope of the "new man," which dates back to early Soviet art and literature. From that time the human body was used to display projections of the coming utopia and to personify its ideals of a perfectly functioning body politic. The movement toward a classless society would free people from the physical debilitations of hunger, poor nutrition, inadequate medical care, and back-breaking manual labor. In turn, workers and peasants who were liberated from the crippling and stunting effects of capitalism would be willing and able to build the new society by virtue of their strength, stamina, vigor, and health. In the worldwide class struggle, the flabby, enervated capitalist that so often appeared in Soviet propaganda would be no match for the superhumans engineered according to Marxist specifications (Clark 1993).

THE NARRATIVE INSCRIBED IN THE MARTYRS MONUMENT

The revolutionary struggle of the world proletariat against the reactionary forces of capitalism is the overarching narrative of Marxism-Leninism.

In Hungary the revolution was launched in 1948, known as the Year of the Turning Point, when the nation was transformed from a bourgeois democracy to a people's democracy. This grand narrative provided the organizing structure for defining the events of October, 1956, in communist Hungary as a *counter*-revolution, with the siege of party headquarters and the senseless slaughter of committed communists as the main act of villainy. Wolfgang Kemp (1996, 58) writes that narratives "seldom come in isolation and are seldom 'original'." The story of the rebels' treachery in Republic Square as embodied in the statue of a dying martyr is vertically integrated into a chain of narratives about the radical transcendence of capitalism that extend back to the writings of nineteenth-century utopian socialists, with their dreams of eliminating competition, private property, and individualism. Labels such as "white terrorists," "Horthyites," and "fascists" allude to previous episodes in the historical struggle of Hungarian communists to establish a workers' democracy, and they positioned the 1956 insurgents as descendants of earlier "reactionary elements."

Moreover, the statue incorporates a narrative that was constructed against the grain of accounts about the October uprising produced by the Western press, particularly *Life* magazine. The thinly veiled glee evident in *Life*'s coverage of the atrocities at Republic Square provided evidence to support all the Cold War rhetoric about the uprising as a sinister plot hatched in the West. *Life* published extensive photospreads that showed the violence in all of its lurid detail, and the accompanying text justified the most heinous actions of the "rebel patriots." For instance, the caption for a grisly full-page photograph of a woman spitting on a victim of lynching reads, "Scornful vengeance is vented by woman who spits at the mangled corpse of a secret police colonel hung head down in Budapest Square of the Republic. Viewing former tormentors' corpses, Hungarians said, 'They shot our children'" ("Patriots Strike" 1956, 42). While American readers may have accepted *Life*'s moral logic of retribution, it only fed into the Kádárian narrative of the "counter-revolution" as an evil plot engineered by the enemies of socialism and justified their revenge on the "counter-revolutionary agents of western imperialism."

Finally, all of the accounts about Republic Square produced within the nation's command culture drew meaning intertextually from each other. The Martyrs Monument could be mute on the subject of the "counter-revolution" because it had absorbed the whole stock of gruesome bodily images that had swirled through the mass media and other public spaces during the "hot" stage of commemoration: fascist hounds slinking around the square, nose to the ground as they reconnoitered the scene; the broken body of a mother who had jumped in desperation; the valiant old veteran of the Popular Front desperately waving a white flag; walls crying tears of blood; unearthed graves and grief-struck families. Most of the victims were twenty- to twenty-two-year-old recruits of the "Internal Forces" (read secret police), hearty young proletarians and peasants in the prime of their lives. The martyr embodied all of these narratives of what had happened on that fateful day, as the strong, healthy body of the new socialist man was subjected to the barbaric forces of reaction.

In their classical, syntagmatic form as theorized by Vladimir Propp (1968), narratives are always about transformations that occur over time. Structurally, a sequence of events takes place in chronological order, moving a character from an initial state of being to some altered state. Roland Barthes (1977, 79) argues that narrative is not confined to the spoken or written tale, where the events unfold over time, but are implicitly present in fixed images as well—the painting, the photograph, the stained-glass window. Here the artists must compress the chain of events into a single pictorial field, where past, present, and future are captured in one frozen moment. In order to capture a present that is replete with memories and expectations, an artist must, in Gotthold Ephraim Lessing's words, "choose the instant that is most laden with significance: that which makes most clear all that has preceded and is to follow" (quoted in Kemp 1996, 64). The choice of the perfect moment must have presented a dilemma for Kalló because of the competing aims of the monument. On the one hand, in his own words, the artist felt compelled to express the *tragedy* that burned inside of him (Lóska 1980, 24). On the other hand, the basic narrative pattern of the proletarian class struggle is characterized by final *victory*, a happy ending.

Béla Ujvári (1978, 10–12) claims that Kalló condensed two elements into the figure: the tragedy of the martyrs' deaths and the inspiration to continue the struggle to build socialism. In other words, Kalló successfully resolved the problem by choosing the instant before the martyr's death as the moment most laden with meaning, capturing both the present loss and the promise of the utopian future. But what is more interesting for us is Ujvári's observation that the tension between these two elements shifted between the time the statue was initially designed and the time it was actually executed in its final form. He writes that the original small-scale model, crafted while the artist was still under the influence of the "counter-revolutionary events," emphasized the physical agony and death throes of the doomed worker. Yet when Kalló created the final product a couple of years later, he played down the motif of martyrdom and death and gave more weight to the continuation of the class struggle by recomposing the arms to suggest more strongly an upward dynamic. While Ujvári suggests that this reorientation took place within the psyche of the sculptor, it reflects the broader politics of forced forgetting as attention was redirected from the past toward the accomplishment of the socialist project.

The *Memorial to the Martyrs of the Counter-Revolution* would carry much of the weight of the Kádár government's version of events at Republic Square during the long years of silence. These decades were not completely devoid of public references to the episode, but the voices were relatively muted. In 1974 Ervin Hollós and Vera Lajtai published *Köztársaság Tér 1956* (Republic Square 1956), an official history based mainly on court documents and the statements of witnesses. The "counter-revolution" was occasionally addressed in documentary films produced by Hungarian Television, and a piece on Republic Square, *Requium—Köztársaság Tér 1956. Október 30*, appeared in 1982. By that time oppositional interpretations of 1956 were beginning to leak out into public spaces, especially the samizdat press. When the Communist Party lost its hegemony, Kalló's monument, like so many others, was quietly hauled away. The quiet years had evidently done their psychological work, making the Martyrs Monument just another part of the landscape.

The symbolic deaths of Mikus's Stalin and Kalló's martyr are very different stories. The life of the Stalin star was short. Fueled by the hard coal of terror, it burned bright for a brief moment and then exploded in a glorious, cleansing fire set by a crowd intoxicated with its own audacity. In the postcommunist imagination, the story of its destruction looms large. The absence of the Martyrs Monument conveys a more complicated set of meanings. It stood in Republic Square for thirty-two years—far longer than the Stalin statue—yet few people today remember it. The statue came down not in a memorable fit of revolutionary zeal, but in the routine of government activity by municipal bureaucrats who aimed to scour the city of its communist iconography. While the public had registered its preference for leaving such monuments in place, the truth is, most people didn't much care.[5]

The abandoned platform in Republic Square speaks volumes about the complex processes of remembering and forgetting, of revealing and concealing, that characterize the formation of historical memory in post-communist Hungary. The symbolic erasure of a once-dominant narrative—in this case the literal removal of a monument—is only the first step in re-remembering the past. The empty space must be filled in, the pedestal must be recycled to support a new narrative. This is not so simple. David Lowenthal writes (1985, 326), "Though the past is malleable, its alteration is not always easy: the stubborn weight of its remains can baulk intended revision." In other words, reconstructions of the past must come face to face with elements of the old narrative. Records, relics, memories, and monuments can be reinterpreted, rearranged, discounted, discredited, explained away, or even hauled away. Their origin or their validity can be questioned. But they cannot be ignored wholesale if the truth claims of the new, victorious regime are to have any legitimacy.

It is perhaps fitting that the entry on the Martyrs Monument in the Statue Park Museum's guidebook is illustrated not by a photograph of the statue, but of a gigantic crater with a crane situated next to it—the hole must be at least thirty feet deep. It appears as if the diggers have reached the water table, but otherwise the crater is empty. Semiologically, the photograph is an iconic symbol of the pit that was dug in Republic Square in the search for underground prisons. At a mythic level, the photograph conveys a sense of the pent-up frustrations that were unleashed on October 30, 1956, particularly when the reader's interpretation is channeled by the written text. The entry briefly describes the rumors about secret cells and tunnels, the digging of the holes, and the mass hysteria that led people to believe they could hear the cries of prisoners as the excavation took place. It concludes, "Needless to say, no cellar prison was ever found." Not unlike the abandoned platform in Republic Square, this image of an empty hole invites the construction of postcommunist narratives that will replace the story told through Kalló's martyr.

CHAPTER FOUR

THE SANCTIFICATION OF HUNGARY'S JEANNE D'ARC

ON OCTOBER 23, 2000, a national holiday commemorating the 1956 revolution, a bronze bust was unveiled in the garden of a private
folklore museum in Budapest. The subject of the statue, Ilona Tóth, was
a twenty-four-year-old medical student executed by the Hungarian government in 1957. Tóth supervised a first-aid station affiliated with the
Péterfy Street Hospital during the uprising. After the Soviets attacked
on November 4, she stayed on, working in the wards by day and in the
basement by night, where she assisted in the production of underground
newspapers. Her alleged crime was the brutal murder of a man she believed to be a secret-police agent. According to official reports, members
of the resistance group discovered a suspicious-looking man lurking
around the premises. They apprehended him, and during the course of his
interrogation, they found a photograph in his pocket that showed him
dressed in an ÁVO uniform. Convinced that he was an infiltrator, they
believed there was no alternative but to get rid of him, and Tóth was
given the job. Prosecutors alleged that the man was actually an innocent
civilian who had had himself photographed in a borrowed uniform "out
of vanity" (Sz. T. 1957).

In the most infamous of the public show trials, Tóth fully confessed to
the terrible murder of István Kollár. First, she testified, she chloroformed
him. Then, not waiting for the drug to take effect, she injected gasoline
into a vein in his neck. When this failed to kill him, she injected air into
his neck, then into his heart. The man was still alive, so one of Tóth's
co-conspirators gave her his pocketknife with which to stab him in the
heart. But she was overcome with chloroform fumes and left the room.
When she returned, her accomplice was standing on the man's neck, suf-
focating him. Tóth examined the captive, and though she believed he was
dead, she stabbed him in the heart to make sure. According to the official

Béla Domonkos's bust of Ilona Tóth (2000).

autopsy report, the fatal wound was the stab to his heart. (Bányász and Szegő 1957; Elszánt Gyilkosok 1957).

Soon after the fall of communism, a group of old classmates and former political prisoners who were convinced of Tóth's innocence began working to clear her name. The Supreme Court examined the case in 1990, following the passage of legislation in 1989 that enabled the invalidation of political convictions. But the justices refused to dismiss the 1957 verdict, echoing the arguments in the original case: Tóth took part in the murder of an innocent man, using a variety of instruments and exploiting her knowledge as a physician. The case was opened again in 1992, but that investigation was suspended in 1994 after the Socialists took control of the government (Györgyi 1999). As things stood in the fall of 2000, Tóth was still legally classified as a murderer. On this basis, requests to erect the bust in the Péterfy Street Hospital's garden or in the courtyard of the medical school she had attended were denied. The folklore museum was intended to be a temporary home for the monument until it could take its rightful place in public.

By the time the statue was dedicated, a new commutation bill was working its way through Parliament. Modeled on the Tóth case, the bill was introduced by Ibolya Dávid, minister of justice in the populist Orbán government. While earlier laws nullified the convictions of people charged with political crimes or with participating in the fighting, the new legislation recognized that many people convicted of "common law criminal actions" in the aftermath of the revolution were actually the victims of the regime's indiscriminate revenge. It thus vacates on procedural grounds the sentences of all those convicted in show trials and summary judgments following the uprising. Parliament adopted the legislation by a vote of 295 to 3 on December 12, 2000, thus, in Dávid's words, providing the missing link in the rehabilitation of the 1956 victims ("Az 1956. Évi Forradalom" 2000; Babus 2000; Nyusztay 2000; Rozgonyi 2000). Based on these new standards, the courts nullified Tóth's conviction, clearing the way for the public display of her image. The statue was transferred from the folklore museum to the Semmelweiss Medical School in the fall of 2001.

As already noted regarding Sándor Mikus's Stalin and Viktor Kalló's martyr, statues do more than represent real or generic figures. In the semiotics of space and time, they provide sites for ritualistic celebrations or commemorations—May Day parades at Procession Square or wreath-laying ceremonies on the anniversary of the siege of the Budapest Communist Party Headquarters. As powerful visual icons, monuments help establish and anchor the ideological meaning that the organizers of such rituals wish to convey: the glory of the socialist revolution or the treachery of the "counter-revolutionaries." But in Tóth's case, attention shifts away from the monument itself to the inaugural ceremony through which it is initially invested with meaning. October 23 was designated a national holiday on May 2, 1990, in the inaugural session of the first democratically elected Hungarian parliament. Thus, Republic Day, which commemorates both the outbreak of the 1956 revolution and the proclamation of the democratic Hungarian Republic in 1989, was first celebrated in 1990. But the holiday has lost its luster in the years since. For the apolitical majority of Hungarians, Republic Day and its highly choreographed state rituals are uninspiring and irrelevant (Kozák 1996; Rab 1997; Szakolczai 2000).[1] The unveiling ceremony, however, was organized around a tightly focused theme, the campaign to rehabilitate Ilona Tóth. Its rhetorical nature allows us to examine the sedimentation of meanings as a relatively new holiday is inserted into a culture and enacted communicatively.

RITUAL AS CULTURAL PRODUCTION

Victor Turner uses the metaphor of a hall of mirrors to convey a sense of the rich, complex production of meaning that takes place through the interaction of the various modes of communication that may be deployed in rituals—song, dance, poetry, the spoken language, the movement and placement of bodies, and the graphic and plastic arts. He writes, "The result is something like a hall of mirrors—magic mirrors, each interpreting as well as reflecting the images beamed to it, and flashed from one to the others" (Turner 1986, 24). The blending and interplay of these communicative layers enables the performance to generate multiple meanings and to serve a variety of functions. Abner Cohen writes (1979, 106), "These performances objectify norms, values, and beliefs; interpret the private in terms of the collective, the abstract in terms of the concrete; confirm or modify relationships, temporarily resolving contradictions; and always recreate the belief, the conviction of the actors in the validity of their roles in society." In other words, cultural performances provide occasions for people to work through the ambiguities and contradictions of life, which are felt particularly keenly during transitional historical periods.

   The unveiling ceremony at the folklore museum offers an opportunity to explore the complex process of cultural production as an observable, public performance whose semiotic field is a dense interweaving of visual, oral, musical, poetic, and natural symbols. Cohen (1979, 90) notes that such symbols can be classified according to a variety of criteria, depending on the purpose of the classification. The purpose, in turn, depends upon the theoretical problem being investigated. In this study, the interest is in cultural-political transformation, the distancing of the nation from the former regime. Of most significance are symbols that distinguish the democratic present from the communist past and symbols that locate the citizen within the fabric of postcommunist public life.

Given these theoretical aims, Christel Lane's work on ritual in the Soviet Union is relevant. He distinguishes between the revolutionary culture of the early Soviet period and the conservative culture of the 1930s aimed at social control. In charting out that distinction, Lane develops a set of axes that are highly suggestive for this investigation: the spontaneous creation of culture versus the deliberate management of culture, and the generation of ritual by its performers versus the sponsorship of ritual by authorities. The tightly controlled, closely choreographed mass spectacle associated with totalitarian culture gave way to a wide range of celebrations on any given holiday with the fall of communism. The patterns Lane describes in his study of Soviet rituals serve as a foil for identifying how the cultural producers of the Tóth statue's unveiling ceremony distanced themselves symbolically from the communist past and made available a conservative, anticommunist cultural identity. (I have modified Lane's analytical framework to include the following categories: the symbolic significance of space, objects, actors, words, and action.)

HUNGARY'S JEANNE D'ARC

As with other mythic elements of the Hungarian revolution, the case of Ilona Tóth was taboo during the long years of silence during the Kádár regime and slipped from the conscious memory of all but her close acquaintances.[2] One of her codefendants, the late writer Gyula Obersovszky, christened her "Hungary's Jeanne d'Arc" in a prison conversation decades ago (Obersovszky 1999, 12). In the postcommunist recovery of the 1956 revolution, this label resonated with efforts to create a cast of heroes, victims, and martyrs. It was picked up and applied by others as the case began to appear in the public discourse of the early 1990s, including conservative commercial and partisan publications (Benedek 1992; Hankó 1992; Pardi 1992). Obersovszky published a series of pieces about Tóth in his periodical, *Vagyok*, during the 1990s. At the end of the decade, he extended these writings into a book entitled *Tóth Ilona: A Magyar Jeanne d'Arc* (Ilona Tóth: Hungary's Jeanne d'Arc), thus further amplifying the designation.

Rhetorically, the label imbues Tóth with the superhuman qualities associated with the nineteen-year-old French martyr—unparalled patriotism, courage, and selflessness. Moreover, the comparison emphasizes her

Ilona Tóth's portrait, second from the right, displayed with those of other revolutionary martyrs in the House of Terror. Photograph by Zsolt Bátori. Courtesy House of Terror Museum, Budapest

innocence as something that the crude agents of the state could never sully. In her splendid book on the image of female heroism associated with Jeanne d'Arc, Marina Warner writes (1981, 269): "the evil represented by the sentence to the stake is entirely external to her; it never touches her purity from the inside. The more terrible it is, the more powerfully it reinforces the idea of her innocence, assailed and yet unvanquished." A constant refrain in the testimonies of Tóth's supporters is that it is utterly unthinkable that such a pure-hearted young woman could have committed the acts with which she was charged (Oláh 1999, 9; Ordódy 1998). One of Tóth's journalistic supporters writes that she knew little about the case until someone handed her a photograph of a clear-eyed young woman looking bravely into the lens of the camera with such sincerity and resolve that the effect was almost mesmerizing. "When I was told that it was Ilona Tóth," she writes, "I immediately felt: This open-faced, fragile medic cannot be a murderer!" (Rozgics 1999). And even those who are convinced that Tóth and her comrades murdered Kollár argue that, given the circumstances, the woman was not a criminal but a hero, one of the true martyrs of the revolution (Eörsi 1999, 2000b, 2000c).

But it is the *distinction* between the two martyrs that was of greatest importance in the campaign to clear Tóth's name: Jeanne d'Arc was a saint, while at the time of the unveiling ceremony, Ilona Tóth was still classified as a sinner. In the foreword to Obersovszky's book, Vilmos Oláh writes (1999, 9), "The French Jeanne d'Arc was burned on the stake in 1431, but the French rehabilitated her in 1456, that is, 25 years later. It appears as if more time is needed in Hungary to bring the truth to light."

The mythic figure of Tóth was further developed through the documentary *Ki Volt Tóth Ilona! "Magasabbak az Egek a Földnél"* (Who was Ilona Tóth? "As the Heavens Are Higher Than the Earth"), broadcast on television on October 23, 1998.[3] Writer Tamás Benedikty-Horvát and director György Ordódy construct a decidedly sympathetic portrait of Tóth, with her former schoolmates describing her extraordinary personal qualities, and forensic and legal experts attesting to her innocence. Visually the film presents a powerful case too, as still photographs of the "clear-eyed young woman" are juxtaposed with newsreel footage of the trial.[4] There the horrors of the communist prisons are inscribed on Tóth's body. She wears a dark, oversized coat that emphasizes her pallor and small frame, her lustrous blonde hair is now dull and matted, her face is drawn, and her gaze is glassy.

Ilona Tóth and codefendant Gyula Obersovszky in court. Years later Obersovszky would christen Tóth "Hungary's Jeanne d'Arc." Courtesy MTI Fotó

The composite picture of Tóth that emerges through public discourse about her case takes on the quality of a heroic legend, as key episodes of her story and attributes of her character are repeated in each telling. The story goes like this: Ilona Tóth was born on October 23, 1932, a clear sign that she was chosen to play a special role in Hungary's history. Her childhood was poor materially but rich spiritually. The young woman's parents divorced around the time of her birth, and her mother raised her on the meager salary of a school teacher, "taking food from her own mouth" to feed her child (Obersovszky 1999, 19). The mother bestowed two special gifts on her daughter: faith in the teachings of the Reform Church and a love of learning. As she grew up, Tóth blossomed into a diligent, intelligent student. She was a daring athlete as well—a fencer, a sky diver, and a glider pilot. The little family's economic straits were evident to her classmates—Ilona owned just one gray skirt and two white blouses. But she was always immaculately clean, washing one of the blouses out each night. Her exemplary qualities were widely admired, and she was elected to leadership positions in student organizations.

As a revolutionary, Tóth tended selflessly to the wounded, whether street fighter or communist, Hungarian or Russian. When she was not caring for the injured, she was making forays to the Austrian border to secure food and medical supplies. The young intern barely slept, relying on caffeine tablets to keep going. And when the uprising was suppressed, she joined the resistance, hiding freedom fighters among the sick and wounded and assisting in the printing and distribution of illegal newspapers, including Obersovszky's *Élünk*. But Tóth's greatest sacrifice— the act that won her the epithet "Hungary's Jeanne d'Arc"—occurred after her arrest, when she took responsibility for the murder of Kollár in a fruitless effort to protect two codefendants charged with participating in the act.[5] The narratives then diverge at this point: By some accounts, Kollár never existed, and the entire murder charge was a fabrication; Tóth's confession was extracted through torture, hypnosis, and drugs. Or, there was such a person, and he happily retired as a colonel in the ÁVO in 1981. Others believe that the charges were essentially accurate with the exception of one important detail: When Tóth thrust the knife into Kollár's heart, he was already dead. As a doctor, she was well aware of that fact, but she readily confessed to the murder to spare her comrades.[6]

As Hungary's Jeanne d'Arc, Tóth's legend is laced with Christian allusions. One vignette depicts a crusty old prison guard consoling a shattered Tóth when the sentence was handed down "around Easter": "You're a good Christian," he comforted her. "You know that Christ, too, arose on the third day" (Hankó 2000, 20). In other anecdotes it was Ilona who comforted her mother by appealing to Christian themes of resurrection and redemption. Visiting Tóth in prison, the anguished mother stated that she could not bear to live if her daughter were executed. "Mother, don't even think about such things," replied Tóth. "Then we wouldn't meet" (Baka 1999, 123). In another story, before Tóth was executed, her despairing mother asked, "Where is Christ, my child?" Ilona responded, "Here, right next to me" (Obersovszky 1999, 108). Religious references are tied to the crusade against communism in more militant renditions of the legend. During her mother's final visit, Tóth reportedly comforted her with these words: "Don't cry, Mother, I will die as a brave Hungarian soldier. You know that the charge is false, and they just want to besmirch the holy revolution" (Hankó 2000, 21). One '56er claims that she became a legend during the brief span of the uprising, recognized as "a guardian angel who flew to earth to protect the bloodied soldiers of the revolution and freedom fight" who were "crushed by three-thousand Bolshevik tanks and three-hundred-thousand blood-thirsty red soldiers" (Várhegyi 1999).

The legend also contains veiled references to Tóth's saintly quality of virginity. According to material published in West Germany in 1986, rumors circulated for years that Tóth was pregnant at the time of her arrest, and she either miscarried as a result of beatings or was forced to undergo an abortion (Polgáry 1986, 15). These stories inflated the horror of the authorities' actions, but they did so at the expense of Tóth's honor. In the discourse of her postcommunist followers, Tóth's purity of body and soul have been restored. Károly Laki (2001), owner of the folklore museum where the statue was erected, has flatly stated, "We know from her autopsy that she was a virgin; she was never with a man." Jocelyn Wogan-Browne's (1994, 24) analysis of medieval constructions of the chaste female body reveals that the virgin is frequently represented as entombed. Locked away in her chamber, cell, or grave, she is preserved intact until her entry into the court of heaven and union with her bridegroom, Christ. Thus, while virginity is "the supreme form of chastity," its power derives from the promise of its own transcendence. Marina Warner makes this point in relation to Jeanne d'Arc. She notes that Jeanne always referred to herself as "Jehanne la Pucelle" (Jeanne the Virgin), and she explains the implications of the term: "*Pucelle* means 'virgin,' but in a special way, with distinct shades connoting youth, innocence and, paradoxically, nubility. . . . It denotes a time of passage, not a permanent condition. It is a word that looks forward to a change in state" (Warner 1981, 22). Accordingly, the heroic figure of Ilona Tóth personifies and concretizes an ideal of the revolutionary as young and spirited, motivated to act through love of country and fellow man. The emphasis on Tóth's purity suggests that when the communists executed her, they took the life of a woman whose productive potential was unfulfilled, thus depriving the Hungarian nation of a piece of its future.

Katherine Verdery (1999, 164) writes that the resurrection of the dead bodies of political victims in postcommunist societies "creates communities of mourners, of 'family' for these 'ancestors,' of those who will be present at the resurrection and included among the 'saved,' and those who will be ejected into damnation." The resurrection of Ilona Tóth's memory through the ceremonial dedication of a monument filled a similar symbolic function. The community of mourners assembled in the folklore museum were invited to project a conservative political ideology and agenda onto the images of suffering and sacrifice associated with Tóth.

SPATIAL CONFIGURATIONS

Christel Lane writes that the settings for Soviet rituals were formed through symbolic "spatial configurations." He uses this term to refer to "buildings, public spaces, monuments and memorials or whole towns that are associated with significant historical events or whole periods" such as the Russian Revolution, the victorious war against fascism, or Stalin's industrialization program. Some of these spatial configurations are so highly saturated with symbolic quality that they "exude it all the time and to such a strong degree that they have become 'holy' or 'sacred' places" (Lane 1981, 223). As discussed in chapter 3, in the communist narrative of the "counter-revolution," Republic Square—the scene of lynchings by the insurgents following their siege of the municipal party headquarters—was singled out for its significance. Much of the memory work following the democratic transition has involved the symbolic reclamation of the sacred sites of the revolution and the preservation of the stories attached to them. Rituals surrounding the October holiday frequently involve the symbolic physical enactment of this reclamation through either the re-creation of the marches and demonstrations that sparked the revolution or the unveiling of plaques and monuments marking the locations of heavy fighting.

Among the various ritualistic elements composing the unveiling ceremony, its spatial configuration is of signal importance: The folklore museum is marked as the *wrong* location for the monument to Ilona Tóth. The rhetorical aim of the ceremony was only partly to honor the memory of the young martyr. More fundamentally, organizers wanted to convince the wider public of her innocence and to effect legislation clearing her name. Authorities had thus far stymied the efforts of Tóth's supporters to sanctify the ground where she actually worked or studied, and the relegation of her likeness to a private garden, located in the suburbs, indicated that something was still amiss in postcommunist public life. People in high places still had the power to deny the innocence of a martyr to communist tyranny.

Meanwhile, the monument's temporary home provided an appropriate setting for the ritual. The folklore museum is located at the end of a quiet dead-end street in Mátyásföld, a pleasant suburb in the eastern reaches of Budapest. In a 2001 interview Károly Laki explained that his passion for collecting Hungarian folk artifacts began when he inherited his grandfather's ornately carved pipe. Over the years he has amassed thousands of objects, including pottery, textiles, clothing, tools, and furniture. Laki first opened the building to the public on March 15, 1973, the 125th anniversary of the 1848 revolution. He received permission to organize programs for children and began exposing them to traditional arts and crafts—music, dancing, and the preparation of *gulyás* ("goulash") over an open fire. Since the fall of communism, the family has also offered programs to foreign tourists to generate a little extra income, but the purpose of the museum, Laki maintained, has little to do with financial benefits. His aim was "to reawaken the Hungarianness" that was snuffed out in the two generations of communist rule. "This is the most important thing," he emphasized.

While a small sign directs the visitor to the folklore museum, the property is unremarkable from the street, blending unobtrusively into the residential neighborhood. As a private collection, the museum is open only by appointment. It has no staff, receives no public funding, and garners no listings in guidebooks to the city. Chapter 5 considers the impulses that drive individuals to establish private museums to exhibit their own personal collections. Here, the lack of public accessibility is the salient issue—as long as the Tóth memorial is relegated to the folklore museum, it will remain largely unseen. This spatial configuration signifies the need to sequester something classified as shameful by official arbiters. In this sense, the fate of the monument is similar to the communist statuary housed in the Statue Park Museum. But the difference is the communist statuary has been condemned for eternity, while the Tóth statue sits in limbo, awaiting redemption.

The dedication ceremony was held in the museum's garden, a highly symbolic space. With its biblical connotations of origins and abundance, the garden is suggestive of myths of ethnogenesis and kinship that assert a territorial and racial commonality among its innocent inhabitants (Schöpflin 1997, 34). Moreover, in the antibourgeois spirit of romanticism, the garden represents a place of respite from the noise and dirt of the industrial city. But the trees that shade this edenic space take on complex meanings within the symbolic field of the unveiling ceremony. In contrast to the ancient associations of trees with life itself, they conjure up their own hideous perversion by a tyrannical regime as the "hanging tree" (akasztófa) or "gallows tree" (bitófa), from which Tóth and so many other victims were hanged.

CONCRETE OBJECTS AS SYMBOLS

Following Victor Turner, Lane (1981, 191) notes that one of the basic properties of symbols is their multivocality, "the accumulation over time of layer upon layer of meaning." This historical sedimentation of meanings that accumulate around symbols is precisely what gives them the power to exert emotional influence. Lane is struck by the *lack* of multivocality in his analysis of the symbolic objects used in Soviet rituals (195). In selecting objects for veneration, cultural strategists disavowed the pre-revolutionary Russian cultural heritage in favor of items inspired by European revolutionary and working-class movements. Objects such as the red banner waved in a parade were foreign to the illiterate peasants and proletarians of revolutionary Russia and thus bereft of any meaning, much less a complex array of associations that build up over time (229).

As a product of the political transformation of 1989, the October 23 holiday is no less an "invented tradition" than is May Day. But in the cultural pluralism of postcommunism, the aesthetics of commemoration is a contested arena that splits along the familiar axis of populist-nationalism and urbanist-cosmopolitanism. While the tastes of the latter are

Entrance to the private folklore museum in Mátyásföld, where Ilona Tóth's statue was erected pending her legal rehabilitation.

eclectic, the former often find inspiration in Hungary's folk arts. In rejecting modernist or postmodernist impulses, populist-nationalists are pursuing a nostalgic historical trajectory that directly links the present with the prewar period. In the conservative period of the 1930s, "veneration of the peasantry as sole unspoilt transmitter of the national character was a cornerstone of the patriotic creed" (Ignotus 1972, 171).

The return to peasant folk culture as the embodiment of Hungarian national identity is reflected in the material objects that symbolically lent meaning to the unveiling ceremony. The museum site is surrounded by a carved wooden fence, with a gated entrance crowned by an arbor. The tradition of wood carving is strongly evocative of Transylvania, the cradle of Hungarian independence.[7] The building itself is made of stucco in the architectural style of a typical village house. Garlands of dried paprika hang from the arches of a narrow veranda, and traditional Hungarian jugs and other pottery are displayed on their ledges. The white-washed walls are decorated with hand-painted folk art in a floral motif.

Behind the main building, a wooden pavilion, carved with folk designs and decorated with garlands of paprika, holds picnic tables. Another outbuilding is crammed with wooden tools and implements that attest to

Tóth statue unveiling ceremony, October 23, 2000. At the lectern is Bishop Károly Takaró, and on the right is museum owner Károly Laki.

the ingenuity of a preindustrial people. The grounds contain objects that are utilitarian as well as symbolic—a stucco oven rescued from a farmstead and a cooking pit, where traditional cuisine is prepared for schoolchildren and foreign tourists. Other objects are purely symbolic. Most noticeably, a number of carved logs or tree trunks are situated around the grounds. They include representations of the seven tribes of Magyars that first settled in the Carpathian basin as well as those of Nimrod and his sons Hunor and Magyar, the mythic fathers of the Hungarian people. Nearby, a pair of wooden carvings represent Laki's mother and father, amplifying the personal, private aspect of this space while establishing its owner's rightful place in Magyar lineage.

The ceremony was held in a small clearing, where a lectern had been set up for the speakers. They were backed by towering evergreens, whose deep colors set off a luridly painted tin crucifix cut in the same pattern as those seen faded and rusting in the countryside. A Hungarian flag bearing the Saint Stephen's coat of arms stood behind the podium.[8] A small wooden sign on the edge of the clearing designated the space as "Heroes' Square," an intimate version of Budapest's famous landmark. The speakers faced two objects. The first was the bust of Tóth. Installed on a concrete pedestal and draped with a white cloth, its ghostly form was reminiscent of a figure being led to the gallows. Next to it was a carved, wooden grave post erected in Tóth's memory at a memorial service held on the fortieth anniversary of her death. With three and a half years separating their placement, the two monuments spoke to the unwavering commitment of Tóth's defenders to clear her name and raise her to the status of national hero. Indeed, the choice of media for the two monuments—the first wood, the other bronze—signifies a strengthening of their determination to accomplish these goals.

The statue was crafted by Béla Domonkos, a commercial sculptor with a small gallery just off the lower end of Váci Street. He was not paid for his work, and he explained in an interview that the money for the materials came from donations, scraped together fillér by fillér.[9] In that same interview, published several days before the ceremony in the Smallholders Party's newspaper, *Kis Újság*, Domonkos spoke about the sad-

The veiled statue of Ilona Tóth, October 23, 2000.

ness he felt as he created the statue: "I formed Ilona with deep love and teary eyes, and now I am deeply touched when I look at her. I can't imagine how the executioner could put a rope around this beautiful young neck." For him, the statue was a talisman through which the spirit of the martyr can confront her killers: "I crafted her expression so that the statue would say, 'Look into my eyes and see that lie, that vile society, that condemned me to death'" (Pósa 2000). Several speakers picked up on this theme of the monument's power to effect justice by resurrecting the soul of Ilona Tóth.

SYMBOLIC SIGNIFICANCE OF ACTORS

Lane (1981, 204–205) writes that in Soviet rituals, the power and presence of public institutions was symbolized by having representatives of those organizations perform ceremonial roles. Their participation pointed to the loci of Soviet power and their cooperative efforts to advance the common utopian goal. In contrast to this ritual, with its staged presentation of state power, only one government official, Justice Minister Dávid, appeared in the cast of characters present at the unveiling ceremony of the Tóth memorial. Nevertheless, the other performers were all linked to public institutions, sometimes antagonistically.

The museum's owner, Károly Laki, served as master of ceremonies. One of the hallmarks of communism was its appropriation of virtually all social networks and associations to further the ideological work of the party. A fervent anticommunist, Laki was characteristically distrustful of organizations. Speaking privately, he emphasized his independence from organized political groups. Indeed, without noting the irony, he claimed that an antiestablishment group, the revanchist Trianon Society, was formed in the museum's wine cellar in 1996. He also acknowledged membership in the Alliance of Former Political Prisoners. (Laki explained that he was imprisoned for his political beliefs in 1951 and again after the revolution, when he spent two years in prison for his role as revolutionary commander of the Budaőrs airfield.) Laki mentioned the Friends of Ilona Tóth Circle but emphasized that his involvement in the memorial service was strictly as a private citizen. While acting as a free agent, "Uncle Károly" was treated with great affection by his guests as a figure respected for his support of conservative causes. Each year, as part of the pageantry surrounding the October 23 holiday, the Society for the Protection of the Hungarian Spirit awards historians, writers, and other cultural producers Certificates of Perseverance for their cultural contributions. In 2000 Laki was honored for his museum work ("Rendületlenül" 2000).

Mária Wittner delivered the opening speech. History has thrust this unassuming woman into the limelight as arguably the most prominent ambassador of the 1956 street fighters. The young, mainly unskilled workers who manned the barricades and manufactured the Molotov cocktails were given the harshest sentences during the mass retaliation (Rainer 1999b, 256). Since the fall of communism, she has spoken in numerous public forums, including the Hungarian parliament and international academic conferences, putting a human face on these victims. Wittner (1994) told her story in an oral history recorded in 1991. Abandoned by her mother, she spent her early childhood in a convent and was transferred to a state orphanage when the communists took power. By the fall of 1956, the nineteen-year-old Wittner was on her own, finding odd jobs cleaning, washing, or shoveling snow, while her infant son remained a ward of the state. When the revolution erupted, she joined the fighters at Corvin Passage. She was wounded during the shooting on November 4, and by the time she was released from the hospital, the uprising was over. She had just begun to work in a factory that made thermos bottles when she was arrested in 1957. Charged with the usual litany of crimes, including the murder of unidentified victims, Wittner was sentenced to life in prison and released only in 1970.

In the oral history, Wittner speaks frequently of Katalin Sticker, her comrade in arms, codefendant, and cellmate. Sticker was taken from their cell and executed in 1959, and the senseless, arbitrary nature of this exercise in "justice" had a profound effect on Wittner. In the waning days of communism, the Committee for Historical Justice held a memorial service for the victims of the reprisals, and Wittner laid a wreath of fifty-six red roses in memory of Sticker, who apparently had no family. Through this initial gesture, she was drawn into the emerging circles of 1956 activists and joined the Alliance of Former Political Prisoners because, as she put it, "that is my place" (Wittner 1994, 29). Although she never met Ilona Tóth, Wittner is one of the central figures in the efforts to have her rehabilitated. It is evident why she would identify with Tóth: both were young women who found themselves hurled to the front lines of a life-and-death struggle for national independence and then trapped in the nightmare of the communist courts. The difference is equally obvi-

ous: Tóth—like Wittner's friend Kati—was hanged, while Wittner's life
was spared for no particular reason.

Ibolya Dávid, minister of justice and leader of FIDESZ's coalition part-
ner, the Hungarian Democratic Forum, gave the keynote address and per-
formed the symbolic function of unveiling the monument. Trained as an
attorney, Dávid has represented her party in Parliament since 1990. She
was just a toddler at the time of the revolution and thus belongs to the
young generation of politicians whose hands are unstained. According to
polls taken at the time of the ceremony, Dávid was among the nation's
most popular politicians (N. Sz. 2001). Her presence as a high-ranking and
highly respected member of the government brought both visibility and
legitimacy to the occasion. But her appearance was more than ceremonial. Following Dávid's appointment to the Justice Ministry, Tóth supporters enlisted her aid in their efforts to have the condemned woman's
record cleared. She reviewed the documentation, and when she became
convinced of Tóth's innocence, she agreed to push the case. Dávid introduced the new commutation legislation on October 12, just days before
the unveiling ceremony.

In planning the ceremony, Laki enlisted the support of Györgyi Kulcsár, the producer of the 1998 documentary on Tóth. Kulcsár worked with
the Justice Ministry, which proposed a short program: Wittner would
make the opening address and Dávid would deliver the keynote speech.
The minister would then unveil the statue, and the ceremony would
end with the singing of the national anthem. But Laki (2001) contended
that "a ceremony is only a real ceremony if there is a beautiful program
that includes children and clergymen, representatives of the various
churches." The program was thus expanded to include groups of schoolchildren and Christian ministers—a Roman Catholic priest, a Reform
Church bishop, and an evangelical pastor.

Laki's insistence on including these two categories of "performers"
reflects more than a simple wish for elaborate pageantry. The inclusion
of children in rituals, Lane claims, reflects a view of history as a relay
race, where the baton is passed from one generation to the next. In the
secular context of communism, it was "a means to abrogate biological
time and to transcend history, thus creating a feeling of collective continuity and purpose" (Lane 1981, 202). Given the orientation of communism toward the utopian future, the casting of children served an important ideological function in conveying an optimistic spirit of progress.
This is equally important at this historical juncture for those who wish

to preserve the memory of the 1956 revolution. As those who directly experienced the events pass on, the young must demonstrate their readiness to honor the past. The casting of the three clergymen points to the centrality of Christianity in postcommunist conservative thought. A legacy of the founder of the nation, Saint Stephen, Christianity is a mark of "Hungarianness" and a way of defining "real" Hungarians against one of their primary others, Jews.

VERBAL SYMBOLS

Lane uses the term "verbal symbols" to refer to ritualistic language meant to arouse the emotions and propel listeners or readers to action. His examples include the swearing of loyalty oaths in military or workers' initiation ceremonies and the recitation of poetic lines by Mayakovsky or Gorky. Dominated by the long, didactic speech, Soviet rituals were weak in verbal symbolism, according to Lane (1981, 203): "Generally speaking, rituals and ceremonies are overloaded with non-symbolic verbal ballast which deadens rather than sensitizes the emotional responses of ritual participants." The original aim of the long holiday speech was the political indoctrination of the uninitiated. In drawing up plans for celebrating the first anniversary of the 1917 revolution, the Moscow Soviet's Popular Education Department called for three days of festivities that would foreground instruction in the basics of socialism: "They should begin with public lectures in the city's districts to explain the meaning and significance of the Revolution to the masses and to review preceding historical epochs" ("From a Report" 1990, 55). With the transition from revolutionary to conservative culture in the Soviet Union, the political speech lost any pretense to transformative power and degenerated into little more than "the padding out of ritual" (Lane 1981, 203).

Terry Eagleton makes an observation that helps us think about the link between verbal symbols in Soviet rituals and in the ceremony at the folklore museum. He notes that radicals and conservatives alike—as opposed to postmodernists—are traditionalists, "it is simply that they ahere to entirely different traditions" (Eagleton 1996, ix). The cultural theorists of the early Soviet period (the radicals) pursued the ultimate modernist project of building a perfect society through "unlimited social engineering, huge and bulky technology, [and the] total transformation of nature" (Bauman 1992, 179). Holiday rhetoric was one of the many cultural fields that were cultivated in pursuit of this dream. The organizers of the unveiling ceremony adhered to a conservative-nationalist tradition, and in their desire to achieve a postcommunist society based on those ideals, they returned to the use of verbal symbolism to stir emotions and drive men and women to action. Yet while speakers in the Soviet system recited lines scripted by the infallible, omniscient Communist Party, the speeches at the folklore museum were delivered in the freewheeling context of political and cultural antagonism.

Károly Laki opened the ceremony with a few words of welcome. Before he introduced the first speaker, he asked the audience to join him in singing the national anthem. Mária Wittner then delivered the opening address, including the reading of a poem about Tóth. Justice Minister Ibolya Dávid gave the major address and then unveiled the statue. The children's performance followed, with elementary and high school students singing and reciting verses. The poems included Bátor Bókai's "Tóth Ilona," written on the fortieth anniversary of her execution; Tibor Tollás's "Túlélők" (Survivers), written in exile on the thirtieth anniversary of the revolution; and Flóra Majtényi's "Mi a Haza?" (What is the Homeland?), an adaptation for children of Emil Ábrányi's 1892 romantic poem. The three clergymen then spoke, weaving biblical readings into their reflections on the day's significance. Finally, Laki offered a few closing remarks, and the ceremony ended with the singing of the "Szózat" (Summons), considered the second national anthem.

The discussion below is confined to the speeches of Laki, Wittner, Dávid, and the clergymen, which were written specifically for this occasion. Together these texts offer a cohesive discourse on the relationship between the communist past and contemporary public life in Hungary. Specifically, the legend of Ilona Tóth is used to exemplify the evils of communism, the heroic character of the struggle against communism in 1956, the incomplete nature of the overthrow of communism in 1989, and the responsibility of citizens in postcommunist Hungary to complete the 1956/1989 revolution. As the following analysis shows, the various speakers emphasize different aspects of this argument based on their own social positions.

THE EVILS OF COMMUNISM

The execution of Ilona Tóth was offered as evidence of the evil nature of communism. After brutally crushing Hungary's glorious revolution, the communists carried out a savage reign of terror, and Tóth was a random victim of this senseless violence. Dávid opened her keynote address with a strong statement of condemnation: "There are statues that never should have been made, and there are deeds that never should have happened. Today, we come together to unveil such a statue. . . . Ilona Tóth would still be among us today, because she was barely twenty-five years old when the communist politicians executed her." [10]

As an attorney and the nation's minister of justice, Dávid attacked the communists' perversion of the law. She cited the Tóth case as a prime example: "The communists used the law as an instrument of deceit and terror more effectively than any other dictatorship. . . . In settling political accounts, they resorted to summary justice and kangaroo courts. Those who found themselves mixed up in this kind of proceeding were in a hopeless situation. Ilona Tóth was subjected to such a show trial."

The criminal proceedings that were conducted during the retaliatory period were designed to assert the iron authority of the communists both within Hungary and before the court of world opinion. Dávid addressed this point as she offered an explanation for why the communists would arrest, convict, and execute an innocent young woman: "They wanted to justify the suppression of the revolution, they wanted to justify their lust for power, they wanted to demonstrate their ability to instill fear in the young." As she continued, she tied the communists' motives in the Tóth case to their underlying traits: "They were always good at this. The communist system turned the logic of justice on its head. Instead of the presumption of innocence, they presumed guilt. Instead of proof, they offered fabrication. . . . This was not the administration of justice, it was a fox-hunt. This is what they did to Ilona Tóth."

While Dávid argued that the communists poisoned civil law, the participating Reform bishop, Károly Takaró, charged them with perverting canonical law. The communists turned the Judeo-Christian moral order upside down, he argued, creating their own version of the Ten Commandments. He went through the commandments one by one, showing how they were inverted by the communists: "Contrary to the first commandment, their chief commandment was, 'There is no God.' They also changed the second commandment: 'He who raises the name [of the Lord] is to be persecuted.' . . . They changed the commandment, 'Thou shalt not kill.' Here, killing was a way of life, a glorious act." As he continued, Takaró emphasized the distortion of the eighth commandment: "Then came the commandment, 'Thou shalt not bear false witness against thy neighbor.' Here, a stunning apparatus was launched. That of the informers, the liars, the falsifiers. They would just point at someone, and he would be taken away. There was nothing written, and there was no investigation."

THE HEROIC STRUGGLE AGAINST COMMUNISM

The second theme, the heroic struggle of the 1956 revolutionaries against communism, was personified through the presence of Mária Wittner and developed in her remarks. Her credentials as a street fighter began on the night of October 23, when she took up a position on the roof of a building across from the radio headquarters and loaded ammunition into the rifles of snipers. She spoke in the first person as she described that day as a page of Hungarian history written in the blood of her comrades: "October 23: . . . The streets of Pest became ours. The kids traded their balls made of rags for Molotov cocktails, unconcerned that the blood they spilled painted the cobblestones of the streets of Pest. Today we remember them, our heroes and martyrs. Our heroes, whose blood flowed on the streets of Pest."

In this short passage, Wittner accomplished several rhetorical aims. First, she established the youth and innocence of the revolutionaries through the mention of children playing ball. This image of children playing in the vacant lots of Budapest resonates with Ferenc Molnár's 1907 novel, *A Pál Utcai Fiúk* (The Paul Street Boys), a classic known and loved by all Hungarians. In Wittner's telling, this idyllic scene of childhood innocence was ripped apart when the first communist bullets were fired on October 23, 1956. Her remark about the substitution of homemade balls (*rongylabda*) with Molotov cocktails—weapons that are equally simple and similarly homemade—underscored the frightening imbalance in firepower as the young street fighters faced off against Soviet tanks. And her reference to the cobblestone streets of Pest situated the 1956 uprising within a European revolutionary tradition going back to Paris in 1789, when the commoners tore up the streets to stone the forces of the ancien régime.

She also mentioned twice that the blood of the revolutionaries ran through the streets. Here she has appropriated the symbolically dense motif of blood from the communists, inverting their old contention that the insurgents were "bloody-handed" aggressors. Or perhaps the more accurate term would be "reappropriated": Her words were surely inspired by Lajos Tamási's 1956 poem, "Piros a Vér a Pesti Utcán" (Red is the Blood in the Streets of Pest):

Red is the blood in the streets of Pest,
The rain beats down, washing the blood,
But it remains on the stones
of the streets of Pest.

Tamási's poem was widely circulated during the uprising, and it is often recited in October 23 rituals. In fact, blood is frequently linked semantically to the nation in artistic renderings of 1956 such as Péter Pócs and László Haris's 1989 poster for the Alliance of Free Democrats. Under the label "301," a reference to the cemetery plot where Imre Nagy and other political victims lay buried, the poster depicts a bleeding map of Hungary. A pair of nails formed in a crucifix are superimposed over the map, thus linking the suffering of Hungarian martyrs with that of Christ. In Wittner's words, as in Tamási's lines or Pócs and Haris's art, blood is the fundamental life force, and its loss is a sign of impending death. But the shedding of blood offers a means of redemption through sacrifice, exemplified through the resurrection of Christ (Linke 1999, 98–101).

It is widely acknowledged that women fought alongside men during the uprising, even if their actions were sometimes secondary, as when Wittner loaded the guns for the male snipers. And while Tóth is often described in traditional female terms—fragile, pure, lovely—her deeds in 1956 were decidedly "masculine." First, she directed a first aid station, though she had not yet completed her training. More important, when her male comrades either bungled the job of killing Kollár or lost their nerve, she took charge and carried out the act like a cool professional— or she at least took responsibility "like a man" for committing the crime. How was the contradiction between war as a masculine-gendered arena and the centrality of women in the episode at hand negotiated through the verbal symbolism of the ritual?

Ibolya Dávid explicitly took up the theme of the heroic role of women in 1956: "As we stand here before the statue that guards the memory of Ilona Tóth, I think about all those girls and women whose courage also commands respect. We know that a large number of women fought like men in the revolution. We know how great their courage was, as they covered for the men of the revolution—fathers, sons, brothers. We know what strength of spirit they needed to manage as the family's sole wage

Péter Pócs and László Haris's 1989 poster for the Alliance of Free Democrats, *301-SZDSZ*. Courtesy Hungarian National Gallery, © 2003 Artists Rights Society (ARS), New York/HUNGART, Budapest

earner, to keep the faith, to survive the deprivation, to raise the children." While Dávid highlights the issue of gender, the standard of revolutionary behavior is masculine—they "fought like men," they "covered for the men." And such was the case with the original Jeanne d'Arc, who cut off her hair and wore men's clothing as a way of attaining the "masculine characteristics" of virtue, reason, and courage (Warner 1981, 147). Marina Warner writes (1981, 155), "Ironically, Joan's life, probably one of the most heroic a woman has ever led, is a tribute to the male principle, a homage to the male sphere of action."

INCOMPLETE OVERTHROW OF COMMUNISM

In the summer of 1989, a national roundtable drew together representatives of the Communist Party and oppositional groups to work out the conditions for the change of political system. In exchange for a smooth, peaceful transition, communist delegates were given verbal guarantees that there would be no witch hunts, no attempts to settle old scores afterward (Romsics 1999, 433–34). In practice, this agreement had two components. First, there would be no purging of former communists from their jobs. Second, there would be no retroactive justice; that is, former officials would not be prosecuted for murder, torture, or other crimes that were either legal when committed or now exempt from prosecution because of statutes of limitations. From the beginning, this compromise galled conservative '56ers, who denounced what was essentially a "negotiated" revolution in their demands for a "total" revolution.

Writing in the early 1990s, Andrew Arato explains their position. Critics of the nature of the 1989 transition claim that the system hasn't really changed, and their evidence "is that many of the same old people continue to occupy important positions in political, economic, and cultural life." But, Arato argues, this criticism "confuses the issue of replacing structures, institutions, and mechanisms of coordination with the issue of replacing individuals" (1994, 196). Nevertheless, "it infuriates victims of the past and their self-appointed spokespeople when individuals with high public visibility retain their posts" (222–23). These sentiments have not abated over the ensuing years. The election of the Socialists in 1994 and 2002 was proof that the old gangsters are never far from the center of power.

In the verbal discourse of the unveiling ceremony, Tóth's legal status as a condemned murderer was offered as proof of the communists' enduring influence. The main theme of Laki's short greeting was the incomplete nature of the revolution as reflected by official resistance to clearing her name: "We first met here on the fortieth anniversary of Ilona Tóth's execution. We have met here on each national holiday since then, and we will continue to do so until her statue is placed in a public setting. The fact that the statue is inaugurated here, and not in a public place, shows that there is still a lot of work to do." He acknowledged Ibolya Dávid's televised public statements indicating that commutation legislation would likely pass. But even with a government receptive to the demands of conservative '56ers, Laki argued, change was moving too slowly because "many people still live among us in the country who are Hungarian citizens, but who work against Hungary."

Dávid alluded to the incomplete nature of the overthrow of communism as well. The context was a lament that the execution of Tóth had ever been permitted to happen, followed by a series of rhetorical questions: "How could this happen? Why did she have to die? Is it we who must answer this?" The correct answer to this last question was embedded in a follow-up question: "Or is it those who are still alive, but who are not among us today?" Dávid then zeroed in on the target: "I am thinking of those who take advantage of the chance for legal oblivion that comes with the passage of time. They are the ones who should answer the questions, as people responsible for their deeds. But I suspect that we wait in vain for an answer." In the meantime, it was up to the people to deliver final justice.

RESPONSIBILITY OF CITIZENS TO COMPLETE THE LONG REVOLUTION

The final theme that ran throughout the speeches was the responsibility of the revolution's survivors and their progeny to complete the act of overthrowing communism that had been so violently interrupted on November 4, 1956. This charge requires that legal and moral wrongs be righted—in the first instance, the rehabilitation of Ilona Tóth and others who were similarly condemned as common criminals. Yet the completion of the revolution demands not only new laws but also new memories. The suppressed truth about 1956 must be brought to light, and the lies and distortions must be unmasked. The monument to Tóth is not only designed to honor a martyred hero but also to serve as a visual cue that would prompt the public to remember "correctly." Addressing this theme, Bishop Takaró asked that the statue proclaim the truth of God, "that every baseness be unveiled, and every deed one day be brought to the scales of justice. And that those whom they wanted to make us forget be unforgettable, and those whom they wanted to be unforgettable, be forgettable."

Dávid spoke to this issue not only as Hungary's minister of justice but also as a representative of the post-1956 generation. Preparing to unveil the bust, she stated: "Honored men and women, the expression of truth is left for the next generation. The expression of truth is our duty. . . . When I unveil this monument, two covers will simultaneously fall from the statue. After a very long time, the cover will finally fall from the mis-carriage of justice committed against the young intern." After Dávid's re-marks came the main action of the ceremony, the unveiling of the statue, which—as her wording suggests—was saturated with meaning.

SYMBOLIC ACTION

According to Lane, symbolic action can be analytically divided into two forms: that which is purely symbolic, and that which has an instrumen-tal as well as a symbolic dimension. In the Soviet context, the latter was far more frequent as a result of the overall aim of the ritual—to hasten action. As examples, Lane mentions the pouring of the millionth ton of steel and the plowing of the season's first furrow (1981, 220–21). The rit-ual at the folklore museum did include actions that were purely sym-bolic. The most prominent example was the sharing of food and drink af-ter the formal ceremony was concluded. Tables were set up in the garden, where the Lakis served traditional Hungarian finger food such as *pogác-sák*, little cheese biscuits, and local wine in handcrafted pottery. Through this offering, the Lakis enacted their role as hosts of the ceremony and de-fenders of Hungarian culture, and the guests' acceptance affirmed their membership in the community.

But the main action—the unveiling of the monument—had an in-strumental as well as a symbolic component. Similar to the moment when a priest raises the host and chalice during mass or a president's wife breaks a bottle of champaign over the bow of a new warship, the un-masking of the monument was the ritual's climactic point. Through these actions, the priest, the first lady, or the politician instill sacred qualities in the person or object acted upon. The young minister of jus-tice asserted that the act of unveiling the monument would unleash its ability to represent the miscarriage of justice, lending force to her leg-islative endeavors on behalf of Tóth. Ill-fated Mária Wittner offered an even more forceful reading of the unveiling as an act that would endow the monument with magical qualities. With the statue's dedication, the spirit of Ilona Tóth would rise from the dead to confront her murderers: "October 23: Ilona Tóth was born 63 years ago today, a medical intern whose executioners burned her on the stake of reprisals after the crush-ing of the revolution. But they could not destroy her soul nor her spirit, because she arose again, like the miraculous sphinx of the saga." Through the miracle that took place that day with the unveiling, she contended, "Ilona Tóth can stand face to face [not only] with her friends, but also with her executioners."

Ironically then, the presentation of the monument was not unlike the ritualistic dedication of the monstrous Stalin statue almost fifty years earlier. A chunk of bronze formed in the likeness of a hero was endowed with some measure of the hero's essence. As the cloth falls, the audience gasps, then applauds, registering its experience of the icon's power. The transformative act does more than invest the monument with sacred qualities. For spectators, the simultaneous experience of this "miracle" binds them together as subjects of the monument's splendor. In the words of Edward Shils and Michael Young (1953, 72), such acts are essentially communal and are thus a means of enacting group solidarity: "They are acts of communion between the deity or other symbols of the highest values of the community, and persons who come together to be in communion with one another through their common contact with the sacred. The fact that the experience is communal means that one of the values, the virtue of social unity or solidarity, is acknowledged and strengthened in the very act of communion."

RITUALIZED CONSENSUS

György Schöpflin argues that ritual is a way of establishing solidarity and an illusion of community in the absence of real consensus: "[It] is more a stylized statement of belief than a fully-fledged internalization of what the ritual supposedly expresses" (1997, 21). His description is accurate with regard to longstanding rituals, but it is less applicable to those in their nascent stage, that is, in the immediate aftermath of social disruption as national identities are actively reformulated. Along these lines, Antoine Prost's (1997, 317–30) analysis of Armistice Day in France reveals how the holiday lost its potency over time as its original planners and participants, veterans of World War I, died off. The ceremonies and other symbolizing activities surrounding the 1956 Hungarian revolution are highly unifying for groups that are predisposed to cohesion as a result of their ideological, generational, and experiential similarities. But for the nation as a whole, they are evidence of deeply rooted cultural tensions. Indeed, as Schöpflin himself points out (1997, 22–23), the frenzied myth making that takes place in times of great social upheaval is an attempt to *impose* unity, to transcend the gaps among diverse groups and create at least the illusion of an ordered society.

The legendary construction of Ilona Tóth exemplifies this feverish, contested stage of identity formation. As the analysis of this dedication ritual shows, Tóth's status as a condemned murderer provided a powerful platform from which to advance a conservative political agenda. The unveiling of her memorial offered an occasion for affirming the beliefs and values of those '56ers and their adherents who defined the revolution as a life-and-death struggle against communism. Through the various narrative strands that composed the ritual, they asserted their moral authority over that of Hungary's postcommunist elected officials, regardless of the party in power. The postcommunist state is to be regarded as legitimate only to the extent that it assumes responsibility for completing the work that was initiated in the streets of Budapest in 1956.

CHAPTER FIVE

MUSEUMS AND THE OBJECTIFICATION OF MEMORY

IN JUNE, 1957, an exhibit documenting the "counter-revolutionary events" of the previous fall opened in Hungary's newly established Contemporary History Museum. Organized by the Institute for Party History, the display was designed to prove that the uprising was the work of reactionary forces bent on destroying the people's republic with the help of the imperialist West. The evidence took the form of material objects: charred red banners, flags with gaping holes where the communist emblem had been cut out, the cover of an American aerial reconnaissance camera recovered by authorities several weeks before the revolt, photographs of "Hungarian fascists" meeting in Munich under the royal Hungarian flag, and photographs that—according to press reviews—depicted "the raging white terror on the streets of Budapest" (Kiállítás Készül 1957; Megnyitották 1957).

With the restoration of Communist Party authority, the "mutilated" flags and incriminating photographs were boxed up and consigned to storage facilities for some thirty years. In the fall of 1989, a month-long exhibit entitled "Objects, Documents, and Photographs, October 23–November 4, 1956" was held in that same museum. Despite the bland title, the display offered a compelling rhetoric of revolutionary dreams and sacrifices to a public for whom 1956 had long been terra incognita. Journalist Béla Kurcz probably spoke for most of the visitors when he wrote in his review of the show, "I admit that it is difficult to escape the power of the things I saw, since I myself only know about what happened through hearsay" (Kurcz 1989). The items brought to light included a Lenin street sign dented by the blows of the hammer that brought it down; a crudely drawn stenciled poster that read "Hungarians! Don't give up! Even tanks can't break the people's will!"; the October 31, 1956, issue of Gyula Obersovszky's newspaper, *Igazság*, proclaiming the victory of the revolution; and photographs that captured the images of triumph and despair—the Stalin monument laying in the street and the makeshift graves in city squares. With the radical revision of the master narrative of 1956, private memory objects took on the status of historically significant national treasures. Thus, in addition to the items hauled up from the museum's storerooms, the 1989 exhibit included recently donated artifacts. Perhaps the most spectacular of these items was the military uniform of the revolutionary defense minister Pál Maléter, who was executed alongside Imre Nagy in 1958. It was presented to the museum by his widow, Judith Gyenes.[1]

At the time of its establishment in 1957, the Contemporary History Museum was charged with collecting artifacts related to the nation's post-1849 period and to the history of the Hungarian and international workers' movements. In 1966 the name of the institution was changed to the Museum of the Hungarian Workers' Movement. As the one-party state imploded in 1989, the last communist government dissolved the museum. Its personnel and collections were absorbed by Hungary's National Museum, where the Lenin street sign, the imposing uniform of the 6 foot, 4 inch Maléter, and the hand of the Stalin monument (mentioned in chapter 2) can be seen today in an exhibit on the rise and fall of the communist regime.

As of 2002, the nation's major official exhibit dedicated to the 1956 revolution was housed in Budapest's Military History Museum. But the only museum devoted exclusively to the revolution is situated in the countryside far from the nation's capital. The 1956 Museum, located in a former schoolhouse about three miles from the small town of Kiskunmajsa, is owned and operated by Gergely Pongrátz. As the product of a "do-it-yourself curator" (Samuel 1994, 27), the 1956 Museum is reminiscent of the "intensely personal and haphazard" cabinets of curiosities first assembled by private collectors during the Renaissance (Alexander 1996, 9). Its owner was a leader of the insurgents at Corvin Passage and was forced to flee the country when the Soviets launched their attack. He returned to Hungary in 1991 after some thirty-five years of exile "to tell the truth about 1956" (Pongrátz 2000).

MUSEUMS AND POPULAR MEMORY

Wolfgang Ernst (2000, 17) argues that museology is more than the academic analysis of the museum as institution; "as a discipline it might

The 1956 exhibit at the Hungarian National Museum, featuring the uniform of
Pál Maléter, minister of defense in the revolutionary government. Photograph by
András Dabasi, Hungarian National Museum

rather be defined as a specific branch of media studies concerned with culture as (literally) 'collective' memory." Firmly rooted in space, the museum is a durable mode of communication biased toward the dissemination of knowledge and information over time (Innis 1951, 33). In the words of Arjun Appadurai and Carol Breckenridge (1992, 36), the museum presents static displays through which group identities are fixed and stabilized as artifacts and are abstracted from their dynamic contexts.

Ordinarily this mode of institutionalizing the past is directed by national governments. In Hungary, for instance, public museums are under the jurisdiction of the Ministry of National Cultural Heritage. But Raphael Samuel argues for the significance of the amateur museum as a site for the construction of collective memory. In an essay entitled "Unofficial Knowledge," he sets out to wrest history from the hands of the professionals and to direct attention to other social actors whose creative energy contributes to our common perceptions of the past: "History is not the prerogative of the historian, nor even, as postmodernism contends, a historian's 'invention.' It is, rather, a social form of knowledge; the work, in any given instance, of a thousand different hands" (1994, 8). In addition to collectors, Samuel's colorful army of popular educators enlists antiquarians, scavengers, balladeers, the writers of historical romances, the animators of the *Flintstones*, and even users of metal detectors, "those electronically equipped cowboys of archaeological excavation" (1994, 18). He contends that an ethnographic approach to the past would highlight these sources of unofficial knowledge. In turn, this would allow scholars to avoid the fashionable but reductionist trend of conceiving of commemorative practices as mere ideology: "historians have become accustomed to thinking of commemoration as a cheat, something which ruling elites impose on the subaltern classes. It is a weapon of social control, a means of generating consensus, and legitimating the *status quo* by reference to a mythologized version of the past. The heritage critics have followed suit, treating nostalgia as a contemporary equivalent of what Marxists used to call 'false consciousness' and existentialists 'bad faith'" (Samuel 1994, 16–17).

Samuel is correct that popular conceptions of the past draw heavily upon unofficial sources of knowledge. But the products of "Clio's underlaborers"—whether historical romances, Hollywood movies, or wax museums—are thoroughly ideological. Those visions of a nation's past that capture the public's imagination do so because they tap into widely shared beliefs and ideas about who we are and where we came from. In turn, these popular representations of the past nourish and stabilize pre-existing ideas about the nation and its people. A number of ideological questions are at issue in competing currents of popular thought about Hungary's 1956 revolution: What social group instigated the uprising? Who were its heroes? Who was to blame for its failure? What are its implications for Hungary's position in the international community today? And who can be trusted, both within and beyond the nation's borders? One set of answers to such questions can be found by examining the 1956 Museum as the product of a self-made museologist. Susan Crane (2000, 68) observes that cabinets of curiosity were "expressions of the tastes and interests of a single collector." As a modern-day cabinet of curiosities, the 1956 Museum reflects the ideology of its owner, a prominent yet controversial figure who personifies a conservative understanding of the revolution and its significance for postcommunist public life.

Comparing the 1956 Museum to the Military History Museum's exhibit "Thirteen Days . . . October 23–November 4, 1956" highlights the ideological work of the private collection. Eilean Hooper-Greenhill (2000, 124) writes that the interpretation of visual culture in museums can be approached from the point of view of the curator or the visitor. The concern here is with curatorial meaning as the production of discourses that interpellate, or offer subjective vantage points, for the visiting public. What is the central narrative of the revolution as created through the selection of objects, the manner of display, and the interpretive work of labels, explanatory panels, or guides in the 1956 Museum and in the Military History Museum? What are the implications of this narrative for postcommunist political values? How is each museum, as a site for the construction and exposition of these values, related to the broader postcommunist political culture in Hungary and popular understandings of the revolution? These questions are addressed through interviews with the designers and through analyses of the exhibits themselves.

INSTITUTIONAL SETTINGS AND ESTABLISHMENT OF THE EXHIBITS

Located in Budapest's castle district, the Military History Museum is one of the city's crown jewels, together with the Széchényi National Library, the National Gallery, and St. Matthias Church. The district, which lies on a hill overlooking the Danube River, has been designated a World Heritage site by UNESCO. The area is restricted to authorized vehicles, so tourists make the trek by foot or public transportation—a funicular ascends from Adam Clark Square on the Buda side of the Chain Bridge, and a bus from Moscow Square carries visitors up through the gothic arches of the Vienna Gate.

The Military History Museum and War History Archives were founded on November 16, 1918, the same day that Hungary proclaimed itself an independent republican state after the collapse of the Austro-Hungarian Empire. Today the museum is part of the larger Institute of Military History that includes a library, archives, map room, and the open-air Weapons History Park. Among the institute's activities is the publication of a quarterly periodical, the *War History Bulletin*. In addition to state funding and revenues from ticket sales, the museum is supported through the Military History Museum Foundation. Its exhibitions include "Soldiers, Castles, Weapons" (a large model of a fifteenth-century castle); "Brighter Than the Chain, the Blade" (1848–49 Revolution); the "Hungarian Royal Army (1922–45)"; and "Sword and Wreath" (military symbols during the last millennium).

In 1990 Gyula Rázsó was named the first civilian director of the Military History Institute and Museum.[2] In an interview following his appointment, Rázsó described what the transition to democracy meant for the institute: "For long decades, the Military History Institute *suffered under the rule of the Political Supreme Group Directorate.* Now it has been given a different role. Among our tasks, in the first instance, is basic historical research, and in the second instance, the expansion, care, and exhibition of our collections" (quoted in Hankó 1990). The exhibit "Thirteen Days" grew out of what was supposed to be a temporary photographic display, "'A People Cried Out . . .' Revolution and Freedom Fight in Hungary, 1956," which appeared in this changed political context. Györgyi Kalavszky Bánffyné organized the photographic display and wrote the text with Col. László Korsós, the current director of the museum. The museum's photographs were supplemented with those from Hungary's wire service, MTI. In an interview Bánffyné explained that the idea for expanding "A People Cried Out" into a fully developed exhibit was triggered by a visitor's donations. The man had been a student at the Technical University in 1956 and had gone into exile in Germany after the uprising was suppressed. On a visit back to Hungary after all those years, he presented the museum with photographs, identification papers, telegrams, and other material related to 1956. The museum directors decided to ask for the public's help in collecting additional material. They issued an appeal through the press, and in response people brought in photographs, documents, and objects, many of which were used to supplement the museum's own holdings, "resulting in a more complex and interesting display" (Bánffyné 2001).[3] This expanded exhibit—renamed "Thirteen Days"—was inaugurated on October 21, 1991.

Bánffyné and her colleagues were well aware of the difficulties they faced in constructing a visual narrative of 1956 that relied on an unfolding historiography. She described the conception of the exhibit: "We began to think that it was possible to try to organize this 'Thirteen Days' exhibit. It took great courage, because we were just beginning the task of processing and writing up the history [of the revolution], so there were still a lot of open questions about what could be accepted as factual. What was it? How did it happen? We decided we would try to show this." The wording here suggests that, as a professional historian and curator, Bánffyné was conscious of the tentative nature of scientific knowledge and the interpretive character of its display. Furthermore, as an employee of a state-run cultural institution, she understood her responsibility to present the public with the closest possible approximation of an elusive and contested truth. In talking about the reactions of visitors to the exhibit, she mentioned a man who wrote in the guest book, "Is this all?": "Now, this person was of the generation who played a role in the revolution, and in his eyes, it was a completely different picture: It was a very, very big thing, a very heroic thing. In a word, he saw it subjectively, while we try, as much as possible [to maintain an objective stance]." In another case, she continued, "someone was here from one of the nests of fighters— I don't remember which one, the Corvin Passage group, the Széna Square group—and that person says, 'The most intensive fighting was here,' and someone from another group says, 'The most significant battles were here.' You can debate this to the end of the world. Big battles were fought here, and there, and there; that's history."

The validity of truth claims is not an issue for Gergely Pongrátz. During long years of exile in the United States, he remained active in the struggle against communism through his involvement in the World Federation of Hungarian Freedom Fighters and similar organizations. He set out his views in his 1982 memoirs, *Corvin Köz 1956*, and he has never wavered from his beliefs: the young street fighters embodied the true spirit of the revolution, and their single-minded goal was the overthrow of communism.[4] For the far right, Pongrátz is a cult figure who personifies an uncomplicated notion of the revolution as the glorious, spontaneous uprising of an oppressed people. His detractors, however, accuse him of playing to the extreme right in the interests of self-promotion, of intolerance toward competing memories and conceptions of 1956, and of distorting the historical record in order to elevate his own role in the uprising. They charge him with attempting to enhance the prestige of the street fighters by diminishing the contributions of other groups—the writers who paved the way for the uprising, the students who triggered it, and the reform communists who endorsed it (Eörsi 1993; Litván 1996, 160; Gyémánt 2000). Most disturbing is his vendetta against the martyred defense minister Pál Maléter, whom he condemns as a traitor who got what he deserved (Pongrátz 1982, 247). Evidently, Pongrátz was never able to forgive Maléter for initially opposing the revolution.[5]

Pongrátz defends himself by admitting that he is indeed biased when it comes to the role and reputation of the freedom fighters. But, he argues, "my account of the historical events is objective, and so far, 'official historians' have not been able to deny its accuracy" (1982, 263). When he returned to Hungary, he explains, the schools were still teaching a twisted version of 1956. While he is not a trained historian, his experiences as leader of the Corvin fighters placed him at the center of the action, and his aim is to describe what he saw. Moreover, he believes that his position as a former commander morally obliges him to set the historical record straight on behalf of the men and women he led. Regarding his enduring responsibility to the freedom fighters, he writes, "the greatest distinction of my life came when these heroes, the Corvinistas, chose me as their commander. This honor demands that as long as I live, I must nurture and protect the spirit and memory of those heroes who sacrificed everything for the homeland" (226). The museum is one mode of preserving that memory, together with his memoirs, a children's camp that he opened in 2001, and a chapel that he is now constructing across the road from the museum.

The 1956 Museum is located on a country road about halfway between Kecskemét and Szeged in the flat, agricultural region of south-central Hungary. For the passing motorist, the white stucco building would disappear into the landscape as just another farmhouse except for the startling site of a tank in the yard. A sign on the face of the building identifies it as the 1956 Museum, and a small, black-marble plaque below the sign states that it was constructed in 1925 as a Roman Catholic elementary school. The property is fenced off, with a graveled parking area to one side. The collections are housed in the two rooms of the former school, and Pongrátz lives in the adjoining teacher's quarters. The museum is open only by appointment, though when Pongrátz is available to show people around, he sticks a handwritten "open" sign on the locked gate next to the bell. The guestbook reveals a steady stream of visitors— groups of school children, Hungarian sightseers, and tourists from Western Europe, North America, and as far away as Australia and Japan.

Originally, Pongrátz planned to establish the museum in Budapest. According to his statements in a newspaper interview, he had found an appropriate facility and secured authorization for its use. Then, after the Socialist Party took control of the government in 1994, the permit to operate a museum was rescinded. At that point he decided to buy his own building (Pósa 2001). He found the old schoolhouse, which was a wreck at the time. The school had been nationalized when the communists took power and then closed in the 1970s. Over the years it was used by the local cooperative farm as an equipment storehouse, a tobacco drying shed, and a bunkhouse. Pongrátz spent several years restoring it, doing much of the work himself. The museum was opened on March 15, 1998, blessed by the Roman Catholic bishop of Nagyvárad (Oradea, Romania).

Directors of "museological collections" in Hungary may apply to the Cultural Heritage Ministry for licenses to operate as museums. The permit also makes them eligible for state funding. The ministry reserves the "museum" designation for those institutes where professionals perform the tasks of collection, research, and public education (Fogyatkozó Látogatók 2000). Pongrátz has not applied. He said there are two reasons why he has not asked for state support: "One of the reasons [is], if the government doesn't put in money, the government has nothing to do with the whole thing. They cannot tell me what to do and how to do it. That's one of the reasons. And the other reason [is], I'm not risking the chance that I'm asking and they're going to say no. . . . I'm not risking it" (2001).

Another potential source of revenue involves creating a foundation. Hungarians can earmark 1 percent of their annual income taxes to any legally constituted, nonpartisan foundation that has existed for at least three years. Pongrátz established his foundation a couple of years ago with an eye toward availing himself of this opportunity. When the organization reaches the three-year eligibility threshold, he will probably seek support from the public. But once again, he has expressed reservations about exposing the museum to interference by outsiders: "I don't know if it's worth it. We're going to put in a couple of newspapers an advertisement and the account number, and we'll see what happens. But you see, this museum is my own property. Nobody can put his nose in what I'm doing over here, and what I'm not doing" (2001). Thus, the 1956 Museum is funded mainly through Pongrátz's own small pension. The only visible source of support is a donation box set on a table along with a few items for sale—1956 T-shirts, lapel pins, decals, and postcards.

György Schöpflin points out that this distrust of the state and of public institutions is characteristic of postcommunist thought. The "hyper-étatism" (Schöpflin 1993, 288) of the bloated communist political system resulted in a deep antipathy toward the state that spilled over into the public sphere as a whole. Leery of politics, public officials, and bureaucratic procedures, people relied on personal connections to get things done (1995, 64). Predictably, this cynical attitude and reliance on unofficial channels has carried over into the postcommunist period. While the 1956 Museum receives no public support and the owner is loathe to apply through regular channels, he does enjoy good relations with individuals in the Ministry of Defense as well as the Military History Institute. Most of the military equipment in the collection, including a Soviet T-55 tank, was acquired through these personal connections. Pongrátz stated: "You see, they don't give me money, but the Department of Defense, when I'm asking for something, they give it [to me]—the tank, the cannons, the mortar" (2001).

The state and the institutions through which it imposes its authority command less respect in postcommunist settings than in older democracies and no longer instill terror. The diffusion of power is a critical component of postcommunist transformation, visible in the cultural as well as the political arena. Artifacts such as the Russian tank undergo a metamorphosis when they are transferred from the Defense Ministry to a private collection. They cease to exist as weapons of totalitarianism and are held up instead as gleaming trophies of the defeat of the communist regime. As Otto Fenichel puts it (1954, 151), an object that once belonged to someone more powerful is a sign that its possessor has robbed something of the power of its original owner. The relationship between the object and its new owner reflects the feeling, "I have acquired something by force or fraud that originally belonged to someone more powerful, but which is now a talisman for me, or which connects me magically with the previous possessor" (149). The question is, what does the voluntary surrender of the trophy to a private collector say about postcommunist political culture? Two other examples of Pongrátz's artifact acquisition through personal channels will help us think this through.

The first involves a large Russian military map of Europe that charts the locations and numbers of army personnel, tanks, and airplanes at the time of the uprising. When asked where he acquired it, the museum owner responded: "From the Soviet Headquarters in 1990. Half give it to me, half steal it. When they showed me this map, I said that I would like to take it. And the person who showed it to me, he turned around and [said], 'I don't hear anything.' So I took the map, and I have it. Very, very valuable; very interesting" (Pongrátz 2000). The second item is a chunk of the Stalin monument. Pongrátz gave a speech at the Military History Institute, and afterward an army colonel went over to him and gave him the relic for his museum. Pongrátz added mischievously: "I always get something! I always get something!" (2001). His exuberance reflects the delight he experiences in expanding his collection to include these items. But this pleasure is not so simple. His acceptance of these objects is a creative act through which he participates in the reinscription of the items' biographies and, by extension, the political culture of the nation. The aura surrounding the tank, the map, and the bronze fragment is a function of the status of the institutions that once owned them. When state and military officials donated the articles to Pongrátz, some measure of the authority and prestige invested in them by these powerful institutions was conferred to him and to his museum (Pomian 1994, 163). For instance, when the Russian map was removed from the Soviet military headquarters and hung on the wall of the 1956 Museum, it affirmed the role of the freedom fighters and their commander in an uprising that eventually culminated in the overthrow of Soviet hegemony. What these examples show, then, is that under the conditions of postcommunism, legitimacy is not always extended from the state to civil society, but rather—in this case—to a well-connected individual who embodies a conservative political ideology.

Nevertheless, Pongrátz's position vis-à-vis the circles of power in Hungary is ambiguous and contradictory. He acknowledges his access to people in high places, but given his enduring distrust of the state, he is more comfortable in the role of outsider. Both Pongrátz and his supporters make much out of the fact that the only museum devoted solely to the revolution is far from the glittering capital and not supported by the state. György Csete, an architect who is designing the chapel across the road, stated in an interview: "I don't know how many people have heard that Gergely built a 1956 museum with his own money and his own hands, with the help of a few construction workers. Because 1956 has no museum in Hungary! This is the shame of shames!" ("A Templomépítők" 2001). In an interview broadcast on Győr television, Pongrátz claimed that this oversight reflects the Orbán regime's attitude toward the revolution: "The government and members of the government speak very beautifully about 1956. Very beautifully. But they don't do anything. They don't do anything about 1956."[6]

OVERVIEW OF THE COLLECTIONS AND THEIR ORGANIZING PRINCIPLES

The Military History Museum presents the revolution as a thirteen-day episode that began with the student demonstrations on October 23 and ended with the Soviet invasion on November 4. The name of its exhibit, "Thirteen Days . . . October 23–November 4, 1956," resonates with the title of one of the classic books about the revolution, Tibor Méray's *Thirteen Days That Shook the Kremlin*. Published in 1959 by the exiled writer, this work in turn is evocative of John Reed's tribute to the Russian Revolution, *Ten Days That Shook the World*. This chain of signification, with its ironic allusion to 1917, reinforces the mythic status of 1956 as the first volley in a long revolution that culminated in the overthrow of the Soviet empire.

In keeping with these literary allusions, the exhibit has been designed as if it were a book that presents the story of the uprising chronologically. Glass showcases containing mainly printed matter and photographs line the walls of the main room, channeling visitors in a clockwise direction.[7] The first of these showcases serves as the title page and prologue to this imaginary book. The title of the exhibit appears in large print, below which is a quote by poet György Faludy that locates the uprising alongside earlier struggles for national sovereignty: "1703, 1848, and 1956: Once every hundred years we stand up against our torturers" These abstract references to a hazy past are given dramatic, tangible form through material synecdoches for the revolution: a chunk of the Stalin monument and a Hungarian flag with a hole in the center. The excised communist emblem, with its bright red star and golden sheaves of wheat, is reminiscent of a publisher's colophon.

Subsequent showcases serve as chapters devoted to each of the thirteen days of the uprising. Structurally parallel, each case bears a date as its title. Next to the date is a bulleted outline of the day's main events. Each list contains about a dozen entries, creating a fairly dense text. Revolutionary posters, flyers, newspapers, and photographs are fastened to

Dated showcases in the Military History Museum's chronological presentation of the revolution, "Thirteen Days . . . October 23–November 4, 1956."

the backboards of these cases. While the displays are dominated by this textual and photographic material, they are made more arresting by small objects that reflect the museum's military focus—pistols, ammunition, model tanks, insignia, and helmets. Larger undated showcases featuring more visually impressive objects such as uniforms, flags, and larger weapons break up the monotony of the dated displays. One of these depicts the "natural habitat" of the street fighters and links the exhibit intertextually to the 1956 Museum. The setting is established through autumn leaves scattered over piles of cobblestones. Machine guns and a helmet with a hand-painted Kossuth emblem are placed on the stones. Two mannequins appear. One is dressed in the worn, tan trench coat that has come to be conventionally associated with the anonymous street fighter. The other is outfitted in a brown leather jacket, black boots, and a dark brown beret. A small label identifies these objects as the clothes worn by Gergely Pongrátz, leading figure of the Corvin Passage fighters, donated to the museum on October 19, 1999.

The presentation of visual evidence confirms an apparently objective account of the past, giving it "the character of inevitability and common sense" (Hooper-Greenhill 2000, 23). As a well-designed exhibit, "Thirteen Days" produces a visual narrative that naturalizes the rhetorical acts of selecting and arranging objects, including the decision to display Pongrátz's leather jacket. The curators consciously set out to construct a balanced and objective account of 1956 that would encompass a range of experiences and memories. Yet they were fully aware of the impossibility of representing a transcendent Truth that would correspond to an unmediated historical reality (Gieryn 1998, 197). When asked about the central message of the exhibit, Bánffyné described an interpretive frame that unifies the nation by drawing upon deeply rooted myths of suffering and unjust treatment (Schöpflin 1997, 29–30): "I don't know if you remember those reproductions of symbolic paintings that are in the hall before you enter the exhibit. One is [the work of] Simon Hollósy. In the other one, a large hawk has downed a little bird. The little bird symbolizes Hungary, and the large hawk the Great Powers around us. The whole exhibit is built around the idea of the paintings."[8]

She then pointed out a set of photographs in the second room of the exhibit. Here allegory is abandoned as the nations symbolized by the hawk are identified through glossy photographs of their leaders. The pictures are divided into two groups. The first is labeled "Those who decided Hungary's fate." High-ranking officials of the Soviet Union, Yugoslavia, Poland, Czechoslovakia, and Romania are represented, together with U.N. Secretary General Dag Hammarskjöld and three Americans: Pres. Dwight David Eisenhower, Secretary of State John Foster Dulles, and Ambassador to the Soviet Union Charles Bohlen. The second group of photographs is labeled ". . . and those who carried it out." All of the individuals depicted here are from the Soviet Union: the commander of the Warsaw Pact, the head of the KGB, the ambassador to Hungary, the military commander in Budapest, etc.

The reference to Hammarskjöld and the Americans requires explanation. One of the cruelest surprises for the revolutionaries was the decision of the United States not to intervene despite Eisenhower's promise of Western assistance should the enslaved peoples of the satellite countries rise up against their occupiers (see, e.g., Lipták 2001, 92). From the standpoint of the United States, the specter of nuclear war made confrontation with the Soviet Union unthinkable. Yet as "the patron saint of the oppressed nations," the United States was in an awkward position (Békés 1997, 56). Eisenhower's National Security Council worked out a compromise position, according to which the United States would try to convince the Soviet Union to allow Hungary to become a neutral nonaligned nation. In turn, the United States would agree not to exploit the

Tivadar Kosztka Csontváry, *Finch Downed by a Hawk* (1893). As employed by the Military History Museum, the iconography suggests that Hungary has been conquered by an unspecified world superpower. Courtesy Janus Pannonius Museum, Pécs, Hungary

situation or to allow Hungary to join NATO, thus recognizing the Soviet Union's security concerns. Eisenhower instructed Dulles to work this message into a campaign speech delivered on October 27. But Dulles— ever the fanatic anticommunist—dropped the references to neutrality and the prohibition on NATO membership and stated only, "We do not look upon these [Eastern European] nations as potential military allies." On October 29 Dulles cabled Bohlen and instructed him to convey this same terse message to Soviet officials. The ambassador complied, thus sealing the fate of Hungary (Granville 1997, 81; Litván 1996, 92–93).

Hooper-Greenhill (2000, 23–48) has shown that assembling portraits into a collection establishes relations of equivalence among the people represented. In the display at hand, the equivalence created by grouping the photographs together under common labels is amplified by their structural uniformity. They are identical in size and format and similar in composition and subject matter. As a result they generate a discourse of culpability that extends beyond the Soviet empire to denounce the betrayal of Hungary by the world's other superpower and by the United Nations, the international organization charged with world peace and security. Bánffyné confirmed this reading as she articulated the curators' aims in arranging these photographs: "Hungary's fate in the twentieth century was decided by the Great Powers. . . . The relationship between the Soviet Union and the United States ultimately determined Hungary's fate. We wanted to show how heroically a small people struggled and fought for freedom, unsuccessfully, but in ways successfully. We wanted to draw attention to the extent to which this small country was a pawn in the games of these Great Powers."

In contrast to the symmetry, unity, and order of the Military History Museum's exhibit, the 1956 Museum strikes the visitor as a less predictable but pleasant mélange. Unimpeded by professional exigencies, the owner has followed his own creative impulses in composing this visual narrative. The result is a collection that appears not so much *organized* as *arranged,* much like a living room designed to display its owner's possessions to best advantage. Stenciled, white-washed walls, parquet floors, and wooden-beamed ceilings provide a warm setting. Museum fittings are supplemented by ordinary furniture—mismatched wooden bookcases and tables of various proportions and finishes. Most of the artifacts are arrayed according to category (weapons, photographs, books, and such), but there are also vignettes where dissimilar items are grouped together for aesthetic effect. In fact, several compositions include fresh or dried floral arrangements.

Assembled according to the whims of its owner, the collection is much more varied than that of the Military History Museum. A good share of the objects on display are weapons, ammunition, and other military equipment that either were used in the armed struggle or are of that vintage. A large number of photographs are also exhibited. Predictably, Corvin Passage is given special attention through enlarged photographs of the site and reproductions of Lajos Győrfi's bronze sculpture, *The Kid from Pest.* This realistic statue of a boy holding a rifle was erected in front of the Corvin Cinema in 1996. It was modeled after a well-known photograph of János Varga, a thirteen-year-old fighter immortalized as Jancsi,

This large flag reportedly flew over the Hungarian embassy in London during World War II. It was donated to the 1956 Museum in Kiskunmajsa by the former ambassador in 1999.

the kid from Pest, in Pongrátz's memoirs.[9] As Boros notes (1997, 126), the figure of the child fighter advances the myth of the revolution as a David-and-Goliath struggle in which innocents armed only with their faith in God faced off against an armored giant. Photographs, paintings, and small-scale models of Győrfi's statue are all on display in the 1956 Museum, as is the text of Antall Andrási's verse "Pesti Srác" (The Kid from Pest).

Yet a striking number of objects are at best tangentially related to the uprising—a half dozen old radios, a reproduction of Ádám Mányoki's por-

Lajos Győrfi's memorial to the young street fighters, *The Kid from Pest* (1996), at the Corvin Cinema in Budapest. Photograph by Zsolt Bátori

trait of Ferenc Rákóczi II, and a corroded brass relief of Lenin. By definition, the term "collection" implies an *interrelated* set of objects (Belk 1994, 317), so what is going on here? To answer this question, it is helpful to look more closely at the modes of acquisition employed by the owner.

As noted above, most of the military equipment was given to Pongrátz by the Ministry of Defense. In most instances, he approached his contacts with a particular class of item in mind—for example, a certain-caliber machine gun. He was similarly purposeful in procuring stock photographs from the archives of the Military History Museum. In other cases, Pongrátz simply happened across items that caught his attention, such as the Russian map. Recognizing their value as authentic historical documents or artifacts, he talked their owners into donating them to the museum. The best example of an object that he stumbled across and then intentionally—indeed, resolutely—fought to acquire is a tattered Hungarian flag with a gaping hole in the center. Pongrátz considers this flag his greatest treasure. His account of its provenance reflects the bases for his evaluation, and his description of how he acquired it demonstrates the creation of national mythology in its most passionate form.

A visitor from the local area came to the museum one day and, as he and Pongrátz sat on the patio talking, told the collector about the flag. The ensign flew across the street from the Stalin monument in 1956, and after the revolution was crushed, its owner—now an old man who lives on a farm a couple of villages away—took it down late one night when the streets were empty. He kept it hidden for over thirty years. Pongrátz immediately wanted to see the flag, so they jumped in the car and drove over. The old man showed it to him and told him that a lot of people had tried to talk him out of it, but he refused to give it away. Pongrátz describes how he pleaded: "I said, 'Pali bácsi [Uncle Pali], sooner or later, you're going to kick the bucket! And after you kick the bucket, this flag is going to the dump. But if you give it to me, it's going to be in a museum fifty years from now!'"

He convinced the man, and the flag now hangs triumphantly in the museum. To its right is the Russian map, and to its left is the royal Hungarian coat of arms and a faded funeral wreath. A tiny slip of paper is pinned to the flag, and the handwritten text identifies it as a gift of "Pál Ördögh, Zsombó, May 10, 2000." The flag is an object of great value by virtue of its historical associations: It flew over the nation's capital in 1956, positioned near the scene of one of the revolution's central mythic events, the destruction of the Stalin monument. As a relic that has been rescued from time and preserved in a museum, it will bear eternal witness to that glorious uprising. Furthermore, its dilapidated physical condition raises it to the status of a sacred object (Guthe 1959, 277; Pomian 1994, 167). Pongrátz remarks: "It's in very bad condition, very *viharvert* [weather beaten]. But that's the nice in it. That's the nice in it." Representing the nation, and by extension, the Hungarian people, the flag is a magnificent display of endurance.

Many of the artifacts in the 1956 Museum were acquired as unsolicited gifts. Some of these allude to 1956—a New Jersey license plate that reads "OKT 23" and a bottle of 1956 Tokaj wine presented to Pongrátz by Democratic Forum politician Sándor Lezsák when Pongrátz was in the hospital following a heart attack. Others have nothing to do with 1956—a sixteenth-century map of Hungary given to Pongrátz years ago by a Hungarian association in Cleveland and a flag that flew over the Hungarian embassy in London during the Second World War given to him by the former ambassador. Then there is the communist kitsch—a ce-

The 1956 Museum owner's most treasured object is a flag that flew near the site of the Stalin monument. Its communist emblem was cut out by an insurgent during the 1956 uprising.

ramic plaque bearing the images of Lenin, Stalin, and Rákosi as well as a gun-metal gray communist emblem that was blazoned on some public building during the Kádár era. These objects are complemented by all manner of ephemera—a poster with a map of pre-Trianon Hungary, a photograph of Cardinal József Mindszenty, and a card that states in several languages "The Hungarian state, the native land, is NOT for sale!"

Puzzled by the eclectic nature of the exhibit and searching for the unifying thread, I asked Pongrátz if he ever *refused* to accept a donation. He answered affirmatively, vaguely stating that people occasionally offer something that isn't appropriate for a museum. When I pressed him about the communist paraphernalia in an attempt to discern why he included these hated images and symbols in his magnum opus to the freedom fighters, Pongrátz would only say about each item, "Somebody brought it to me." Complimented on the pleasant visual arrangement and told that, with no formal training, he must have a good eye, Pongrátz corrected me, "Heart.A *bad* heart!" He chuckled at this reference to his history of heart attacks, but I finally understood. This seemingly capricious collection locates the revolution within a broader conservative ideology of traditional, Christian nationalism that comes from the heart. While the museum owner has carefully and methodically assembled a narrative of 1956 through the material culture available to him, he has done so on the basis of principles that are held at a deeply intuitive and emotional, rather than cognitive, level and derive from the authenticity of experience.

The conservative ideology that frames the production of culture in the 1956 Museum requires elaboration. Analyses of conservatism in postcommunist Central and Eastern Europe tend to emphasize its most extreme, protofascist, anti-Semitic forms. (In Hungary this usually means focusing on ultraconservative writer and politician István Csurka.) Sabrina Ramet (1999, 18–19) writes that at the core of radical-right beliefs is "an ideological and programmatic emphasis on 'restoring' supposedly traditional values of the Nation and imposing them on the entire Nation or community." Pongrátz's concept of nation has organic undertones, but it is neither hostile nor exclusionary. He describes his Armenian ancestry in *Corvin Köz*, writing that while his blood is Armenian (his forefathers arrived in Transylvania in the fourteenth century), his heart is Hungarian (Pongrátz 1982, 27–28). He has publicly argued against giving minorities special status, contending that everyone in Hungary should be treated alike. After all, he reasons, Gypsies, Jews, Romanians, Slovaks, and Magyars fought side by side in 1956, and they now rest together in Section 301 of the New Public Cemetery, united for eternity by their sacrifices.

Pongrátz's train of thought regarding this illustrates the centrality of the 1956 revolution in the conservative ideology he makes available to the public through the discourse of the 1956 Museum. Crucifixes and irredentist posters may *decorate* the museum, but these are not what animate the owner. In conversations, he ignored the 1919 dismemberment of Hungary by imperialistic French president Georges Clemenceau and helpless American president Woodrow Wilson (Ignotus 1972, 147), reserving his wrath for Eisenhower, Dulles, and Bohlen: "We were sold out by the United States government. The Hungarian revolution started on the 23rd of October. On the 28th of October, Imre Nagy declared victory. The Russian troops left Budapest. [The Nagy government] started to talk with the Russians [about withdrawing from the country]. . . . The next day, the 29th of October, the telegram was sent to Charles Bohlen." Pulling a copy of his book from the shelves and reading the infamous line from Dulles's cable to Bohlen, Pongrátz then cried out in despair: "What was the purpose of [sending] that telegram the day after we won the revolution? [Of telling] the Russians, 'We don't want Hungary; Hungary is yours!'?" Many years later, he continued, Boris Yeltsin visited the United States and stated on television that the downfall of communism started in 1956 in Hungary. "So these kids," he added, "they weren't making only Hungarian history; they were making world history. Thanks to these kids, the whole communist system collapsed" (Pongrátz 2000).

Both of these exhibits, then, locate the revolution within a narrative of oppression, triumph, betrayal, and ultimate victory. This theme is subtly but forcefully written into the carefully scripted exhibit of the Military History Museum. The eclectic nature of the 1956 Museum's holdings, together with their more whimsical arrangement, invites a more imaginative reading that centers around the romantic image of the courageous and selfless young street fighters.

THE PRESENTATION OF THE COLLECTION

Museum collections are presented to visitors through either self-guided or personally conducted tours. The Military History Museum is self-guided, with the exhibits designed to enable visitors to understand the information and ideas that the curators want to convey (Alexander 1996, 197; Hooper-Greenhill 2000, 172). Attendants are sometimes seated in the main room of the "Thirteen Days" exhibit, and at other times they wander in and out as they patrol the wing. Their ability as well as their willingness to interpret the material on display varies. Occasionally, the head of visitor service is on duty, and he enjoys explaining the historical background of objects to viewers. More often, the attendants serve simply as guards. When asked whether there were information sheets about the exhibit translated into English, German, or other foreign languages, one elderly attendant replied that she had no idea and suggested going to the main information desk.

As we have seen, "Thirteen Days" was originally devised to impart information to a public whose knowledge about what took place in 1956 was at best incomplete. Thus, its function is primarily didactic. Michael Belcher (1991, 62) notes that the educational functions of didactic exhibits are not left to the objects themselves but are carried out by other interpretive media. Here the planners relied heavily on the written word. Three types of text were employed: labels and explanatory information written expressly for the exhibit; newspapers, posters, and other printed materials produced and circulated during the revolution; and excerpts from literary works that allude to 1956. Examining these texts reveals that the lessons to be mastered extend beyond the factual. A shared national identity is made available, with the written material providing a common historical text whose rhetoric emphasizes Hungarian self-determination.

The most prominent items in the first category, information written by the curators for the exhibit, are the detailed lists of events that took place on each of the days of the uprising. In addition to charting the demonstrations and strikes, the military maneuvers and the armed struggles, these tablets record the achievement of democratic civil liberties—the reconstitution of political parties, the formation of workers' councils, and the establishment of independent newspapers and radio stations. The theme of vulnerability and betrayal also appears here:

October 29: • The Minister of Defense announces that Soviet troops will begin to withdraw from Budapest the following day.
            • U.S. Ambassador to Moscow, Bohlen, informs the Soviet leadership that his government has no plans concerning Hungary.
October 31: • Radio Miskolc [in Eastern Hungary] reports that Soviet troops have reversed direction and are marching into Hungary.
            • U.S. President Eisenhower expresses admiration for the Hungarian people but states that he does not view the new leadership as a political coalition.

Other facts that appear on the lists are historically insignificant, but they correspond to symbolically powerful photographs and help create a seamless exhibit. One example appears in the list of events occurring on October 29: "Stalin Boulevard, Stalin Bridge, and Stalin Square are renamed Hungarian Youth Boulevard, Árpád Bridge, and Dózsa György Boulevard." A photograph in that day's showcase depicts a man on a ladder hanging a handmade sign on the wall of a building. The sign reads "Teréz Boulevard," the precommunist designation of Lenin Boulevard. A second example is an entry in the list of events for November 2 that reads, "The Writers Union starts a collection for the families of the fallen." The showcase contains the familiar photographic image of a wooden box overflowing with cash, sitting unguarded on a sidewalk. Above the box is a poster reading, "The honor of our revolution allows us to take up a collection for the families of our martyrs IN THIS MANNER." As these examples demonstrate, the *word* is made visible in countless photographs: the cold, chiseled inscription on a defaced monument to the Soviet liberators, the artful graffiti that weaves together Hungary's call to arms with a demand that the Russians go home (Talpra Magyar, Hí a haza; Minden Ruszki, Menjen haza!). The presentation of such photos alongside tablets of historical "facts" establishes a semiotic loop of text-image-text that draws the viewer into the imagined past, where the people arose to reclaim and rename the urban landscape as a site of moral action.

The second type of text, the revolutionary newspapers, posters, and flyers, offers a more fragmented yet compelling narrative. The appeal of these documents is partly a function of their graphic design. Compared to the uniform lists of events, they are simply more interesting visually. In addition, their tone conveys the atmosphere of exhilaration, optimism, and nervous energy that marked the thirteen days. This is true even of those documents that foreshadow the treachery that was to come, for example, an appeal issued by a group called the Revolutionary Hungarian Youth. Printed in both Russian and Hungarian, the flyer implores, "Soviet Soldiers! You drove the German fascists out. Would you want to follow in their footprints now? Do you want to crush an independent Hungary? We cannot believe this. Don't shoot! Go home!"

The authenticity of these documents is of even greater significance than their content. Crudely laid out and clumsily printed, they force viewers to reflect upon the circumstances of their production—the urgent need to disseminate information quickly, the risks involved in subverting the Communist Party's control of public information. These documents also invite contemplation about their consumption by a public trying to stay abreast of rapidly unfolding developments. There is a performative dimension to the act of reading old newspapers or posters that takes museum visitors back to the streets of Budapest in the autumn of

1956. As they stand before the showcases and survey the material, they stand in for the original readers, reenacting their dreams of national neutrality and sovereignty.

The third type of text used in the Military History Museum's exhibit, excerpts from the literature on the revolution, is overtly rhetorical. The selected passages lend emotional intensity to the historical facts as they amplify the exhibit's organizing theme of vulnerability and betrayal. November 4, the final day of the uprising, is represented by photographs of Russian tanks rolling in, and the absence of Western intervention is captured by two literary excerpts. One of these is the last stanza of Gábor Görgey's poem "Requiem, 1956," written in November of that year. The lines are a bitter allusion to the frantic radio messages that were broadcast from Hungary when the Soviets attacked. As Görgey's words suggest, these desperate pleas for help were met with only token gestures of support:

> Hello world! Hello! Hello! Can't you hear?
> Then I'll scream it out:
> > There must be freedom! Freedom!
> > Do you understand? Give it to us at last!
> Send us wreaths and beautiful, colorful ribbons,
> We expect truckloads of wreaths and powdered milk:
> We like to bury our dead with ribbons and glass beads, our
> > be-ribboned, be-ribboned dead.[10]

The second excerpt is from Albert Camus's speech "Kádár Had His Day of Fear," delivered on March 15, 1957, at a meeting in Paris organized by the Anti-Fascist Solidarity Committee to mark the Hungarian holiday. Camus's uncompromising stand as a leftist who condemned tyranny in any form led him to take a strong public position on behalf of the Hungarian revolutionaries, expressed in dozens of speeches, articles, petitions, letters, and telegrams. In the postcommunist commemorative discourse of 1956, his words are recited more often than those of any other international figure. János Szávai helps us understand their resonance for a public bent on distancing itself from the communist past when he writes that Camus rejected the era's fashionable moral relativism. As a passionate believer in the European concepts of justice and freedom going back to the Greeks, Camus addressed the Hungarian revolution as if it were an ancient tragedy: The oppressed rose up against tyranny, and the victory of tyranny, the defeat of the oppressed, could only be temporary (Szávai 1996, 966–67). The passage on display echoes the sentiments of the Görgey verse and carries through the theme of betrayal: "I am not one of those who want the Hungarian people to take up arms again, to commit itself to an uprising doomed to be suppressed before the very eyes of the Western world which will not spare either its applause or its Christian tears but in the end will go home and put on its slippers like football fans after the Sunday match."[11]

Walter Benjamin (1968, 67) once observed that "the phenomenon of collecting loses its meaning as it loses its personal owner. Even though public collections may be less objectionable socially and more useful academically than private collections, the objects get their due only in the latter." The emotional power of the collection displayed in the Military History Museum is indeed blunted by its abstraction from the lived social world. Housed in glass showcases and frozen in time, even Camus's indictment loses intensity. In contrast to the impersonal, didactic character of the "Thirteen Days" exhibit, the 1956 Museum is highly evocative. Belcher (1991, 60–61) writes that the evocative exhibition "is about arousing emotions in the visitor by creating an atmosphere and possibly a 'theatrical' style of presentation." The romantic aura that permeates the 1956 Museum is largely a function of the curatorial presence of its owner.

Michael Billig (1990, 62) draws our attention to the construction of memory through conversations about the past in which one or more of the discussants participated in the events. In this interactive mode of commemoration, the past is discursively recalled and recreated with each telling, as when a family leafs through a photo album and talks about the people and places whose images are preserved there. Something similar takes place in the 1956 Museum, with Pongrátz serving as the patriarchal storyteller. As he guides his visitors through the artifacts, he brings the past to life through his personal recollections of what happened almost a half century ago. Visitors participate in the discursive reconstitution of the past through a process Gillian Roberts and Janet Bavelas (1996) call semantic collaboration. In keeping with conventional practices of conversation involving museum guides, Pongrátz is granted extended time to speak. But the act of "listening" is an essential component of the production of meaning. At times, visitors offer their own recollections or comments based upon their knowledge of history. Yet most are too young to recall the events, and few of them are experts in the subject. Instead, they move the conversation along through verbal and nonverbal communicative acts that affirm Pongrátz's stories and tacitly invite him to continue—nodding, asking questions, and voicing surprise.

The interactive nature of making meaning is important to keep in mind, for it helps us understand the guided tour as a mode of presentation through which the public is ideologically insinuated into the worldview of the museum owner. Perhaps the best example of this dialogic process in my experience as an interlocutor involves Pongrátz's story about a pair of revolutionaries depicted in one of the photographs on display. He identified the subjects as Hard Hat and Bag Man, the *noms de guerre* of a father and son who fought together in 1956 and were hanged together in 1958. Pongrátz's account did not end with this cruel fact. His voice cracked, tears ran down his cheeks, and he asked in despair, "Why did they have to hang them?" He paused to collect himself, looking to me for answers. My sympathetic silence and eye contact, probably a typical response, signaled the achievement of shared emotions as we jointly contemplated mankind's capacity for senseless cruelty.

The homelike setting of the 1956 Museum contributes to the dialogic accomplishment of meaning. Visitors treat their host with deference and respect and seldom challenge either his version of the past or his right to articulate it. Indeed, Pongrátz's presence as a living mediator between past and present is seen by both him and his guests as a crucial component of a trip to the museum. He described his status as a living relic: "I get a lot of calls, and they tell me, 'The bus is coming,' I don't know, 'Tuesday,' and [they ask] if I'm going to be here. Because that's the only reason they're coming, if I'm here. . . . [M]y presence is as much important as what they see. The explanation I give them. And, what's the word? Authentic. I'm an authentic freedom fighter" (2001). His claims are reinforced by entries in the guest book such as, "I never had a more authentic tour guide than the hero of '56, the pride of our nation, the commander of the Corvin Passage, Gergely Pongrátz."

The tour is conducted according to a loosely structured but standard script consisting mainly of descriptions of objects and their use during the uprising. Notwithstanding Pongrátz's emotional accounts of individuals who were killed in the fighting or reprisals, his delivery is remarkably factual, even dispassionate, in tone. This stems from his belief that objects speak for themselves, "an old but persistent museum fallacy" (Hooper-Greenhill 2000, 49). According to this prestructuralist epistemology, the object embodies a unified, stable, and unchanging meaning, and the task of the curator is simply to present it in an ideologically neutral way. The etymological connection of the word "object" to "objectivity" is evident in this rendering. According to scientific or journalistic notions of objectivity, an external world of objects independent of human experience, perception, or history is "out there" waiting to be "discovered."

Of course, a more culturally informed concept of museum artifacts locates them within human history and emphasizes their profoundly political and rhetorical character. Eilean Hooper-Greenhill (2000, 108–9) writes that objects enable reflection and speculation. They are invested with deeply held feelings and associations and give material form to abstract ideas such as "nation" or "sacrifice." Specific histories and personal experiences are recalled through their observation, and they are used to construct mythic identities of hero and villain. For instance, the treachery of the Russians is foregrounded in Pongrátz's description of a machine gun as he discursively articulates the object to a well-known historical episode: "This is a machine gun that was installed on the Soviet tanks, and it was very, very dangerous, because the Russians, they shot everything that was moving. People standing in line for bread; they even shot them. Fifteen dead and twenty-five wounded, this machine gun" (2000). In a second example, a Molotov cocktail reveals the ingenuity of the freedom fighters in Pongrátz's telling: "That's a Molotov cocktail. I don't know why they call it Molotov cocktail. The Russians, the only thing they had to do with it, they received it. Nothing else. But the first Molotov cocktail, how it was born: We were on József Körút [Boulevard] 82, right on the second floor. We were then about eight kids, and on the Körút, right under us, was a tank." He explains that the tank had been disabled, and he was throwing hand grenades at it, but they would not explode. "My brother Andy, he took his handkerchief, and he came over and said, 'Greg, pour a little gasoline on the handkerchief.' I asked him, 'What do you want?' He said, 'You'll see.' So I poured gasoline on the handkerchief, he put the corner of the handkerchief in the neck of the glass, and he said, 'Now put in the cork.'" His brother then told him to go to the window, light the handkerchief, and throw the bottle at the tank. He did as he was instructed, and the result was an enormous explosion: "BOOM!! . . . Everybody was yelling, 'The tank is burning! The tank is burning!' That was the first Molotov cocktail" (2001).

The claim that the Corvin Passage fighters invented the Molotov cocktail is a bold one. Absent any knowledge of the history of guerilla warfare, Pongrátz relies entirely on experiential memory to craft his interpretation of the object. Within his mental world, the weapon *was* created at 82 József Boulevard in 1956. Visitors may doubt the claim that the Corvinistas invented the device, but this does not diminish the thrill of hearing what their outmatched ancestors accomplished with a bottle, a rag, some gasoline, and a match. As Samuel argues (1994, 16), popular memory tends to crystallize around extraordinary events and larger-than-life personalities because they stir the imagination. Nevertheless, the museum owner's audacity is remarkable. Harking back to the earlier builders of cabinets of curiosity, Pongrátz is convinced that all knowledge about 1956 can be gathered under one small roof. Objective reality is located in the artifacts and reflected in the photographs, and Truth can be faithfully rendered through their presentation. György Schöpflin locates this "epistemological certainty" within the thought world of postcommunist conservatism: "there is a strong, sometimes unshakable belief in the 'single truth,' that it is possible to know with absolute certainty and reject epistemological doubt. . . . Correspondingly, there is a rejection of ambiguity, the dogmatism of which is at times close to morbid, as if the very idea that there could be more than one answer to a particular question was inherently threatening. Coupled with this is the unstated belief that the world is black and white, that there is only one answer to questions, in a word that things are knowable in a one-dimensional fashion" (1994, 194).

The curators of the Military History Museum recognized the need to sort carefully through various factions' competing truth claims about 1956. They avoided endorsing any single position by offering a narrative of national unity in the face of external oppression and betrayal. In the guided tour of the 1956 Museum, the revolution centers around the heroic struggle of the freedom fighters. This one-dimensional narrative both draws from and feeds back into a conservative ideology that claims to have a corner on truth.

Faded photographs, yellowed newspaper clippings, and crumbling ruins all evoke a sense of mourning. They all represent what are ultimately fruitless efforts to safeguard memories and defy the passage of time. In the exhibits analyzed here, one composition captures the melancholy and trauma of Hungary's 1956 revolution with particular force. It resides in the 1956 Museum. The focal point is a mannequin wearing men's clothes—a brown wool jacket, a plaid shirt, black trousers, and a brown fur hat. While the clothes look vaguely old, neither their vintage nor their

Clothing worn by András Pongrátz when he escaped from Hungary in November 1956, now on display in the 1956 Museum.

style is remarkable. The outfit is functional, assembled with an eye toward warmth and comfort. The figure is wearing the red, white, and green armband of a street fighter, and an automatic rifle is strapped across his chest. A mortar and a wooden box with mortar shells are placed in front of the figure, as if it were using these arms to defend a position. A vase of red, white, and pink chrysanthemums sits on the floor just to the left of the box of shells, and a potted plant sits on the right.

An enlarged photograph of the bombed-out buildings in Corvin Passage covers the walls behind the figure. While the composition is free standing, if the viewer faces the figure head on, he appears to be framed by a vaulted entrance to Corvin Passage. Thus, there is no mistaking his affiliation with the Corvinistas. The weaponry is labeled, though the clothes and figure are not. As it turns out, Gergely Pongrátz's younger brother, András, was wearing these clothes when he escaped across the border in late 1956. This information is presented verbally as Pongrátz gives his tour, as he mentions flatly, "My brother Andy, he was wearing those clothes during the revolution" (2001).[12]

As with any museum display of a partisan's clothing, the freedom fighter's outfit invites the visitor to imagine the courage and ingenuity of the wearer as he faced untold dangers. Yet there is one aspect of the composition in the 1956 Museum that makes it unbearably sad, and that is the visible traces of its own construction. Unlike more professional installations, this one is awkward, amateurish. Reminiscent of P. T. Barnum's mermaid hoax, the mannequin has been assembled of different pieces: the face is white, while the hands are flesh colored. And like a baby doll that cannot hold its bottle, the figure cannot clasp the rifle: the fingers are held stiff and straight in front of the body, with the rifle tucked behind the right wrist. The cobblestones, autumn leaves, torn-down street signs, and other conventional elements of the street fighters' natural habitat in the Military History Museum or the National Museum are perhaps clichéd, but they do not arrest the viewer's attention. Here the vase of chrysanthemums departs entirely from professional display practices. Viewers are not only reminded of a shrine, they are forced to realize that someone has *made* this shrine. And therein lies the unintended emotional power of this display and of the 1956 Museum as an institution: It speaks to the human drive to honor and preserve the past regardless of the limitations of the composer.

CHAPTER SIX

SCULPTING HEROES IN A POST-RADICAL AGE

WHEN THE SOVIET ARMY attacked Hungary on November 4, 1956, Imre Nagy, his political supporters, and their families took refuge in the Yugoslav embassy, just down the street from where the Stalin monument had stood. A couple of weeks later, János Kádár signed a document guaranteeing their safe passage home. He provided a bus for their convenience, and despite some misgivings, they climbed aboard. Instead of taking them home, the Russian driver delivered them to a military compound on the outskirts of Budapest. From there they were deported to Romania and held in an isolated resort used by Communist Party officials. In the spring of 1957, security police arrested Nagy and most of the other men. Their wives and children still were not allowed to return home, and they learned about the men's fate only in August, 1958. Nagy's wife, Mária; his daughter, Erszébet; and the other adults were instructed to send the children out to play and to report to the dining room. The guards unceremoniously tossed a couple of Hungarian newspapers on the table, and the women read the announcement of the Justice Ministry: Nagy and three co-conspirators had been executed for plotting to overthrow the government, while a fifth defendant had died in prison of an unspecified illness.[1]

By the time Nagy was put to death, the mass retaliations had suppressed all remnants of resistance, but authorities still dared not transport the remains of the martyred prime minister beyond the prison walls. Thus, the bodies were buried next to the gallows, and a truckload of old office furniture was dumped over the site to cover up any traces of the graves (Pajcsics 1999). Three years later the coffins were dug up and reburied after nightfall in unmarked graves in Section 301, a remote, weed-choked corner of Budapest's New Public Cemetery. In addition to the remains of prison inmates who either died in custody or were executed,

Section 301 contained dissected cadavers as well as the carcasses of experimental and zoo animals (Dornbach 1994, 13–14; Susa 2000, 177). The earthly remains of Imre Nagy and his colleagues lay in this unhallowed ground for almost thirty years. Family members' requests for information as to their whereabouts were repeatedly rejected.

In the summer of 1988, the reform-communist prime minister Károly Grósz visited the United States, where he publicly stated that the families of Nagy and his fellow martyrs would finally be permitted to bury their dead. The problem was, nobody knew exactly where the bodies were. Anticipating the thaw in Cold War relations, the Interior Ministry had already began to search for the remains. Following Grósz's announcement, the problem became more urgent, and the agent assigned to the case was ordered to complete the task as quickly as possible. Digging through mountains of top-secret material, he happened across a dossier labeled "Hornets' Nest." There he founds maps and documents that revealed that Nagy had been buried in Section 301, Row 23, Plot 9, under the name of Piroska Borbíró, a woman born in the village of Párkánynánás in 1908. With family members watching, the bodies of Nagy and his comrades were disinterred in the final days of March, 1989. The scene offered grim testimony to the barbarity of the post-1956 criminal-justice system. The bodies had been stuffed in croker sacks fastened with wire and then placed face down in crude wooden boxes. The boxes, wrapped in tarpaper, had largely rotted away. Aluminum tags around the ankle bones corresponded to the entries in prison records, confirming the men's identities (Pajcsics 1999; Susa 2000, 177).

On June 16, 1989, thirty-one years to the day after their deaths, Imre Nagy and his fellow martyrs were given a funeral. Some two hundred thousand mourners gathered in Heroes' Square for a majestic, solemn ceremony that lasted four hours and was broadcast throughout the nation by Hungarian Television. Then, in a private service, the families returned their dead to Section 301, which had been transformed into a national memorial site. The Nagy funeral is widely regarded as the most important symbolic event in the collapse of Hungarian communism (Tóbiás 1999; Garton Ash 1990). It has been characterized as "the closing day of the Kádár era" (Szilágyi 1999a, 131), "the symbolic burial of the post-1956 regime" (Kis 1999, 28), and "the day the nation buried communism" (Mink 1999, 19). This conclusion of an era was symbolically accomplished through the long-awaited consecration of the men who had initiated the long revolution. In Péter György's words (2000, 255), "The heroes again became heroes."

Or did they? By definition, a hero is a famous figure widely recognized and revered for epitomizing the virtues of the culture. While the deeds attributed to a hero may be apocryphal, like the story of George Washington and the cherry tree, they belong to the store of common historical knowledge. Yet as István Rév remarks (1995b, 27), Imre Nagy was brought back to life from anonymity when he was placed on the bier in Heroes' Square. The communist government had published a series of White Books establishing the official historical narrative on the uprising soon after its suppression. The final volume, *The Counter-Revolutionary Conspiracy of Imre Nagy and His Accomplices*, claims to "prove beyond all doubt that well before the counter-revolution erupted, a secret underground organization led by Imre Nagy existed for the purpose of overthrowing the state" (Magyar Népköztársaság 1958, 3). Having completed the case, the producers of official knowledge then erased Nagy from history books aimed at the masses, apart from fleeting references to his "revisionist" premiership of 1953–54 and his "treasonous" activities in 1956 (see, e.g., Blaskovits 1978, 122–23). As a result, "Nagy was the unknown hero for those hundreds of thousands who came to bury him" (Rév 1995b, 27). The enigma surrounding Nagy is reflected in Ferenc Pintér's well-known funeral poster, *Remember at the Bier of Imre Nagy*. Resembling the negative of a photograph, Nagy's disembodied head is silhouetted in white against a black background. His distinctive mustache and bushy eyebrows appear in black, but the face is otherwise featureless. Two empty circles, one red and one green, represent Nagy's signature pince-nez. As James Aulich and Marta Sylvestrová describe the poster (1999, 100), "Imre Nagy reappears as a ghostly presence, his meaning refusing the constraints of realism."

As mentioned throughout this book, the transformation of a nation's political order demands a new constellation of cultural symbols that express the values of the new regime and legitimize its authority. The identification of new national heroes is a key component of this symbolic work. Recognized for actions that can be readily dramatized, for example, defending the fatherland against foreign and domestic tyranny, they provide models for conduct, inspiring succeeding generations to emulate their courage and sacrifice (Edelman 1988, 43). Typically, revolutionary leaders are elevated to the status of foundational mythic figures, as was the case with Lenin, Gandhi, and José Martí. As *the* symbol of the Hungarian revolution (Rainer 1995), Imre Nagy would appear to be a perfect candidate for the position of postcommunist foundational hero. Yet his reputation has remained somewhat ambiguous and contentious, mainly

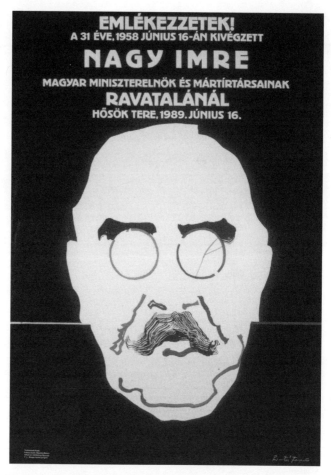

Ferenc Pintér, *Remember at the Bier of Imre Nagy* (1989). The image was originally produced for a poster announcing the symbolic burial of Imre Nagy and his
fellow martyrs in Paris's Pére-Lachaise Cemetery on June 16, 1988. With revised
text, it was recycled the following year when it finally became possible to hold
the actual funeral in Hungary. Courtesy Hungarian National Gallery

because he was a committed communist. In a 1996 public opinion poll,
Budapesters were asked to name individuals associated with the events
of 1956. Seventy-eight percent of them listed Nagy, but only 56 percent
of those surveyed counted him among the positive actors in Hungarian
history; another 28 percent were uncertain; and 6 percent judged him
negatively ("A Mai Közvélekedés" 1996).

Against this backdrop, a privately financed memorial to Imre Nagy
was unveiled in Martyrs' Square on June 6, 1996, the centennial of his

birth. Created by Tamás Varga, son of renowned sculptor Imre Varga, the monument features a life-sized representational statue of the prime minister. The bronze figure is dressed in a homburg and top coat, with an umbrella tucked under its arm. Nagy's identity is established by his mustache and spectacles. The figure stands in the center of a bronze bridge that spans a water-filled marble pool; its hands rest on the railing of the bridge. The monument is located at the center of an axis formed by two landmarks: The Hungarian Parliament, with its towering gothic spires, lies just to the northwest, and an obelisk that pays tribute to the Soviet liberators, the last such monument remaining in the city, stands in the center of Freedom Square, just to the southeast. The figure of Nagy is positioned so that the Soviet monument is behind him, and he is looking pensively over his left shoulder toward parliament.

Tamás Varga's life-sized statue of Prime Minister Imre Nagy (1996).

Varga's monument to Imre Nagy in Martyrs' Square near the Hungarian Parliament.

Semiotically, the composition employs conventional signs whose meanings are widely shared. The hat, coat, and umbrella suggest that the figure is an average city dweller in the middle of the twentieth century. The bridge, a common aesthetic motif, symbolizes transition or passage. The Hungarian Parliament is an architectural metaphor for the nation. In the composite, these elements offer a coherent visual narrative that activates and amplifies a patriotic reading of the former prime minister: Imre Nagy was an ordinary man whom fate singled out to lead the nation. A lifelong communist who believed to the depths of his soul in proletarian internationalism, Nagy was no less ardent in his love for the Hungarian motherland. After a lifetime of trying to reconcile the tensions between communism and patriotism, he reached a crossroads in October, 1956. Forced to choose between his competing loyalties, Nagy chose the nation.

The sense of closure is strong in figurative statuary, where a likeness of the referent is literally carved in stone or cast in bronze. But from a structuralist standpoint, the meaning of any text is constantly reworked and regenerated through its intertextual relationships. As David Lidov puts it (1999, 172), "Whatever happens, whatever we invent, we can extend language to talk about it." Varga's monument can be understood as a "primary text" that tells a self-contained story about Nagy while repeating, embellishing, and challenging other narratives. As a primary text, it also serves as a palimpsest for the inscription of meaning by other cultural producers. To put it in the language of semiotics, the monument mobilizes "secondary texts." Following John Fiske (1987, 117–24), the term is used here to refer to discourse *about* the monument, specifically, the reviews of art critics and the verbal responses of the sculptor.

As discussed below, critics savaged the monument as deeply political, a charge that Varga vigorously denies. The aversion to politics displayed by both the critics and the sculptor is characteristic of postcommunism, a reaction to the overinflation of politics and its extension into all spheres of life in the communist system (Schöpflin 1995, 65–67). More fundamentally, however, faith in the efficacy of politics and the political subject has been abandoned throughout the West in what Terry Eagleton (1996, 25) refers to as the "post-radical age." He writes that in the postmodern imagination, the subject can barely "fasten its own shoelaces, let alone topple the political state" (16). From this perspective, the celebration of revolutionary heroes who are ready to lay down their lives for the fatherland comes across as an outmoded relic of nineteenth-century romanticism. As Barry Schwartz and T. Bayma put it (1999, 962), "To die in the name of something greater than oneself—something that precedes and survives one's own existence—is a traditional idea." The following analysis looks more closely at the critical discourse surrounding the monument and Varga's account of his artistic intentions as a way of further elucidating this distrust of politics and political heroes. Since the critics as well as the sculptor draw from the lore surrounding Nagy in crafting their arguments, a biographical sketch of Nagy is first needed.

IMRE NAGY

Even in life, Imre Nagy was an extraordinarily ambiguous figure. His biographers consistently write about "the dualism of his personality" (Molnár 1989, 170) and the liminality of his character as a man caught between Moscow and Budapest, between the Communist Party and the Hungarian nation. He was a Muscovite communist and a Hungarian patriot (Unwin 1991, 4), a professional revolutionary and an indomitable humanist (Molnár 1966, 168). Tugged in opposing directions by political tides, he was "a go-between and peacemaker" (Molnár 1989, 186), "a bridge between the authorities and the people" (Molnár and Nagy 1983, 84).[2]

Nagy was born in Kaposvár in 1896, a time when an aristocracy loyal to the Habsburgs still controlled much of the nation's land in the form of large, feudal estates. The vast majority of the rural workforce was either landless day laborers and farm servants or owners of small plots that were hardly large enough to sustain life (Hanák 1991, 143). Among all the nations of Europe, only Romania suffered a comparable imbalance in the distribution of land (Romsics 1999, 22). Nagy's background was that of the poor, landless peasantry; as a result, he would be centrally concerned throughout his life with land reform, agrarian policies, and the plight of the peasant.

Drafted in World War I and sent to the Russian front, Nagy was captured. He joined the Bolshevik Party while in prison and fought with the Red Army during the Russian Revolution. He returned to Hungary in 1921 and worked as an organizer of agricultural workers in his native Somogy County. He was imprisoned several times for his illegal activities and emigrated to the Soviet Union in 1930. Joined by his wife and daughter, he remained there until the end of World War II, devoting most of his time to the study of agricultural issues.

Soon after returning to Hungary, Nagy was appointed minister of agriculture in the provisional government. As such, he was a chief architect of the postwar land reforms that dismantled the great feudal estates of the Esterházys and Festeticses and gave the land to the peasants. When the communists seized power, they launched an aggressive campaign aimed at the rapid and complete collectivization of land. Nagy objected, advocating a more gradual, voluntary approach. Because of his opposition, he was stripped of his various positions within the government and party hierarchy. He then taught agricultural economics before being brought back into politics as minister of food in 1950. With this assignment, János Rainer writes (1997, 145), "the former defendant of democratic agrarian policies became the faceless executioner of Rákosi's most vicious offensive against the peasantry."

In his two-year tenure as minister of food and then requisitions, Nagy was responsible for a complex set of agricultural policies collectively referred to as the system of requisitions. Central to these was the obligatory delivery of agricultural products—wheat, corn, eggs, milk, poultry, meat, lard, wine, and such. In part, the system was designed to address urgent food shortages. But the quotas were highly unrealistic—often impossible to meet—and the methods of extraction from noncompliant producers were brutal. The term "attic sweeping" (*padlássöprés* or *padláslesöprés*) evoked nightmarish images of the search and seizure of hidden food or grain and now is used as shorthand for the broader persecution of the peasantry.[3] The more fundamental intention of the system of requisitions was to liquidate the kulaks. Unable to meet the harsh production demands, peasants were forced to move to the cities and accept industrial work. Those who remained inevitably came into conflict with the authorities and became the victims of terror. Proceedings were launched against hundreds of thousands of peasants for the crime of "endangering the public supply" in the late 1940s and early 1950s because of their failure to satisfy the requisition demands (Rainer 1996, 476–79).

Nagy became prime minister in 1953 during the climate of de-Stalinization. Beyond implementing modest structural reforms, his program set a new tone in which the excessive Sovietization of Hungarian life was played down in favor of national identity. Miklós Molnár (1989, 179–80) claims that "the psychological liberation of national consciousness was a conscious and deliberate initiative" that reflected Nagy's enduring, authentic patriotism: "Expressions such as the education of 'little Hungarians' in the schools, or the 'hearts of ten million Hungarians throbbing in unison' came naturally to his lips, as did quotes such as 'if the earth be God's hat, our fatherland is the bouquet pinned to it.'"[4] Tibor Méray (1959, 18) provides a sense of the changed climate of everyday life: "The people could once more feel free, speak out, live, seek some diversion. Thousands of little artisans were again able to obtain licenses to work. Blacksmiths and barbers reopened their shops. . . . The young people listened openly to jazz; Budapest's pretty women resumed their use of rouge and eye-shadow."

Although he was thrown out of office in 1955, Nagy had won the nation's heart as a man of the people. Playwright Gyula Háy writes (1990, 456): "When the authorities only dared to go out into the streets in curtained automobiles, Imre Nagy went around on foot. And the other pedestrians and tram and bus riders understood his unspoken words." An important element of the mythology surrounding Nagy involves his return to civilian life as a modest, ordinary man. Méray relates (1959, 45):

> [H]e would walk daily down Orsó Street to Pasaréti Avenue, the route of the Number Five blue omnibus, which would already be

jammed when he boarded it at Virágárok or Áron Gábor Street. He would ride to the end of the line, to Vörösmárty Place in the heart of the city. . . .

Some days he would take with him two little children, the daughter and son of his daughter Zsóka. He would seat them on the terrace of Gerbeaud's confectionery, on Vörösmarty Place, and order a cream puff or ice cream for them.

Nagy's actions during the 1956 uprising have been the subject of debate. Communist Party leaders brought him back into the fold and appointed him prime minister in a desperate attempt to gain control of the situation, and despite his unwavering opposition to their policies, he accepted in the spirit of maintaining party discipline. For the first few days, he pursued a course aimed at restoring order, though his supporters emphasize that he was not responsible for attacks on demonstrators or the Soviet intervention. His measured approach was a function partly of his loyalty to the party and partly of his careful, deliberative nature. Rainer (1997, 149) writes that he was caught off-guard, while Molnár and Nagy (1983, 131) claim that he was out of touch with what was going on in the streets. Whatever the explanation, the prime minister undeniably hesitated and wavered in the initial days of the revolution.

A decisive shift in Nagy's stance took place on October 28. In a radio address he rejected the Politburo's position that the uprising was a counter-revolution, characterizing it instead as "a great national and democratic movement embracing and unifying all our people." He ordered a cease fire, announced that the Soviets had agreed to a troop withdrawal, and pledged that the government would "immediately begin to realize the people's just demands" (quoted in Lasky 1957, 115). Two days later he announced that the one-party system would be abolished, and he formed a cabinet modeled after the postwar coalition government. With wording that foreshadows Varga's likeness of Nagy on the bridge, Molnár and Nagy (1983, 144) write that by taking this step, "Imre Nagy crossed the Rubicon." When news reached Nagy that eastward-bound Soviet forces had reversed direction, he announced the withdrawal of Hungary from the Warsaw Pact. The last time the Hungarian public heard him speak was his radio announcement at dawn on November 4 stating that the nation was under attack.

CRITICAL RESPONSES TO THE MONUMENT

Critical responses to the Nagy monument are framed within broader concerns about transitional politics and public art. Tibor Várnagy (1996, 42) argues that the "great cleansing"—the removal of communist monuments—was a mistake that was compounded as equally politicized statuary replaced Imre Varga's tribute to Béla Kun or Viktor Kalló's mortally wounded martyr. In a piece that appeared in the art periodical *Balkon*, he writes (1996, 42): "after most of the statues produced in the former system were spirited away at great expense and untold energy, we immediately tried to fill in the empty space. It's no wonder we haven't been successful in depoliticizing public monuments over the past few years, since they've become instruments for seeking justice and atonement." In the flurry of statue building since the political transformation, he continues, almost no aesthetically significant memorials to the revolution have appeared.[5] Instead, cheap, sentimental schlock has cropped up all over the country, with Varga's monument to Imre Nagy a prime example. Péter György concurs (2000, 22, 332), castigating the monument as kitsch in his book on public memory and 1956.

As Matei Calinescu (1987) points out, the concept of kitsch has both aesthetic and ideological dimensions: it is *bad* art, embodying banality and triteness, and it is *diversionary* art, offering easily digestible products that can only deliver "vicarious experience and faked sensations" (Greenberg 1957, 102). Reviewers criticized Varga's monument on both of these counts. First, judging the work on its aesthetic merits, they point to what Calinescu (1987, 251) would call its "stylistic overdetermination," or, less generously, its "aesthetic overkill." György (2000, 332) describes the composition as a theatrical scene that looks as if it were constructed of pieces from the prop room of *Madame Butterfly*. For Julianna P. Szűcs (2001), writing in *Népszabadság*, its dizzying eclecticism offers a chain of associations leading from Japanese gardens (*japánkert*) through garden dwarfs (*kerti törpe*) to dwarf papas (*törppapa*), that is, Father Smurf. The elements of the composition are all wrong: The bridge is clumsy, heavy, and oversized; the pool of water is shallow, dirty, and stagnant (Várnagy 1996, 41). The statue of Nagy is particularly unsatisfactory. Extending his allusion to Puccini's opera, György (2000, 332) charges that Varga has represented Nagy as "a slightly dull, romantic, minor civil servant enjoying a well-deserved retirement, who is perhaps musing about . . . the adventurous sex life of Captain Pinkerton." In combination, these awkward elements fail to convey the psychological and political turmoil that Nagy and the nation experienced in 1956.

The most scathing criticism of the monument links it ideologically to statuary created during the middle and late Kádár period. As discussed in chapter 2, the imposing monuments of high socialist realism were surrounded by sacred protective zones whose transgression instilled awe and terror (Yampolsky 1995, 94). As the political climate softened, these unapproachable, grandiose overstatements were rejected in favor of "deheroized" statuary that was smaller in scale and designed to feel more human (Rényi 2000; Wehner 1986, 66–78). In Szűcs's words (2001), "the statue stepped down from its overly high pedestal and positioned itself in proximity to viewers, attracting them with its playthings and practically inviting them to paw it." The ideological effects of such "Disneyfied" (György 2000, 22) monuments was to infantilize citizens by drawing them into a sphere of amusement and fantasy. In a tone dripping with ridicule, Szűcs (2001) describes Varga's "charming" composition as a contemporary example of the genre: "You can saunter across the bridge and lean against the railing. You can stand next to the figure and ruminate with it; you can put your arm around its shoulders and pretend to be pals with it. You can spit into the water from the bridge, or blow soap bubbles, or hide under it." She concludes that if this kind of statue—infantile, saturated with petty-bourgeois sentiments, and stylistically straight out of the Kádár era—can be erected in 1996, "then it reveals that this age doesn't know what to do with Imre Nagy."

While Szűcs charges that the monument diverts attention from a lack of consensus about the prime minister, she never mentions any specific points of contention over his memory. Tibor Várnagy (1996, 43), however, dredges up Nagy's role as Rákosi's minister of food and requisitions, arguing that the monument is an affront to "the people still living among us for whom the name of Imre Nagy brings to mind personal memories of attic sweepings rather than '56." In his two-volume, definitive biography of Nagy, János Rainer (1996, 478) acknowledges the psychological trauma inflicted on the peasantry by the agricultural policies that Nagy oversaw and the inheritance of bad memories by succeeding generations. But he claims his subject was always remembered as the "father of agrarian reform" and as the respected prime minister of 1953–54, not as the overlord of the attic sweepers: "this dark period of his life, when he was implementing the most hated Stalinist measures, somehow 'dropped out' of the collective memory of the Hungarians and was not held against him later" (Rainer 1997, 145). Assuming Rainer is correct, Várnagy's appeal to the victims of terror is a red herring. His real target is not the minister of food and requisitions—in fact, it is not Imre Nagy at all—but rather the persistent construction of heroes—any heroes—and a public art reflecting that conservative tendency.

AN ARTIST'S DEFENSE

Tamás Varga claims that the monument's deficiencies are a function of the constraints imposed by the donors coupled with his own lack of experience.[6] Plans for the monument were initiated by the late Andrew Sarlos, a Hungarian-born investor who was one of Canada's wealthiest citizens.[7] Initially, it seems odd that the man who "pioneered the concept of the hostile takeover in Canada" (McGraw-Hill Ryerson 2000) would be the driving force behind a monument to an ardent believer in radical economic democracy. Indeed, the same year that Sarlos, Hungarian-Canadian businessman Béla Fejér, and Hungarian entrepreneur Sándor Demján financed the monument to Imre Nagy, they opened the Polus Center, the largest shopping mall in East Central Europe. Located on the site of a former Soviet military base on the outskirts of Budapest, the shopping and entertainment center reportedly "seethes with Americana," with sections designated as Wall Street, Rodeo Drive, and Sunset Boulevard (Agovino 1998).

But Sarlos's autobiography clarifies his motivations. As a twenty-one-year-old air force officer in training, he was caught up in the purges of the early 1950s and spent a year in Rákosi's prisons, where, he writes, he "endured brutality and privations far beyond the boundary of common decency" (1993, 19).[8] When Imre Nagy was appointed prime minister in 1953, Sarlos was among the thousands of political prisoners who were released. His gratitude and affection are obvious when he describes Nagy as "the highly respected, gentle economist whom we knew as the instigator of some valued land reforms, . . . a prime minister committed to finding remedies for Hungary's various illnesses" (21). At the time of the 1956 uprising, Sarlos was an economics student at Karl Marx University. He participated in the demonstrations on October 23 and joined the National Guard in response to the Soviet attack on November 4. Stationed in City Park near where the Stalin statue had stood, his unit was quickly overwhelmed and disbanded on November 7. He left Hungary the following day (28–32).

Sarlos returned to his native country only in the 1980s, when he became centrally involved in Hungary's economic transition both as an advisor and investor. In fact, he and the other donors originally planned to erect the statue of Nagy in front of the Bank Center, one of their Budapest properties whose tenants included Citibank, the World Bank, and the U.S. embassy. Eventually, the venue was changed to the more ideologically neutral terrain of Martyrs' Square. But, as Imre Nagy's daughter and her husband recall, Sarlos's conception of the monument as a representational figure held sway (Boros 1995, 41). Nagy was to be cast as "Imre bácsi"—Uncle Imre—a figure who could be easily understood by the masses. This is the design Varga was commissioned to create.

In addition to the demand that he produce a realistic likeness of his subject, Varga was forced to collaborate with József Finta, a renowned architect who worked with the donors on several big projects, including the design of West End, the huge shopping complex at Nyugati Railroad Station that devoured several city blocks. According to his original concept, Varga states, Martyrs' Square would have retained something of its slightly seedy character, thus evoking the 1950s. But the architects insisted on converting the area into a carefully manicured, landscaped space replete with the most expensive, beautiful paving stones available. It was also they who insisted on the pond, according to the sculptor. He favored a leaner, sparer composition and unsuccessfully argued that the surfeit of design elements and decorations would detract from what ought to be its central component, the statue of Nagy. Varga does fault himself for his failure to articulate his vision in negotiations with the architects, blaming it on his relative youth and obscurity.

While the sculptor tacitly admits that the monument may be unremarkable artistically, he vigorously rejects the critics' claim that it is political, offering two responses to this charge. First, he argues that he has no particular attachment to 1956 or to Nagy and therefore had no political agenda in taking on the project. In the context of this defense, Varga discusses the significance of the bridge. For him, it is evocative of the sense of danger and tension experienced by the nation during his lifetime. Second, he claims that his creative intention was to represent the *human* side of Nagy. In advancing this argument, Varga appeals to the folk-heroic legends surrounding the prime minister, claiming that these capture the essence of who Nagy was. As the following analysis shows, both arguments involve a rejection of politics as sectarian and confrontational in favor of dimly remembered but widely shared historical memories.

THE BRONZE BRIDGE

Born in 1953, Tamás Varga cannot recall the revolution. But, as he describes his childhood memories, "1956" was always in the air, shrouded in secrecy and mystery, the subject of muffled whispers and cryptic allusions. As with all children of his generation, Varga was socialized into a convoluted set of communicative norms that dictated what topics could be broached and how in various social settings: within the family, in the presence of guests, among friends, and in school. The revolution loomed large within this communicative dynamic as a central reference point for evaluating a person's moral character. As he explains, the range of possibilities for public action was extremely narrow during the 1950s, so the uprising presented citizens with an unparalleled opportunity to take a stand. As a result, people's behavior in 1956 became the litmus test for judging their courage, honesty, and integrity.

Varga states that this tense atmosphere made a deep impression on him, and while he has no particular attachment to 1956 as a historical event or to Imre Nagy as a historical figure, he was driven to express visually the sense of secrecy, mystery, and danger that surrounded his memories of that time. And this is where the bridge comes in. For Varga, the bridge—or more precisely, *the texture of its surface*—is the most interesting element of the monument. He denies any intentional metaphoric connections between the bridge and either the dichotomies of Nagy's personality or the choices he faced. Instead, the bridge relates to the artist's own childhood memories of instability, uncertainty, and hidden perils. The bed of the bridge is made of bronze plates, each about a square yard, which are cast in diamond-shaped patterns that alternate between open gratings and solid metal. In addition, there is a small gap between each plate. This design was intended to evoke the sense of danger experienced by a child (or adult, for that matter) who, walking across a bridge made of wooden slats or metal grating, is never certain that he will not slip between the cracks and disappear into the churning waters below.

Conflating 1956 with images of Budapest's devastation at the end of World War II, Varga describes the inspiration for the creation of the bridge: "I cannot identify definitively which bridge remains in my head—whether it was the Chain Bridge, lying destroyed in the Danube. But there was this bridge that you could walk on, and you could see through the grating, or it was a temporary bridge between Parliament and Buda.[9] Whether this was a dream or a nightmare, I don't remember."

By incorporating the open grate for the bed of the Nagy monument's bridge, Varga sought to convey a sense of peril. Photograph by Zsolt Bátori

Curiously, Varga's fusion of 1956 and World War II appears in Budapest's City History Museum as well, where the two events are treated as one in an exhibit entitled "The Resurrection of a City Twice Leveled by Bombs (in 1945 and 1956)." An excerpt on the main panel reads, "The occupying German forces withstood the onslaught of Soviet troops on the offensive until the very end. The result was almost complete annihilation of the city. All its bridges were demolished. . . . In 1956 Budapest once again became the capital of revolutions, the city that in barely more than a decade was shot to rubble for the second time by the Soviet army." By linking these episodes, the sculptor and the museum curators offer the public an elliptical memory of shared suffering, deprivation, and loss at the hands of successive waves of conquerors. The destruction of all seven of Budapest's bridges by the retreating Germans is a well-known story that captures the longer tragedy of Hungarian history synecdochically. While the spans had been repaired by the time Varga was born,[10] widely reproduced photographs documented the scenes of destruction, attesting to the treachery of the enemy and the resiliency of the Hungarians: slabs of concrete pavement poking out of the Danube at forty-five-degree

angles, wooden pontoon footbridges, queues of pedestrians waiting for
ferries, and the magnificent lions that sit at the foot of the Chain Bridge
lying in ruins (see, e.g., Kosáry 1971, 714–15). Indeed, the City History
Museum exhibit contains a full-sized replica of one of the Chain Bridge's
damaged lions. Thus, Varga's visual allegory of the man on the bridge
glosses over politics to locate Nagy at the center of a precarious national
history marked by periodic catastrophe, destruction, and recovery.

THE BRONZE BÁCSI

In his analysis of the construction of Abraham Lincoln as an American
hero, Barry Schwartz (1990) contrasts epic heroes with folk heroes. Using
language that is reminiscent of the art critics' distinction between "classic" and late socialist statuary, he bases the distinction on the accessibility of the figure to the public. Like the commanding monuments of the
early communist period, epic heroes are distant and untouchable, sepa-

Budapest's magnificent Chain Bridge was destroyed in World War II. A replica of
one of the damaged lions that sits at the foot of the bridge appears in the Budapest History Museum. Photograph by Zsolt Bátori. Courtesy Budapest History
Museum Photographic Collection

rated from the common person by an "impassable barrier." Schwartz writes: "Epic heroes are not the kind of beings we may cozy up to. We do not come close to them, let alone touch them, with impunity" (98). But folk heroes—like the modest statues dating from the 1970s—are readily approachable: "As embodiments of the common life, folk heroes are imitable as well as touchable. They are also 'touching' in that they evoke sentiments which become central to their own public identities" (98).

Varga makes a distinction between Nagy the politician and Nagy the man that parallels Schwartz's delineation of the cool, distant epic hero and his folksy counterpart. He acknowledges the fact that his artistic subject was a leading political figure whose actions altered the course of Hungarian history. But he argues that Nagy's greatness lies in the fact that despite his historical significance, he lived his life as an ordinary man. Thus, Varga's intention was to abstract Nagy from politics and to represent his human side, to craft him as a folk hero. By constructing Nagy as an eminently approachable, touchable figure, the artist tapped into and extended the popular folklore surrounding Nagy as a simple, unpretentious man of the people, the doting grandfather who took his grandchildren out for ice cream. In conversation, Varga repeats the legend of Nagy taking public transportation to work, then adds: "Maybe today this story seems ridiculous. Why did he travel by tram when he could have used a black Volga? Maybe it doesn't seem important, but it is, because it tells us something about the everyday behavior of the man."

Thus, for Varga, Nagy was an extraordinary individual *despite* his political role. By presenting him in an accessible manner, Varga hoped to rescue and preserve the memory of a man whose simplicity and humility contrasted sharply with the vanity and ruthlessness associated with politicians. Then, once he has freed Nagy from the burden of his political past, his communist convictions are no longer relevant or divisive. As Varga puts it, the content of Nagy's beliefs is unimportant. What matters is that he was honest about his principles and consistently stood up for them, ultimately sacrificing his life for what he believed in: "Maybe he believed in communism, but nobody can question his good intentions."

THE ECLIPSE OF POLITICS?

Murray Edelman describes two conflicting perspectives regarding the political leader as historical subject. The first position, epitomized by

Thomas Carlyle's work on heroes, holds that "the actions of leaders determine the course of events; history is biography" (Edelman 1988, 44). In contrast, the poststructuralist argument views leaders as nothing more than a creation of language. According to this view, leadership is "an epiphenomenon, a byproduct of more fundamental historical and social processes" (45). The discourses examined herein reflect these two positions. For the sculptor, Imre Nagy is one of Carlyle's Great Men, a humble leader who sacrificed his life for the nation. For the critics, however, heroism is an ideological construction, an unwanted remnant of an earlier, conservative period. Ironically, what is left out of these opposing positions is a socialist humanist position on human agency along the lines of Marx's famous dictum that man makes his own history but under conditions not of his own choosing. Such an approach would recognize Imre Nagy's place in Hungarian history as a man who, against all odds, set the nation on an irreversible course toward political democracy, but whose vision of economic equality recedes ever further into the past.

As noted above, political apathy is characteristic of both postcommunism and postmodernism. In contemporary Hungary, politics is further burdened by the lingering traces of the post-1956 compromise—the public's tacit agreement to be silent, to forget. Along these lines, the philosopher Mihály Vajda has described the Kádár regime as "a very bad farce" whose effects are still being felt today: "Undoubtedly, Hungarians had it better than Czechs or East Germans during those twenty years, but this was the most demoralizing regime, precisely because the limits were vague. Here, you could steal, cheat, be a crook, and the response was, 'That's okay, just don't get involved in politics.' I believe we still see the remnants of this today. There is no solidarity, no strength of character in this country" (in Szilágyi 1999b, 182). Couple that legacy of passive compliance with the rancor surrounding public life today, and it is easy to see why politics garners little respect.

More optimistically, however, I maintain that politics in the broader sense of praxis—free, creative activity through which people transform the world and realize their potential—inheres in the construction of the visual and verbal narratives we have examined. In her attempt to keep alive the Greek ideals of civic virtue, citizenship, and political participation as cherished expressions of the human condition, Hannah Arendt locates freedom in the performance of action. People are free, she writes (1968, 153), "as long as they act, neither before nor after; for to *be* free and to act are the same." For Arendt, the polis is a space where freedom can appear through the performing, communicative act, "tangible in words which can be heard, in deeds which can be seen, and in the events which are talked about, remembered, and turned into stories before they are finally incorporated into the great storybook of human history" (154–55). Despite the undeniable turn away from politics, then, the acts of storytelling encountered in this book support Walter Fisher's (1997, 311–13) faith in people's intelligence, their capacity for authenticity, their ability to argue, and their desire for understanding.

In her discussion of "statue politics" in postcommunist Eastern Europe, Katherine Verdery (1999, 5) writes that the erection of a monument arrests the bodily decay of the person represented, altering the temporality associated with him and "bringing him into the realm of the timeless or the sacred." Given the illusory nature of the public consensus Nagy achieved through his funeral, something further was needed to sanctify him, to corral the ambiguous, amorphous, and sometimes contradictory meanings associated with him. Varga's sculpture was intended to anchor a particular memory of Nagy in time and place, one that foregrounds his decency and humanity.

Imre Nagy's smoking jacket displayed in a cell that held political prisoners. A tear, repaired by hand, is visible on the sleeve. The exhibition appears in the Hungarian National Museum. Photograph by Zsolt Bátori

But perhaps the critics are right; perhaps the age of monuments is over. The avant-garde sculptor György Jovánovics, who designed the abstract monument to 1956 near the grave of Imre Nagy, has said that he entered that competition only reluctantly because of his distaste for memorials as a genre. To his way of thinking, monuments are an inferior mode of expression because "they draw upon conservative, outmoded, nineteenth century artistic elements and are based upon counterfeit claims" (quoted in Mihancsik 1994, 203).

Of all the visual texts that have contributed to the emerging mythology surrounding Nagy, the most successful are those that capture his tragedy with economy and subtlety. Two examples: First, in the National Museum, just across from the exhibit that contains the Stalin monument's hand and Pál Maléter's uniform, there is a mockup of the jail cell where Imre Nagy was incarcerated. His elegant, brown smoking jacket sits on a modest wooden bench. If one looks closely, one can see a rip on the sleeve, carefully but clumsily mended. Second, looking again at Pintér's funeral poster, one will see a faintly visible crack in the left lens of Nagy's pince-nez. Both details, hardly visible, speak worlds about the violence that was visited upon a man who dared to challenge hierarchical power and about the endurance of the human spirit.

THE PERSISTENCE OF NARRATIVE

FOLLOWING THE SYMBOLIC BURIAL of communism in 1989, Hungary implemented democratic political structures that have proven to be remarkably stable and secure. But the political cultural ferment that was
unleashed is as heated as ever, and the legacy of the 1956 revolution remains a primary catalyst in the formation of citizens' sense of self and
nation. The active, sustained production of political cultural identities
through visual narratives linked to 1956 is evidenced by the fact that the
kind of postcommunist memory work examined throughout this book
has not abated. One of the most visible dimensions of this ongoing flux
is the shifting locations of the *lieux de mémoire*. The monuments, exhibits, and sacred objects refuse to stay in place.

One example involves the rehabilitation of Ilona Tóth. After her name
was cleared, the statue was moved to the entrance of the Semmelweiss
Medical School, where it was ceremoniously dedicated by FIDESZ deputy leader Zoltán Pokorni and Justice Minister Ibolya Dávid on November 1, 2001. This official revaluation of Tóth's reputation touched off
a whole new round of public debates, sparked by Péter Kende's editorial
in *Népszabadság,* "Statue for a Murderer?" (2002). He claims that no
one has ever proved that the original charges were factually inaccurate.
Therefore, he argues, "No matter how beautiful Ilona Tóth was as a figure
representing the 1956 revolution, she still killed a man. Thus, she should
not have been rehabilitated, or if she were, then at least a statue should
not have been erected in her honor." The local assembly of Budapest's
Sixteenth District, where Tóth lived, threatened to boycott *Népszabadság* for publishing the vicious opinion of a single individual about one of
its distinguished citizens ("Kegyeletsértő Népszabadság" 2002). So, while
Tóth was absolved legally, the question of her guilt or innocence is still
hotly contested in the court of public opinion.

No longer banned from public space, Ilona Tóth's monument was transferred to the entrance of the Semmelweiss Medical School in 2001. Photograph by Zsolt Bátori

Other examples abound: The eighty-seven-year-old widow of Sándor Mikus protested when a portion of the Stalin monument—a one-hundred-foot section of the base's stone relief—was taken out of storage and built into the House of Terror without her permission (Dobozi 2002). When the Budapest City Council's Cultural Committee upheld her position, conservatives lashed out against the committee's chairman, Free Democrat Ferenc Körmendy, for "treating the Soviet executioner responsible for the deaths of millions of people so kindly" (K. 2002). In the meantime, another portion of Mikus's relief lays on the ground at the Statue Park Museum, where it weathers the elements as museum administrators seek funding for its preservation. In addition, the Military History Museum recently closed its "Thirteen Days" exhibit and now advises potential visitors to see the 1956 display in the House of Terror. Gergely Pongrátz's leather jacket was transferred to the House of Terror, but otherwise, there is little to see in its visual pastiche that is specifically related to the uprising.

Speaking in the twilight of communism, György Konrád (1989,327) alluded to the memory of 1956 as a moral force that would guide the nation in the struggle to effect democratic changes. He stated: "We will achieve the original goal, national and social freedom. We have a memory that we can cling to. We remember that once we tried. Over the course of thirty-one years, this memory became noble. It became classic, like a good novel." When Konrád offered these reflections in 1987, memoirs and historical accounts of the revolution and its terrible aftermath were circulating in samizdat form and would soon spill over into officially sanctioned public discourse. With the communist tyranny of the 1950s as their setting, these stories of honor, sacrifice, and victimization clearly delineated the forces of good and evil. The transformations that were negotiated in 1989 afforded no opportunity for the courageous, heroic actions associated with 1956, and perhaps for that reason, symbolic action became the main strategy for staking out political and moral positions.

Portions of the stone relief that once circled the pedestal of the Stalin monument now line the walls in the House of Terror Museum. In the foreground are busts of Stalin and Mátyás Rákosi. Photograph by Zsolt Bátori. Courtesy House of Terror Museum, Budapest

A section of the stone relief from the Stalin monument awaits installation at the Statue Park Museum. Photograph by Zsolt Bátori. Courtesy http://www .szoborpark.hu

A passage in Géza Ottlik's novel *Iskola a Határon* (School on the Border) anticipates the mythic role that 1956 is destined to play in years to come. The protagonist, a military-school cadet in the 1920s, mentions that the four hundredth anniversary of the Battle of Mohács, where Hungary suffered its first major defeat by the Turks, was approaching. He then muses about the irony of commemorating defeat: "Perhaps it seems strange to celebrate defeat, but those who would celebrate victory here, the powerful Ottoman Empire, no longer exist. The traces of the Tartars as well as the tough Habsburg Empire also vanished, practically before our eyes. We're accustomed to celebrating major battles that we lost but survived. Perhaps we're also accustomed to thinking of defeat as more exhilarating, made of denser stuff, more important than victory—in any case, we regard it as our more authentic quality" (Ottlik 1959b, 422–23). As time goes by and memories of 1956 give way to history, the narratives examined here are likely to take on a far less contentious cast. As visual renditions of the well-thumbed classic Konrád imagines, they will contribute to the familiar story of defiance, endurance, and survival despite the endless history of defeat.

NOTES

INTRODUCTION

1. ÁVO is an acronym for Államvédelmi Osztály (State Security Department). The organization was renamed Államvédelmi Hatóság (State Security Authority) in 1948. Officially, the acronym ÁVH was used thereafter, but in everyday speech the secret police remained the hated ÁVO.

2. The entire speech appears in the appendix of Pető 2001.

3. János M. Rainer (1999a, 445) refines the notion of collective national amnesia when he writes that the silence of the Kádár era hardly means that people had forgotten what happened. The silence may have signaled acquiescence, he argues, but it did not imply public approval of the regime nor acceptance of its explanations about the "crimes" committed by Imre Nagy and thousands of others. Besides, he points out, the silence was far from complete. The "counter-revolution" was taught in history classes, and it was the subject of television documentaries and journal articles on major anniversaries. Gábor Gyáni (2001) also disputes the myth of total amnesia, noting that 1956 leaked into public consciousness in countless ways. For instance, Russian soldiers stationed in Hungary were a visible reminder of the uprising they had suppressed. Another reminder was the absence of the hundreds of thousands of people who emigrated in 1956, leaving behind family members and friends who felt the loss. Even the experience of living under the relative comfort of "goulash communism"—the palatable dictatorship dished up by Kádár in exchange for an end to political dissention—was an indirect reminder of the uprising.

4. György Litván (2000) has catalogued the dominant myths and legends specifically associated with the 1956 revolution.

CHAPTER I

1. Schönherz was arrested and executed during World War II as a result of his involvement with the illegal Communist Party. A political exile, Bolgár served as an officer in the Soviet Army during World War II and participated in the liberation of Hungary. After the war he represented Hungary as a diplomat to Czechoslovakia and then to Great Britain.

2. Art historian Géza Boros (1993) assembled excerpts from a number of news articles, editorials, conference papers, legislative proceedings, and competition entries that chronicle the development of the idea of Statue Park Museum. His collection is an excellent entry into the debates.

3. In the case of disagreements, the city had veto power over the districts. Ákos Tömöry (1991, 74) provides a chart that lists the monuments by district and indicates the recommendation of both bodies to either remove the work or leave it in place.

4. In a 1992 public opinion poll, residents of Budapest were asked to indicate their preferences regarding the fate of ten types of monuments. Lenin statues were regarded most negatively, but the results were still surprisingly positive. Only 9 percent of respondents believed the Lenins should be destroyed, and only 12 percent believed they should be warehoused; 46 percent would put them in the Statue Park, and 33 percent would leave them in place. Other works that were viewed somewhat negatively were memorials to Soviet heroes and statues of Marx and Engels. Those monuments that were seen most positively represented noncommunist leftist political figures, antifascist resisters, and Captain Osztapenkó, a Soviet soldier killed by the Germans during World War II. The Osztapenkó statue was an important landmark on the road to Lake Balaton, and its removal caused the greatest public consternation. See "A Múltat Végképp Eltörölni?" 1992.

5. I am thinking in particular of Imre Varga's memorial to Béla Kun. András Rényi (2000) argues convincingly that not only is the work important aesthetically but also Varga never intended it to be a monument to the ideals of Kun or the Hungarian Soviet Republic. It is a clever farce, a parody of a monument. After all, Rényi points out, it was erected in 1986, by which time the idea of a monument to communism was absurd to anyone. See also Boros 1999.

CHAPTER 2

1. The Austro-Hungarian Empire had been a self-contained unit with a common currency and an extensive internal market. Its breakup thus threw the Hungarian economy into turmoil. The crisis was intensified with the peace treaty in that the territories Hungary lost had been a major source of raw materials. By 1920, agricultural production was about 50–60 percent of its prewar level, and industrial production was about 35–40 percent (Romsics 1999, 130).

2. This account is drawn from documentary footage that appears in Márta Mészáros's 1987 film, *Napló Szereleimnek.*

3. In the months leading up to the completion of the mammoth project, the press had kept the public informed about the monument's progress, pointing with pride to its projected size. A newspaper article in October reported: "We can illustrate with an example how huge the statue will be. The coat pocket is 1.2 meters long, and the diameter of a button is more than 10 centimeters" ("Így Készül" 1951).

4. Some of the domestic-culture tsars were hardly more sophisticated. In a radio interview in 1986, György Nonn recalled being appointed deputy minister of popular culture in the early 1950s. Rákosi summoned him and personally informed him of the appointment. Taken aback, Nonn protested that he knew nothing about literature, the cinema, or culture in general. The new deputy minister was told that knowing nothing about culture was no excuse; he was to stop being difficult and get to work (Radio Free Europe 1986, 25).

5. The line "Meghalt a cselszövő, elmúlt a rút viszály" is from the first great Hungarian national opera, Ferenc Erkel's *Hunyadi László*. Composed in 1844, the opera was set in the fifteenth century to avoid problems with Austrian censors. *Hunyadi László* contrasts the heroic Transylvanian Hunyadi family with the weak Habsburg boy-king László V, a pawn of his manipulative relative Ulric Cilli. The death of the traitorous Cilli at the hands of Hunyadi's supporters precipitates the joyous lyrics. On the Hunyadi family, see Held 1985, 172; on the cultural-historical significance of the opera, see Tyrrell 1994, 246–49.

6. The appearance and disappearance of symbols on this site is actually even more layered. Nine years after the Stalin monument was toppled, István Kiss's massive monument to the 1919 Hungarian Soviet Republic—the "Running Fool" that now resides in the Statue Park Museum—was erected here. László Prohászka claims that this monument did stand on the site of the former alter (1994, 170). The crucifix and sign commemorating the Regnum Marianum Church were erected when the Kiss monument was removed. In 2000 a group of high school students sawed down the crucifix and sign and painted a red star on the monument's base. The perpetrators happened to be Jewish, and their school—which prides itself on its openness to diverse cultures, religions, and worldviews—was attacked in the right-wing press as "anti-Christian," "anti-Magyar," and "a nest of Bolshevism" (Varró 2000, 14).

CHAPTER 3

1. A 1978 survey revealed a total of 128 memorials to "the fallen heroes who fought against the counter-revolution." Most were plaques and most honored specific individuals. Of the seven statues identified in the survey, only the Kalló monument was not connected to a particular person (Boros 1997, 10).

2. In a radio interview many years later, Marosán admitted that party leaders had been uncertain that the assemblies could be pulled off, and they were partly an experiment in the leadership's ability to command mass participation in public ceremonies prior to organizing May Day festivities. Orders went out that every member of the party and the Communist Youth Alliance was required to attend and to bring one other person along. He estimated that there were seventy to eighty thousand people in Republic Square alone (Rapcsányi 1983, 16–17). Marosán also discusses the event in his memoirs (1989, 206–12).

3. Hungarian writer Géza Ottlik (1959a) lampoons this fact in his novel *Hajnali Háztetők* (Rooftops at Dawn). The title of the book refers to the designation the protagonist gives his painting when—in 1956—authorities force him to alter the descriptive title, "Portrait of Man with Violin, Seated Nude, and Undercover Prostitute."

4. As Géza Boros explains (1997, 12), the issue of names was tricky. József Moharos (1960) argued that names should not be engraved on the pedestal: If the monument were to commemorate all martyrs to the working-class movement, it would be impossible to list them all. If it were to commemorate the 1956 martyrs, it would be difficult to determine what names should be included. In 1983 the question was finally settled when a sixty-five-foot wall with a relief and the names of military, security, and party personnel who died in the square on October 30, 1956, was added to the site.

5. In a 1992 poll that measured public opinion about the fate of public statues and monuments, respondents were asked specifically about memorials to the communist victims of 1956. Fifty-four percent said they would leave them where they are, 34 percent would transfer them to the Statue Park, 8 percent would warehouse them, and 4 percent would destroy them ("A Múltat Végképp Eltörölni?" 1992).

CHAPTER 4

1. On the subject of invented holidays, my friend Zsuzsa tells a story suggesting that for ordinary people, October 23 means little more now than the anniversary of the Russian Revolution meant in the old days: "My mom went to the farmers' market early on the morning of the 23rd to buy some beans because she wanted to make soup. Only a handful of grannies were selling their produce, and my mom and the other women couldn't figure out why. After a while, one of them remembered: 'Today is October 23rd; this is a holiday.' Another woman added, 'You know, they celebrate this day now instead of November 7th.'"

2. As always, the injunction against addressing 1956 was not total, especially in the early years when it was still being milked for propaganda purposes. A chapter on the Tóth case appears in László Szabó and István Pintér's *Szenzációk Nyomában*, which deals with how the foreign press purportedly distorted the "counter-revolution." Polemical in the extreme, the book sheds little light on Tóth as a historical figure, either hero and antihero. Outside of Hungary, the case was doggedly pursued by a Swede, Paul Karlsson, who published a book in 1983 attesting to Tóth's innocence. As far as I have been able to determine, it was never translated from Swedish into either a major language or Hungarian.

3. The financing and broadcast of the film reflect the politics of the Tóth case. Györgyi Kulcsár (2001), the producer, stated that work began on the film in 1991 with enough support from the Hungarian Historical Film Foundation to do the shooting. Then, when the Socialists were elected in 1994, public funding dried up. The filmmakers appealed to various Hungarian groups in

Canada and the United States, which donated most of the funds necessary to complete the project. The rest of the money was donated in small amounts by individual Hungarians. Hungarian Television refused to air the documentary, citing Tóth's legal status as a condemned murderer. It was thus broadcast on Duna Television, which is also public but has greater autonomy and, given its mandate to promote Hungarian culture beyond the borders, has a more nationalist orientation.

4. The case of Tóth et al. was the first of the major trials in the postrevolution reprisals. Resembling the show trials of the early 1950s, the proceedings were designed to demonstrate the authority of the Communist Party and were open to both foreign and domestic journalists. In the court of international opinion, however, this clumsy attempt at propaganda backfired. The world was horrified to see not only a young female medic before the bench but also the renowned writers Gyula Obersovszky and József Gáli. Indeed, the death sentences of the writers were commuted after an international outcry (Kőszeg 1989, 33; Rainer 1989, 40–41).

5. The case followed the common practice of amalgamating defendants and charges regardless of whether they were actually connected in any way. This trial involved three mini-cases—two unrelated murders and the publication of *Élünk* (Gyenes 2000). Ferenc Gönczi and Miklós Gyöngyösi were executed as Tóth's accomplices in the murder of Kollár. Obersovszky and Gáli were charged with knowing about the killing in addition to publishing subversive material. Altogether, the number of defendants in the Tóth case was twelve, "just like the apostles" (Obersovszky 1999, 67).

6. In addition to the Obersovszky book and the documentary film mentioned above, competing narratives have been constructed through the writings of István Benedek (1992), László Eörsi (2000b, 2000c, 2002), Ildikó Hankó (1992, 2000), Gábor Jobbágyi (2002), Mária Rozgics (n.d., 1998, 1999), and others. Among those who are convinced of Tóth's innocence, Pál Gyenes (2000) is remarkable for his moderate tone. The 1956 Institute has posted some fifteen articles on the case on its Web site (http://www.rev.hu). These provide a good entry into the debates.

7. With the Ottoman advances in the sixteenth century, Hungary came to be divided into three parts: one area was under Habsburg rule, a second was under Turkish domination, and a third—Transylvania—was an independent principality. Thus, according to historical consciousness, Transylvania represents a place where Hungarian culture was preserved for 150 years against the alien Germanic and Turkish influences. Partly for this reason, the loss of Transylvania to Romania as part of the Treaty of Trianon, the peace settlement imposed by the Allies at the end of World War I, was viewed as a violation of Hungary's sacred territorial integrity. In a sense, both Hungary and Romania can legitimately lay claim to this contested territory. It was part of the Kingdom of Hungary for over 1,000 years, but the largest ethnic group, at least for the past two centuries, has been Romanian (Ignotus 1972, 37).

8. While the official red, white, and green Hungarian flag is unadorned, it is not unusual to see variations that have either the Kossuth or Saint Stephen's crest in the center.

9. A fillér was worth $\frac{1}{100}$ of a Hungarian forint. With inflation, it became practically worthless, and its use was discontinued several years ago.

10. All of the quoted passages are translated from audiotape recordings I made at the ceremony.

CHAPTER 5

1. Oral histories provided by Judith Gyenes (Gyenes 1998; Maléterné 1990) offer a chilling glimpse into the reprisals as experienced by the families of its direct victims. At the time of the revolt, she was working at the National Plant Species Experimental Institute. When her husband was arrested, she was fired and forced to work as an unskilled manual laborer. With only twenty-four hours' notice, she had to vacate her apartment and move into a two-room flat already occupied by a family of six. An ÁVO who lived in the same building taught his children to spit on her and taunt her as "the murderer's wife." Gyenes was informed of Maléter's execution by her sister and brother-in-law, who heard it on the radio.

2. As of this writing in 2001, the institute is once again headed by a military officer, Maj. Gen. József Holló.

3. All of Bánffyné's remarks are from Bánffyné 2001.

4. *Corvin Köz 1956* was originally published in the United States. Pongrátz published a second edition in Hungary in 1992, adding a new conclusion, "And What Has Come to Light since Then."

5. According to László Eörsi, Pongrátz's hatred of Maléter grew out of envy. Following the announcement of a ceasefire on October 28, Maléter's reputation soared. The public could hardly imagine that victory had been achieved by young, untrained civilians and attributed success instead to the soldiers of the Kilián Barracks, above all, to Maléter. The Pongrátz wing of the Corvin leadership could not and still cannot stomach the fact that Maléter's prestige was created at the expense of their own fame and glory (Eörsi 2000a, 96). For more information and other opinions on the subject, see Horváth 2002, 11–13 and passim; Koncz 1999, 178; and Szabó 1999.

6. The program was first broadcast in October, 2000. I watched it on videotape in Pongrátz's home and do not know the title of the program or the exact date of its broadcast.

7. The exhibit includes a second room that is less unified thematically and will not be analyzed in detail here. Half of the room is set up for the presentation of programs, though it is rarely used as such. Display cases mainly feature memorabilia.

8. The paintings, Hollósy's *Rákóczi March* (1899) and Tivadar Kosztka Csontváry's *Finch Downed by a Hawk* (1893), express the rise of national sentiments and aspirations for political independence that dominated Hungarian public life in the late nineteenth century. Bánffyné aptly described the allegorical Csontváry painting. Hollósy's work depicts a rag-tag crowd running toward the viewer of the canvas. It pays tribute to Ferenc Rákóczi II, the national hero who led the peasants against the Hapsburgs in the 1703 uprising

alluded to in the Faludy quote that introduces the exhibit. Both paintings can be seen on the Fine Arts in Hungary Web site (http://www.kfki.hu/keptar).

9. Jancsi disappears from home to join the fighting group at Corvin Passage. His angry mother comes looking for him, and he begs not to be turned over to her. She eventually spies him, but when Pongrátz tells her about the heroic deeds of these children who refuse to go home, she relents, tearfully telling him: "The life of these children is in your hands. For the love of God, look after them. What you've achieved over the last several days is the seventh wonder of the world. But the eighth wonder will be if you can hang on to the victory you've achieved" (Pongrátz 1982, 191-92). János Varga survived, but he was sentenced to thirteen years imprisonment in the Mária Wittner case (Boros 1997, 124).

10. Görgey's poem is published in his 1994 collection, *21 Vers*. For the text of radio messages broadcast from Hungary subsequent to the Soviet invasion, see Lasky 1957, 228–41; and Varga 1989, 493–514.

11. The full speech is available in English in Camus 1960, 157–64. I have used an English translation given to me by Bánffyné.

12. I asked Pongrátz why he donated his leather jacket to the Military History Museum instead of displaying it in his own collection. He responded that he did not want to be accused of making the museum a shrine to himself: "The museum is for the revolution," he said, "not for me." He was reluctant to display even his brother's clothing and chose not to label it because he did not want to seem self-aggrandizing.

CHAPTER 6

1. Only much later would they learn the details. Imre Nagy, Pál Maléter, and Miklós Gimes, a journalist who served as a liaison between the press and the government during the uprising, had been hanged on June 16, 1958. József Szilágyi, the head of Nagy's secretariat, was tried separately and hanged on April 24, 1958. Géza Losonczy, minister of state in the revolutionary government, suffered a nervous breakdown in prison and died on December 21, 1957, as a result of forced feeding during a hunger strike. The widows of Géza Losonczy and József Szilágyi were among those held in Romania. Their oral histories appear in Ember 1989, 21–33, 97–123.

2. The dualism and liminality of Nagy's character are captured in the titles of Miklós Molnár and László Nagy's biography. The work was first published in Paris in 1959 as *Imre Nagy, Réformateur ou Révolutionnaire?* Two years later a Hungarian edition was published in Brussels under the title *Két Világ Közt: Nagy Imre Útja* (Between Two Worlds: The Path of Imre Nagy).

3. In 1954 László Bertók, then a high school student, alluded to the attic sweepings in his poem, "Quiet Life":

They took all of our grain.
My mother cried; my father was silent.

> My brother stole a handful of our own oats
> for the horse.
> We sit in the light of the evening lamp,
> and ponder what remains:
> An empty attic, and in my father's eyes
> an unexpressed thought.

With this verse used as evidence against him, Bertók was arrested and imprisoned for his writings. He tells the story in his memoirs (Bertók 1994).

4. The latter lines are from a poem by Sándor Petőfi. When Nagy fell from grace, his inclusion of these words in a speech was used as evidence of his chauvinism. See Méray 1959, 26.

5. He mentions two exceptions: Gábor Bachmann and László Rajk's staging for the Nagy funeral and György Jovánovics's monument to 1956 in the New Public Cemetery. For information on these works of art, see Zsófia Mihancsik's (1994) interview with Rajk and Jovánovics.

6. All of the sculptor's remarks are based on Varga 2001.

7. On the background of the monument, see Géza Boros's (1995) interview with Erzsébet Nagy and János Vészi. On Sarlos, see his autobiography (Sarlos 1993) and David Olive's (2000) profile.

8. The entire squadron was arrested and charged with planning to defect with their aircraft to Yugoslavia (Sarlos 1993, 17).

9. Varga is evidently thinking of the old Kossuth Bridge, torn down in 1961. It crossed the river where the red metro line now links Kossuth and Báttyány Squares and was the first permanent bridge to reopen after the war.

10. The one exception is Elizabeth Bridge, which was rebuilt between 1960 and 1964. On the reconstruction of Budapest's bridges, see Dragonits et al. 1971, 138.

BIBLIOGRAPHY

Note: The abbreviation "OSA" refers to the Open Society Archives, Central European University, Budapest.

"A Helyi Önkormányzatok és Szerveik, A Köztársasági Megbízottak, Valamint Egyes Centrális Alárendeltségű Szervek Feladat- és Hatásköreiről." 1991. Évi XX. Törvény. Available on the Hungarian Parliament's Web site (http://www.mkogy.hu).

"A Magyar Szabadságért Elesett Hősök Emlékművét: Felavatták a Köztársaság Téren." 1960. *Népszabadság*, November 1, p. 3.

"A Mai Közvélekedés Nagy Imréről." 1996. *Népszabadság*, June 17, p. 5.

"A Múltat Végképp Eltörölni?" 1992. *Népszabadság*, October 16, p. 6.

"A Templomépítők Szent Emberek." 2001. *Igazunk '56* IV/4:27.

Aczél, Tamás. 1952. "Sztálin Szobra—A Béke Jelképe." *Szovjet Kultúra*, January, 6.

———. 1994. "Kezdők az Oxford Streeten: Kísérletek egy Korszak Idézésére." In *Évkönyv III*, ed. János Bak et al., 69–93. Budapest: 1956 Institute.

Aczél, Tamás, and Tibor Méray. 1959. *The Revolt of the Mind: A Case History of Intellectual Resistance behind the Iron Curtain*. Westport, Conn.: Greenwood.

Agovino, Theresa J. 1998. "How Much Shopping Can One City Do?" *Metropolis*, May, http://www.metropolismag.com/html/content_0598/ma98buda.htm.

Alexander, Edward P. 1996. *Museums in Motion: An Introduction to the History and Functions of Museums*. Walnut Creek, Calif.: AltaMira.

Aman, Anders. 1992. *Architecture and Ideology in Eastern Europe during the Stalin Era: An Aspect of Cold War History*. New York: Architectural History Foundation / Cambridge, Mass.: MIT Press.

Anderson, Benedict. 1991. *Imagined Communities: Reflections on the Origin and Spread of Nationalism*. London: Verso.

Andrási, Gábor, Gábor Pataki, György Szűcs, and András Zwickl. 1999. *The History of Hungarian Art in the Twentieth Century*. Trans. John Bátki. Budapest: Corvina.

Appadurai, Arjun and Carol A. Breckenridge. 1992. "Museums Are Good to Think: Heritage on View in India." In *Museums and Communities: The*

Politics of Public Culture, ed. Ivan Karp, Christine Mullen Kreamer, and Steven D. Lavine, 34–55. Washington: Smithsonian Institution Press.

Aradi, Nóra. 1974. *A Szocialista Képzőművészet Jelképei.* Budapest: Kossuth Könyvkiadó / Corvina Kiadó.

Arato, Andrew. 1994. "Revolution, Restoration, and Legitimization: Ideological Problems of the Transition from State Socialism." In *Envisioning Eastern Europe: Postcommunist Cultural Studies,* ed. Michael D. Kennedy, 180–246. Ann Arbor: University of Michigan Press.

Arendt, Hannah. 1968. *Between Past and Future.* New York: Penguin.

Aulich, James, and Marta Sylvestrová. 1999. *Political Posters in Central and Eastern Europe, 1945–95: Signs of the Times.* Manchester: University of Manchester Press.

"Az 1956. Évi Forradalom és Szabadságharc Utáni Leszámolással Összefüggő Elítélések Semmisségének Megállapításáról." 2000. Évi CXXX. Törvény. Available on the Hungarian Parliament's Web site (http://www.mkogy.hu).

B. R., Zs. 1978. "Önmaga Mestere Volt: Mikus Sándor 75 Éves." *Esti Hírlap,* August 12. OSA fonds 300, subfonds 40, ser. 6, box 123, file Mikus Sándor.

B. T. 1957. "A Végtisztesség Előtt. . . ." *Népszabadság,* March 3. OSA fonds 300, subfonds 40, ser. 1, box 1300, file 56-os forradalom/1957 (3 of 9).

Babus, Endre. 2000. "A Múlt Fátyla." *HVG* (online at http://hvg.hu), November 4.

Baka, Andrásné. 1999. "Baka Andrásné, Ny. Tanár Levele." In *Tóth Ilona, A Magyar Jeanne d'Arc,* by Gyula Obersovszky, 121–23. Budapest: Codex Print Kiadó.

Bakhtin, Mikhail. 1984. *Rabelais and His World.* Trans. Helene Iswolsky. Bloomington: Indiana University Press.

Bánffyné, Györgyi Kalavszky. 2001. Interview with author. Budapest. February 7.

Bányász and Szegő. 1957. "Tóth Ilona Vallomása a Domonkos Utcai Gyilkosságról." *Népakarat.* February 19, p. 8.

Barthes, Roland. 1972. *Mythologies.* Trans. Annette Lavers. New York: Hill and Wang.

———. 1977. *Image, Music, Text.* Trans. Stephen Heath. New York: Hill and Wang.

Bauman, Zygmunt. 1992. *Intimations of Postmodernity.* London: Routledge.

Bayer, Zsolt. 2000. *1956: ". . . Hogy Legyen Jel."* Budapest: XX. Század Intézet és Történeti Hivatal.

"Begyógyítjuk az Ország Sebeit." 1957. *Magyar Nemzet,* October 31. OSA fonds 300, subfonds 40, ser. 1, box 1301, file 56-os forradalom/1957 (9 of 9).

Békés, Csaba. 1997. "The 1956 Hungarian Revolution and the Great Powers." In Cox 1997, 51–66.

Belcher, Michael. 1991. *Exhibitions in Museums.* Washington: Smithsonian Institution Press.

Belk, Russell W. 1994. "Collectors and Collecting." In *Interpreting Objects and Collections,* ed. Susan M. Pearce, 317–26. London: Routledge.

Benedek, István. 1992. "Tóth Ilona Elmeszakorvosi Leleteinek Értékelése." *Magyar Fórum*, September 24, pp. 14–15.

Benjamin, Walter. 1968. *Illuminations*. Trans. Harry Zohn. New York: Schocken.

Berecz, János. 1986. *Ellenforradalom Tollal és Fegyverrel, 1956*. 3d ed. Budapest: Kossuth Könyvkiadó.

Berger, John. 1969. *Art and Revolution: Ernst Neizvestny, Endurance, and the Role of Art*. New York: Vintage International.

Berger, Peter L. 1994. "Observations on the Transition in East-Central Europe." In Kovács 1994, 293–98.

Bertók, László. 1994. *Priusz*. Budapest: Századvég Kiadó.

Billig, Michael. 1990. "Collective Memory, Ideology, and the British Royal Family." In *Collective Remembering*, ed. David Middleton and Derek Edwards, 60–80. London: Sage.

Bíró, Béla. 1995. "Átmenet, de Hová? Beszélgetés Schöpflin Györggyel." *2000 Irodalmi és Társadalmi Havi Lap* (November): 3–6.

Blair, Carole, Martha S. Jeppeson, and Enrico Pucci Jr. 1991. "Public Memorializing in Postmodernity: The Vietnam Veterans Memorial as Prototype." *Quarterly Journal of Speech* 77:263–88.

Blaskovits, János. 1978. "A Szocializmus Alapjainak Lerakása Magyarországon (1948–1962)." In *Míg Megvalósul Gyönyörű Képességünk, a Rend: A Magyar Munkásmozgalom Története, 1918–1978*, ed. Sándor Borbély and Béla Esti, 113–32. Budapest: Móra Ferenc Könyvkiadó-Kossuth Könyvkiadó.

Boldizsár, Iván. 1951. "Sztálin Szobra Budapesten." *Irodalmi Újság*. December 20, p. 1.

Bonnell, Victoria E. 1997. *Iconography of Power: Soviet Political Posters under Lenin and Stalin*. Berkeley: University of California Press.

Boros, Géza. 1993. "A Lenin-Kertektől a Tanú Térig." *Kritika* 8:11–13.

———. 1995. "Hol Lesz Nagy Imre Szobra? Beszélgetés Nagy Erzsébettel és Vészi Jánossal." *Kritika* 6:40–41.

———. 1997. *Emlékművek '56-nak*. Budapest: 1956 Institute.

———. 1999. "Köztéri Művészet Magyarországon I–II." *Beszélő* (online at http://www.beszelo.hu), June 15.

Bown, Matthew Cullerne, and Brandon Taylor, eds. 1993. *Art of the Soviets: Painting, Sculpture and Architecture in a One-Party State, 1917–1992*. Manchester: Manchester University Press.

Bozóki, András. 1994. "From Soft Communism to Post-Communism (Authoritarian Legacy and Democratic Transition in Hungary)." In *Transition to Capitalism? The Communist Legacy in Eastern Europe*, ed. János Mátyás Kovács, 121–46. New Brunswick, N.J. Transaction.

Brooks, Jeffrey. 2000. *Thank You, Comrade Stalin! Soviet Public Culture from Revolution to Cold War*. Princeton, New Jersey: Princeton University Press.

"Budapest Dolgozói Kegyelettel Emlékeztek Meg az Ellenforradalom Mártírjairól." 1959. *Népszava,* October 31. OSA fonds 300, subfonds 40, ser. 1, box 1301, file 56-os forradalom/1959 (2 of 2).

Calinescu, Matei. 1987. *Five Faces of Modernity: Modernism, Avant-Garde, Decadence, Kitsch, Postmodernism.* Durham, N.C.: Duke University Press.

Camus, Albert. 1960. *Resistance, Rebellion, and Death.* Trans. Justin O'Brien. New York: Vintage.

Clark, Toby. 1993. "The 'New Man's' Body: A Motif in Early Soviet Culture." In Bown and Taylor 1993, 33–50.

Cohen, Abner. 1979. "Political Symbolism." *Annual Review of Anthropology* 8:87–113.

Condee, Nancy. 1995. "Introducation." In *Soviet Hieroglyphics: Visual Culture in Late Twentieth Century Russia.* ed. Nancy Condee, vii–xxiii. Bloomington: Indiana University Press.

Connerton, Paul. 1989. *How Societies Remember.* Cambridge: Cambridge University Press.

Coquin, François-Xavier. 1989. "L'Image de Lénine dans L'Iconographie Révolutionnaire et Postrévolutionnaire." *Annales* 44 (2): 223–49.

Cox, Terry, ed. 1997. *Hungary 1956—Forty Years On.* London: Frank Cass.

Crane, Susan. 2000. "Curious Cabinets and Imaginary Museums." In *Museums and Memory,* ed. Susan Crane, 60–80. Stanford: Stanford University Press.

Dobozi, Pálma. 2002. "Terror Háza: Önkény az Önkény Házában?" *Magyar Hírlap* (online at http://.magyarhirlap.hu), January 19.

Dornbach, Alajos. 1994. *The Secret Trial of Imre Nagy.* Westport, Conn.: Praeger.

Doty, William G. 2000. *Mythography: The Study of Myths and Rituals.* 2d ed. Tuscaloosa: University of Alabama Press.

Drábik, János. 2003. "Az Érem Másik Oldala." *Leleplező* 5/2:132–35.

Dragonits, Tamás, Lajos Füle, Pál Granasztói, et al., eds. 1971. *Városépítés Magyarországon a Felszabadulás Után.* Budapest: Műszaki Könyvkiadó.

Eagleton, Terry. 1996. *The Illusions of Postmodernism.* Oxford: Blackwell.

Edelman, Murray. 1988. *Constructing the Political Spectacle.* Chicago: University of Chicago Press.

Eleőd, Ákos. 1993. "A Szoborpark (Műleírás)." *2000 Irodalmi és Társadalmi Havi Lap* July, 60–61.

"Elszánt Gyilkosok, Megrögzött Ellenforradalmárok." 1957. *Népszabadság,* February 19, p. 8.

Ember, Judit. 1989. *Menedékjog—1956: A Nagy Imre-csoport Elrablása.* Budapest: Szabad Tér Kiadó.

"'Én is Egy Voltam Közülük. . . .': Elkészült a Köztársaság Téri Emlékmű Szobra." 1959. *Esti Hírlap,* August 20. OSA fonds 300, subfonds 40, ser. 1, box 1301, file 56-os forradalom/1959 (1 of 2).

Eörsi, László. 1993. "Széljegyzetek egy Memoárhoz." *Kritika* 2:46–47.

———. 1999. "Válogatás 1998 Történelmi Dokumentumfilmjeiből." In *Év-*

könyv VII: Magyarország a Jelenkorban, ed. Éva Standeisky and János M. Rainer, 363–74. Budapest: 1956 Institute.

———. 2000a. "Corvin Köz 1956." *Beszélő,* September–October, pp. 95–98.

———. 2000b. "Érvek Helyett Csúsztatás." *Magyar Hírlap,* December 4, p. 7 (Tóth Ilona files, 1956 Institute).

———. 2000c. "Tóth Ilona Pere Nem Volt Koncepciós." *Magyar Hírlap,* October 30, p. 7 (Tóth Ilona files, 1956 Institute).

———. 2002. "Tóth Ilona és Kultusza." *Népszabadság,* April 4, p. 12.

Ernst, Wolfgang. 2000. "Archi(ve)textures of Museology." In *Museums and Memory,* ed. Susan Crane, 17–34. Stanford: Stanford University Press.

Esbenshade, Richard S. 1995. "Remembering to Forget: Memory, History, National Identity in Postwar East-Central Europe." *Representations* 49: 72–96.

Farmer, Sarah. 1995. "Symbols That Face Two Ways: Commemorating the Victims of Nazism and Stalinism at Buchenwald and Sachsenhausen." *Representations* 49:97–119.

Fenichel, Otto. 1954. "Trophy and Triumph." In *The Collected Papers of Otto Fenichel.* 2d ser. New York: W. W. Norton, 141–62.

Fischer, Ernst. 1963. *The Necessity of Art: A Marxist Approach.* Trans. Anna Bostock. New York: Penguin.

Fisher, Walter R. 1997. "Narration, Reason, and Community." In *Memory, Identity, Community: The Idea of Narrative in the Human Sciences,* ed. Lewis P. Hinchman and Sandra K. Hinchman, 307–27. Albany: State University of New York Press.

Fiske, John. 1987. *Television Culture.* London: Methuen.

"Fogyatkozó Látogatók." 2000. *HVG* (online), June 24.

Foss, Sonja. 1986. "Ambiguity as Persuasion: The Vietnam Veterans Memorial." *Communication Quarterly* 34 (3): 326–40.

Foucault, Michel. 1972. *The Archeology of Knowledge.* Trans. A. M. Sheridan Smith. New York: Pantheon.

———. 1980. *Power/Knowledge: Selected Interviews and Other Writings, 1972–1977,* ed. Colin Gordon; trans. Colin Gordon, Leo Marshall, John Mepham, and Kate Soper. New York: Pantheon.

Frigyesi, Judit. 1998. *Béla Bartók and Turn-of-the-Century Budapest.* Berkeley: University of California Press.

"From a Report on the Organization of Celebrations for the First Anniversary of the October Revolution in the Newspaper *Izvestiya.*" 1990. In *Street Art of the Revolution: Festivals and Celebrations in Russia 1918–33,* ed. Vladimir Tolstoy, Irina Bibikova, and Catherine Cooke Trans. Frances Longman, Felicity O'Dell, and Vladimir Vnukov, 55. London: Thames and Hudson.

Fulford, Robert. 1999. *The Triumph of Narrative: Storytelling in the Age of Mass Culture.* New York: Broadway.

G. J. 1950. "A Legboldogabb Magyar Szobrászművész." *Magyar Nemzet,* December 24, p. 7.

Garton Ash, Timothy. 1985. "The Hungarian Lesson." *New York Review of Books*, December 5, pp. 5–9.

———. 1990. *The Magic Lantern: The Revolution of '89 Witnessed in Warsaw, Budapest, Berlin, and Prague.* New York: Random House.

Geréb, Sándor, and Pál Hajdú. 1986. *Az Ellenforradalom Utóvédharca 1956. November–1957. Március.* Budapest: Kossuth Könyvkiadó.

Gieryn, Thomas F. 1998. "Balancing Acts: Science, *Enola Gay*, and History Wars at the Smithsonian." In *The Politics of Display: Museums, Science, Culture*, ed. Sharon Macdonald, 197–228. London: Routledge.

Görgey, Gábor. 1994. *21 Vers.* Budapest: Belvárosi Könyvkiadó.

Granville, Johanna. 1997. "In the Line of Fire: The Soviet Crackdown on Hungary, 1956–57." In Cox 1997, 67–107.

Greenberg, Clement. 1957. "Avant-Garde and Kitsch." In *Mass Culture: The Popular Arts in America*, ed. Bernard Rosenberg and David Manning White, 98–110. New York: Free Press.

Gregory, Stanford W., Jr., and Jerry M. Lewis. 1988. "Symbols of Collective Memory: The Social Process of Memorializing May 4, 1970, at Kent State University." *Symbolic Interaction* 11 (2): 213–33.

Guthe, Carl E. 1959. *The Management of Small History Museums.* Bulletins of the American Association for State and Local History, vol. 2, no. 10. Madison, Wisc.: American Association for State and Local History, 257–326.

Gyáni, Gábor. 2001. "1956 Elfelejtésének Régi-Új Mítosza." *Élet és Irodalom.* February 9, p. 8.

Gyémánt, Mariann. 2000. "Csöndes és Hangos Ötvenhatosok: Mécs Imre a Szelektív Emlékezetről." *168 "ra*, October 19, pp. 30–31.

Gyenes, Judith. 1998. "Gyenes Judith Maléter Pálné." *Rubicon* 4 (5). Insert, "Remény, Bizonytalanság, Megtorlás": ix–xii.

Gyenes, Pál. 2000. "Fellebbezés Tóth Ilona és Társai Ügyében." *Magyar Hírlap*, November 16, p. 7 (Tóth Ilona files, 1956 Institute).

Györgyi, Kálmán. 1999. Letter from Kálmán Györgyi, attorney general, to Tibor Helcz, president of the World Alliance of Former Hungarian Political Prisoners, USA, April 21, http://w3.datanet.hu/~mkapu/20001109/toth.htm.

György, Péter. 2000. *Néma Hagyomány: Kollektív Felejtés és a Kései Múltértelmezés 1956 1989-ben (A Régmúlttól az Örökségig).* Budapest: Magvető.

Halbwachs, Maurice. 1992. *On Collective Memory.* Ed. and trans. Lewis A. Coser. Chicago: University of Chicago Press.

Hall, Stuart. 1992. "The West and the Rest: Discourse and Power." In *Formations of Modernity*, ed. Stuart Hall and Bram Gieben, 275–320. Cambridge: Polity Press / Open University.

———. 1997a. "Introduction." In *Representation: Cultural Representations and Signifying Practices*, ed. Stuart Hall, 1–11. London: Sage / Open University.

―――. 1997b. "The Work of Representation." In Hall, *Representation*, 15–64.

Hanák, Péter, ed. 1991. *The Corvina History of Hungary from Earliest Times until the Present Day*. Budapest: Corvina.

―――. 1998. *The Garden and the Workshop: Essays on the Cultural History of Vienna and Budapest*. Princeton: Princeton University Press.

Hankó, Ildikó. 1990. "Stratégia Helyett Politika." *Magyar Nemzet*, October 1. OSA fonds 300, subfonds 40, ser. 1, box 1243, file múzeumok 1 989–93.

―――. 1992. "Mártír vagy Bűnös volt Tóth Ilona?" *Magyar Nemzet*, November 18, p. 7.

―――. 2000. "Tóth Ilona Védelmében." *Demokrata*, November 9, pp. 20–21 (Tóth Ilona files, 1956 Institute).

Haraszti, Miklós. 1987. *The Velvet Prison: Artists under State Socialism*. New York: Basic Books.

Háy, Gyula. 1990. *Született 1900-ban*. Budapest: Interart.

Hegedűs, András B., and Zsuzsanna Kőrösi. 1996. "Szikrák Futottak a Csizmák Peremén: Hogyan Emlékezünk 1956. Október 23-ra?" *Népszabadság* (online at http://www.nepszabadsag.hu), October 22.

Held, Joseph. 1985. *Hunyadi: Legend and Reality*. Boulder, Colo.: East European Monographs. Distributed by Columbia University Press.

Hinchman, Lewis P., and Sandra K. Hinchman. 1997. "Introduction." In *Memory, Identity, Community: The Idea of Narrative in the Human Sciences*, ed. Lewis P. Hinchman and Sandra K. Hinchman, xiii–xxxii. Albany: State University of New York Press.

Hobsbawm, Eric. 1990. *Nations and Nationalism since 1780: Programme, Myth, Reality*. Cambridge: Cambridge University Press.

Hollós, Ervin, and Vera Lajtai. 1974. *Köztársaság Tér 1956*. Budapest: Kossuth Könyvkiadó.

Holz, Wolfgang. 1993. "Allegory and Iconography in Socialist Realist Painting." In *Art of the Soviets: Painting, Sculpture and Architecture in a One-Party State, 1917–1992*, ed. Matthew Cullerne Bown and Brandon Taylor, 73–85. Manchester: Manchester University Press.

Hooper-Greenhill, Eilean. 2000. *Museums and the Interpretation of Visual Culture*. London: Routledge.

Horváth, Miklós. 2002. *Maléter Pál*. 2d ed. Budapest: H&J Kiadó.

Hungarian Radio. 1957. "A Budapesti Pártbizottság Székházának Ostroma." Radio Free Europe's Monitoring Service, March 5, pp. 204–207. OSA fonds 300, subfonds 40, ser. 1, box 1300, file 56-os forradalom/1957 (3 of 9).

Ignotus, Paul. 1972. *Hungary*. New York: Praeger.

"Így Készül a Sztálin-szobor." 1951. *Magyar Nemzet*, October 7. OSA fonds 300, subfonds 40, ser. 1, box 1243, file műemlék 1951–59.

Innis, Harold A. 1951. *The Bias of Communication*. Toronto: University of Toronto Press.

Jackson, John Brinckerhoff. 1980. *The Necessity for Ruins, and Other Topics*. Amherst: University of Massachusetts Press.

Jobbágyi, Gábor. 1998. Szigorúan Titkos Emlékkönyv/Top Secret Memoir, 1956. Hungary: Szabad Tér Kiadó.

———. 2002. "Ténymegállapítás: 'Mindkét Oldalt Néma Talp.'" *Magyar Nemzet*, February 5, p. 6.

K. 2002. "Sztalinért Kampányol az SZDSZ." *Magyar Fórum* (online at http://www.magyarforum.hu), January 24.

Karlsson, Paul. 1983. *Dömd pa Förhand: Ilona Tóth-processen i Budapest*. Viken, Sweden: Eremit.

Karp, Ivan. 1992. Introduction to *Museums and Communities: The Politics of Public Culture*, ed. Ivan Karp, Christine Mullen Kreamer, and Steven D. Lavine, 1–17. Washington: Smithsonian Institution Press.

Katona, Imre. 1974. Foreword to Hollós and Lajtai 1974, 7–11.

"Kegyeletsértő Népszabadság." 2002. *Helyi Hírek XVI. Független Folyóirat*, May. Accessed through the 1956 Institute's Web site (http://www.rev.hu), "Tóth Ilonával Kapcsolatos Írások a Sajtóban."

Kemp, Wolfgang. 1996. "Narrative." Trans. David Britt. In *Critical Terms for Art History*, ed. Robert S. Nelson and Richard Shiff, 58–69. Chicago: University of Chicago Press.

Kende, Péter. 2002. "Szobor egy Gyilkosnak?" *Népszabadság*, April 22. Accessed through the 1956 Institute's Web site (http://www.rev.hu), "Tóth Ilonával Kapcsolatos Írások a Sajtóban."

Kennedy, Michael D. 1994. "An Introduction to East European Ideology and Identity in Transformation." In *Envisioning Eastern Europe: Postcommunist Cultural Studies*, ed. Michael D. Kennedy, 1–45. Ann Arbor: University of Michigan Press.

"Kiállítás Készül az Ellenforradalom Dokumentumaiból." 1957. *Népszabadság*, May 29. OSA fonds 300, subfonds 40, ser. 1, box 1300, file 56-os forradalom/1957 (5 of 9).

Kis, János. 1989. *Politics in Hungary: For a Democratic Alternative*. Trans. Gábor J. Follinus. Boulder, Colo.: Social Science Monographs.

———. 1999. "1989: A Víg Esztendő." *Beszélő*, October, pp. 22–46.

Koncz, Lajos. 1999. "A Barikád Köszöni Jól Van. . . ." *Beszélő*, October, pp. 178–79.

Konrád, György. 1984. *Antipolitics*. Trans. Richard E. Allen. New York: Harcourt Brace Jovanovich.

———. 1989. "Tisztelgő Sorok." In appendix of *Ellenzékben*, by Miklós Vásárhelyi, 322–27. Budapest: Szabad Tér Kiadó.

Konrád, György, and Iván Szelényi. 1979. *The Intellectuals on the Road to Class Power*. New York: Harcourt Brace Jovanovich.

Kosáry, Domokos, ed. 1971. *Magyarország Története Képekben*. Budapest: Gondolat Könyvkiadó.

Kőszeg, Ferenc. 1989. "Huszonöt Év Után" (1983). In *Halottaink 1956*, ed. János Balassa et al., 1:30–35. vols. Budapest: Katalizátor Iroda.

Kovács, János Mátyás, ed. 1994. *Transition to Capitalism? The Communist Legacy in Eastern Europe*. New Brunswick, N.J.: Transaction.

Kozák, Gyula. 1996. "Ünneprontás." *Beszélő*, October, pp. 70–76.

Kulcsár, Györgyi. 2001. Interview with author. Budapest. January 26.

Kurcz, Béla. 1989. "Kiállítás '56 Tizenkét Napjáról." *Magyar Nemzet,* October 11, p. 6.

Laki, Károly. 2001. Interview with author. Budapest. January 23.

Lampland, Martha. 1990. "The Politics of History: Historical Consciousness and the Hungarian Revolutions of 1848/49." *Hungarian Studies* 6 (2): 185–94.

Lane, Christel. 1981. *The Rites of Rulers: Ritual in Industrial Society—The Soviet Case.* Cambridge: Cambridge University Press.

Lasky, Melvin J., ed. 1957. *The Hungarian Revolution: The Story of the October Uprising as Recorded in Documents, Dispatches, Eye-Witness Accounts, and World-wide Reactions.* New York: Praeger.

Lidov, David. 1999. *Elements of Semiotics.* New York: St. Martin's.

Linke, Uli. 1999. *Blood and Nation: The European Aesthetics of Race.* Philadelphia: University of Pennsylvania Press.

Lipták, Béla. 2001. *A Testament of Revolution.* College Station: Texas A&M University Press.

Litván, György. 1992. *Az 1956-os Magyar Forradalom Hagyománya és Irodalma* (Előadások a Történettudományi Intézetben, no. 19). Budapest: A Történettudományi Intézet.

———, ed. 1996. *The Hungarian Revolution of 1956: Reform, Revolt, and Repression, 1953–1963.* New York: Longman.

———. 2000. "Mítoszok és Legendák 1956-ról." In *Évkönyv VIII,* ed. Zsuzsanna Kőrösi, Éva Standeisky, and János M. Rainer, 205–18. Budapest: 1956 Institute.

Lodder, Christina. 1993. "Lenin's Plan for Monumental Propaganda." In *Art of the Soviets: Painting, Sculpture and Architecture in a One-Party State, 1917–1992,* Matthew Cullerne Brown and Brandon Taylor, 16–32. Manchester: Manchester University Press.

Longworth, Philip. 1994. *The Making of Eastern Europe.* New York: St. Martin's.

Lóska, Lajos. 1980. "Egy Művész Ötven Után: Beszélgetés Kalló Viktorral." *Művészet* 6:24–27.

Lowenthal, David. 1985. *The Past Is a Foreign Country.* Cambridge: Cambridge University Press.

Lukacs, John. 1988. *Budapest 1900: A Historical Portrait of a City and Its Culture.* New York: Weidenfeld and Nicolson.

Magyar Népköztársaság. 1958. *Nagy Imre és Bűntársai Ellenforradalmi Összeesküvése.* Budapest: Minisztertanács Tájékoztatási Hivatala.

Maléterné, Judit Gyenes. 1990. "Pali" (1985). In *Doku 56: Öt Portré a Forradalomból,* ed. Zsolt Csalog, 297–358. Budapest: Unió Kiadó.

Marosán, György. 1989. *A Tanúk Még Élnek.* Budapest: Hírlapkiadó Vállalat.

Martin, Wallace. 1986. *Recent Theories of Narrative.* Ithaca, N.Y.: Cornell University Press.

McGraw-Hill Ryerson. 2000. "The Daring Ambitions of Canada's Corporate Elite." Press release about publication of David Olive, *No Guts, No Glory.*

Available online at the McGraw-Hill Ryerson Web site (http://www
.mcgrawhill.ca).

"Megnyitották 'A Magyarországi Ellenforradalom' Című Kiállítást." 1957.
Népakarat, June 23. OSA fonds 300, subfonds 40, ser. 1, box 1300, file 56-
os forradalom/1957 (6 of 9).

Méray, Tibor. 1959. *Thirteen Days that Shook the Kremlin: Imre Nagy and
the Hungarian Revolution.* New York: Frederick A. Praeger.

———. 1969. *That Day in Budapest: October 23, 1956.* Trans. Charles Lam
Markmann. New York: Funk and Wagnalls.

Meštrovič, Stjepan G. 1994. *The Balkanization of the West: The Confluence
of Postmodernism and Postcommunism.* New York: Routledge.

Mihancsik, Zsófia. 1994. "Nagy Imre Temetése, és az 56-os Emlékmű Szüle-
tése." *Budapesti Negyed* 2 (3): 187–218.

Milosz, Czeslaw. 1960. Introduction to *On Socialist Realism*, Abram Tertz
[pseud.]. New York: Pantheon.

Mink, András. 1999. "Miért 1989?" *Beszélő*, October, pp. 17–21.

Moharos, József. 1960. Memo to János Hantos, August 24. Exhibit on Representation of the Counterrevolution, Open Society Archives, Central European University, Budapest, 1996. Available online at http://www.osa.ceu
.hu/galeria/index_hu/sites/ellenforradalom/megemlekezes.html.

Molnár, Miklós. 1966. "The Heritage of Imre Nagy." In *Ten Years After: The
Hungarian Revolution in the Perspective of History*, ed. Tamás Aczél,
153–74. New York: Holt, Rinehart, and Winston.

———. 1968. *Victoire d'une Défaite: Budapest 1956.* Paris: Fayard.

———. 1989. "Imre Nagy." In *Hungarian Statesmen of Destiny, 1860–
1960*, ed. Pál Bődy, 169–89. Highland Lakes, N.J.: Atlantic Research and
Publications.

Molnár, Miklós, and László Nagy. 1983. *Reformátor vagy Forradalmár volt-e
Nagy Imre?* Paris: Magyar Füzetek Kiadása.

Morley, David, and Kevin Robins. 1995. *Spaces of Identity: Global Media,
Electronic Landscapes, and Cultural Boundaries.* New York: Routledge.

MTI. 1957. "Pályázati Felhívás az Ellenforradalmárok által Meggyilkolt Kom-
munista Mártírok Emlékművére." *Népszabadság*, March 31. OSA fonds
300, subfonds 40, ser. 1, box 1300, file 56-os forradalom/1957 (4 of 9).

MTI. 1958. "A Budapesti Dolgozók Kegyelettel Emlékeztek Meg az 1956-os
Ellenforradalmi Támadás Mártírjairól." *Népszabadság*, October 31. OSA
fonds 300, subfonds 40, ser. 1, box 1301, file 56-os forradalom/1958 (1 of 1).

Murányi, Gábor. 1999. "Sztálin-őrület '49." *HVG* (online at http://hvg.hu),
December 18.

N. Sz. 2001. "A Felmérések Szerint Most Kedveltebbek a Kormánypárti
Politikusok." *Magyar Hírlap* (online at http://.magyarhirlap.hu), February 28.

Nora, Pierre. 1989. "Between Memory and History: Les Lieux de Mémoire."
Representations 26:7–24.

Nyusztay, Máté. 2000. "Ötvenhatos Megtorlás: Semmis Ítéletek." *Népszava*
(online at http://www.nepszava.hu), December 13.

Obersovszky, Gyula. 1999. *Tóth Ilona, A Magyar Jeanne d'Arc.* Budapest: Codex Print Kiadó.

Oláh, Vilmos. 1999. "Egy Hely Betöltetlen a Márványtáblán: Tóth Ilonáé." In *Tóth Ilona, A Magyar Jeanne d'Arc,* by Gyula Obersovszky, 7–9. Budapest: Codex Print Kiadó.

Olive, David. 2000. *No Guts, No Glory: How Canada's Greatest CEOs Built Their Empires.* Toronto: McGraw-Hill Ryerson.

Ómolnár, Miklós, ed. 1989. *Tizenkét Nap, Amely—1956 Október 23–November 4: Események, Emlékek, Dokumentumok.* Budapest: Szabad Tér Kiadó.

Ordódy, György, dir. 1998. *Ki Volt Tóth Ilona! "Magasabbak az Egek a Földnél."* Unio Civilis–Hunnia.

Örkény, Antal, and György Csepeli. 1994. "Social Change, Political Beliefs, and Everyday Expectations in Hungarian Society: A Comparative View." In *Transition to Capitalism! The Communist Legacy in Eastern Europe,* ed. János Mátyás Kovács, 259–74. New Brunswick, N.J.: Transaction.

Ottlik, Géza. 1959a. *Hajnali Háztetők.* Budapest: Magvető.

———. 1959b. *Iskola a Határon.* Budapest: Magvető.

Pajcsics, József. 1999. "A 301-es Parcella Titkai." *Magyar Hírlap,* June 16. Available online at http://tausz.tripod.com/sajto.htm.

Pardi, Anna. 1992. "Tóth Ilonáról." *Magyar Fórum,* October 22, p. 12.

"Patriots Strike Ferocious Blows at a Tyranny." 1956. *Life,* November 12, pp. 34–43.

Pető, Andrea. 2001. *Rajk Júlia.* Budapest: Balassi Kiadó.

Plachy, Sylvia. 1993. "Graveyard of the Statues: Communist Heroes, in Perspective," *New York Times Magazine,* May 2, p. 46.

Polgáry, Sándor, ed. 1986. "A Tóth Ilona-per: 'Eleve Elítélve.'" *Nemzedékek,* October, 8–18 (Tóth Ilona files, 1956 Institute).

Pomian, Krzysztof. 1994. "The Collection: Between the Visible and the Invisible." In *Interpreting Objects and Collections,* ed. Susan M. Pearce, 160–74. London: Routledge.

Pongrátz, Gergely. 1982. *Corvin Köz 1956.* Rev. ed. Budapest: By the author.

———. 2000. Interview with author. Kiskunmajsa. June 8.

———. 2001. Interview with author. Kiskunmajsa. August 26.

Pósa, Zoltán. 2000. "Anyám, Ne Sírj Ezek Előtt!" *Kis Újság,* October 20, p. 9.

———. 2001. "Csak a Végeredmény Számít." *Magyar Nemzet,* June (clipping from personal files of Gergely Pongrátz).

Pótó, János. 1989. *Emlékművek, Politika, Közgondolkodás.* Budapest: MTA Történettudományi Intézet.

Pozsonyi, István. 1998. "Kádárék Terrorral Ünnepeltek." *Magyar Fórum,* March 12. Available online at http://www.miep.hu/forum/1998/11/xI111 .pdf.

Prohászka, László. 1994. *Szoborsorsok.* Budapest: Kornétás Kiadó.

Propp, Vladimir. 1968. *Morphology of the Folktale,* trans. Laurence Scott. Bloomington: American Folklore Society and Indiana University.

Prost, Antoine. 1997. "Monuments to the Dead." In Pierre Nora, ed., *Realms of Memory: The Construction of the French Past,* vol. 2, *Traditions,* ed. Lawrence D. Kritzman and trans. Arthur Goldhammer, 307–30. English-language ed. New York: Columbia University Press.

Rab, Krisztina. 1997. "Mégis, Kinek az Ünnepe?" *Magyarország,* October 23, pp. 6–7.

Radio Free Europe. 1986. "Hungarian SR/11" (special monitoring report), October 31. OSA fonds 300, subfonds 40, ser. 1, box 1313, file 56-os forradalom/SR 1956–86.

Rainer, János M. 1989. "Adatok az 1956-os Forradalmat Követő Megtorláshoz." In *Halottaink 1956,* ed. János Balassa et al., 2:20–54. 2 vols. Budapest: Katalizátor Iroda.

———. 1995. "Nagy Imre, A Forradalom Jelképe." *Rubicon* 6 (8): 6–14.

———. 1996. *Nagy Imre. Politikai Életrajz.* Vol. 1, 1896–1953. Budapest: 1956 Institute.

———. 1997. "The Life Course of Imre Nagy." In *Hungary 1956—Forty Years On,* ed. Terry Cox, 141–51. London: Frank Cass.

———. 1999a. *Nagy Imre. Politikai Életrajz.* Vol. 2, 1953–58. Budapest: 1956 Institute.

———. 1999b. "The Reprisals." In *Encounters: A Hungarian Quarterly Reader,* ed. Zsófia Zachár, 249–59. Budapest: Hungarian Quarterly Society, Balassi Kiadó.

Rajk, Lászlóné. 2001. "Rajk Lászlóné Beszéde a Partizánvitán." In appendix of *Rajk Júlia,* by Andrea Pető, 246–50. Budapest: Balassi Kiadó.

Ramet, Sabrina P. 1996. "Eastern Europe's Painful Transition." *Current History* 95 (599): 97–102.

———. 1999. "Defining the Radical Right: The Values and Behaviors of Organized Intolerance." In *The Radical Right in Central and Eastern Europe since 1989,* ed. Sabrina P. Ramet, 3–27. University Park: Pennsylvania State University Press.

Rapcsányi, László. 1983. "Állam-miniszter 1956–57-ben: Interjú Marosán Györggyel." *História* 2:13–17.

"Rendületlenül." 2000. *Magyar Fórum,* October 26, p. 4.

Rényi, András. 2000. "A Légből Kapott Monumentum." *Mozgó Világ* 2:99–113.

Rév, István. 1995a. "Identity by History." In editors' introduction to "Identifying Histories: Eastern Europe before and after 1989," ed. Stephen Greenblatt, István Rév, and Randolph Starn, 8–10. Special issue, *Representations* 49:1–14.

———. 1995b. "Parallel Autopsies." *Representations* 49:15–39.

Révai, József. 1951. *Révai József Elvtárs Felszólalása a Magyar Dolgozók Pártja II. Kongresszusán, 1951 Február 26-án.* Budapest: A Magyar Dolgozók Pártja Központi Vezetősége Agitációs és Propaganda Osztály.

Roberts, Gillian L., and Janet Beavin Bavelas. 1996. "The Communicative Dictionary: A Collaborative Theory of Meaning." In *Beyond the Symbol Model: Reflections on the Representational Nature of Language,* ed. John Stewart, 135–60. Albany: State University of New York Press.

Romsics, Ignác. 1999. *Hungary in the Twentieth Century,* trans. Tim Wilkinson. Budapest: Corvina.

Rosenfield, Lawrence J. 1980. "The Practical Celebration of Epideictic." In *Rhetoric in Transition: Studies in the Nature and Uses of Rhetoric,* ed. Eugene H. White, 131–55. University Park: Pennsylvania State University Press.

Rozgics, Mária. N.d. "Védő és Vádlott Egyaránt Áldozat." *Napi Magyarország* (clipping from personal files of Károly Laki).

———. 1998. "Miért Félnek Tóth Ilonától?" *Napi Magyarország,* October 22, p. 12.

———. 1999. "Tóth Ilona Mártírhalálára." *Napi Magyarország,* June 26, p. 15 (Tóth Ilona files, 1956 Institute).

Rozgonyi, Ernő. 2000. Speech to Hungarian Parliament, 170. Ülésnap (November 8). Available at the Hungarian Parliament's Web site (http://www.mkogy.hu).

Samuel, Raphael. 1994. "Unofficial Knowledge." In *Theatres of Memory,* vol. 1, *Past and Present in Contemporary Culture,* 3–39. London: Verso.

Sarlos, Andrew. 1993. *Fireworks: The Investment of a Lifetime.* Toronto: Key Porter Books.

Schöpflin, György. 1993. *Politics in Eastern Europe, 1945–1992.* Oxford: Blackwell.

———. 1994. "Conservatism in Central and Eastern Europe." In Kovács 1994, 187–202.

———. 1995. "Post-Communism: A Profile." *Javnost* 2 (1): 63–72.

———. 1997. "The Functions of Myth and a Taxonomy of Myths." In *Myths and Nationhood,* ed. György Schöpflin and Geoffrey Hosking, 19–35. London: Hurst.

Schwartz, Barry. 1982. "The Social Context of Commemoration: A Study in Collective Memory." *Social Forces* 61 (2): 374–402.

———. 1990. "The Reconstruction of Abraham Lincoln." In *Collective Remembering,* ed. David Middleton and Derek Edwards, 81–107. London: Sage.

Schwartz, Barry, and Todd Bayma. 1999. "Commemoration and the Politics of Recognition." *American Behavioral Scientist* 42 (6): 946–67.

Sennett, Richard. 1994. *Flesh and Stone: The Body and the City in Western Civilization.* New York: Norton.

Shils, Edward, and Michael Young. 1953. "The Meaning of the Coronation." *Sociological Review,* n.s., 1 (2): 63–81.

Sinkó, Katalin. 1992. "Political Rituals: The Raising and Demolition of Monuments," trans. Ervin Dunay. In *Art and Society in the Age of Stalin,* ed. Péter György and Hedvig Turai, 73–86. Budapest: Corvina.

Skoda, Lajos. N.d. Letter to Béla Kelen. Exhibit on Representation of the Counterrevolution, Open Society Archives, Central European University, Budapest, 1996. Available online at http://www.osa.ceu.hu/galeria/index _hu/sites/ellenforradalom/megemlekezes.html.

Stites, Richard. 1985. "Iconoclastic Currents in the Russian Revolution: Destroying and Preserving the Past." In *Bolshevik Culture: Experiment and Order in the Russian Revolution*, ed. Abbott Gleason, Peter Kenez, and Richard Stites, 1–24. Bloomington: Indiana University Press.

Susa, Éva. 2000. "Identification of Hungarian Historical Persons." *Acta Biologica Szegediensis* 44 (1–4): 175–78.

Sz. Kürti, Katalin. 1995. "Szoborsorsok Debrecenben." *Debreceni Szemle* 3 (online at http://www.atomki.hu/debrecen/debreszem), September.

Sz. T. 1957. "Elkészült a Vádirat Tóth Ilona, A Gyilkos Szigorló Orvosnő és Társai, Obersovszky Gyula és Gáli József Ügyében." *Népakarat*, January 18, p. 4.

Szabó, László, and István Pintér. 1960. *Szenzációk Nyomában*. Budapest: Táncsics Könyvkiadó.

Szabó, Miklós. 1999. "Az Ellopott Barikád." *Beszélő* (online at http://www.beszelo.hu), February.

Szakolczai, Attila. 1994. "A Forradalmat Követő Megtorlás Során Kivégzettekről." In *Évkönyv III*, ed. János Bak et al., 237–56. Budapest: 1956 Institute.

———. 2000. "Október Huszonharmadikánk." *Népszava*, October 21, p. 7.

Szávai, János. 1996. "Albert Camus és a Magyar Forradalom." *Magyar Szemle* 10:962–69.

Székely, András. 1980. "Mikus Sándor." In *Harmincöt Év; Harmincöt Művész*, ed. Nóra Aradi, 236–45. Budapest: Corvina Kiadó.

Szíj, Rezső. 1977. *Mikus Sándor*. Budapest: Corvina Kiadó.

Szilágyi, Sándor. 1999a. "Adalékok a Nagy Imre-újratemetés Történetéhez." *Beszélő*, October, pp. 130–35.

———. 1999b. *A Hétfői Szabadegyetem és a III/III: Interjúk, Dokumentumok*. Budapest: Újmandátum Könyvkiadó.

Szörényi, László. 1989. "Leninkert." *Hitel*, July 5, p. 62.

Szűcs, György. 1994a. "Not to Praise, but to Bury." *Hungarian Quarterly* 35 (135): 100–107.

———. 1994b. "A 'Zsarnokság' Szoborparkja." *Budapest Negyed* 3:151–65.

Szűcs, Julianna P. 2001. "Nagy Imre a Gyermekek Között." *Népszabadság* (online at http://www.nepszabadsag.hu), January 4.

Tertz, Abram [pseud.]. 1960. *On Socialist Realism*. New York: Pantheon.

Tismaneanu, Vladimir. 1994. "Fantasies of Salvation: Varieties of Nationalism in Postcommunist Eastern Europe." In *Envisioning Eastern Europe: Postcommunist Cultural Studies*, ed. Michael D. Kennedy, 102–24. Ann Arbor: University of Michigan Press.

———. 1998. *Fantasies of Salvation: Democracy, Nationalism, and Myth in Postcommunist Europe*. Princeton: Princeton University Press.

Tóbiás, Áron. 1999. "Új Történelmi Időszámítás." *Magyar Nemzet*, June 15, p. 7.

Tolstoy, Vladimir, Irina Bibikova, and Catherine Cooke, eds. 1990. *Street Art of the Revolution: Festivals and Celebrations in Russia, 1918–33*. New York: Vendome..

Tőkés, Rudolf L. 1996. *Hungary's Negotiated Revolution: Economic Reform,*

Social Change, and Political Succession. Cambridge: Cambridge University Press.

Tömöry, Ákos. 1991. "Emlékművi Vetélés." *HVG,* December 7, pp. 73–75.

Trapp, Frank Anderson. 1987. *Peter Blume.* New York: Rizzoli.

Turner, Victor. 1986. *The Anthropology of Performance.* New York: Performing Arts Journal Publications.

Tyrrell, John. 1994. "Russian, Czech, Polish, and Hungarian Opera." In *Oxford Illustrated History of Opera,* ed. Roger Parker, 237–78. Oxford: Oxford University Press.

Ujvári, Béla. 1978. *Kalló Viktor.* Budapest: Képzőművészeti Alap Kiadóvállalata.

Unwin, Peter. 1991. *Voice in the Wilderness: Imre Nagy and the Hungarian Revolution.* London: Macdonald.

Urbán, Károly. 1993. "Révai: A Kultúrdiktátor." *Rubicon* 7 : 10–13.

Urbán, László. 1989. "Hungary in Transition: The Emergence of Opposition Parties." *Telos* 79 : 108–18.

Váli, Ferenc A. 1961. *Rift and Revolt in Hungary.* Cambridge, Mass.: Harvard University Press.

Váradi, Júlia. 1994. "Szoborpark-történet: Váradi Júlia Beszélgetése Eleőd Ákos Építésszel." *Magyar Építőművészet* 94 (2): 19–24.

Varga, László. 1989. *A Forradalom Hangja: Magyarországi Rádió Adások 1956. Október 23–November 9.* Budapest: Századvég Kiadó.

Varga, Tamás. 2001. Interview with author. Budapest. January 30.

Várhegyi, Sándor. 1999. "Tóth Ilona." *Igazunk '56* 2 (9): 13.

Várnagy, Tibor. 1996. "Gondolatok az 'Úúúúúúúúúj' Köztéri Szobrászatról és a Pipa." *Balkon* 9 : 41–43.

Varró, Szilvia. 2000. "Díszei Hullanak." *Magyar Narancs,* December 21, pp. 13–15.

Verdery, Katherine. 1999. *The Political Lives of Dead Bodies: Reburial and Postsocialist Change.* New York: Columbia University Press.

Warner, Marina. 1981. *Joan of Arc: The Image of Female Heroism.* Berkeley: University of California Press.

Wehner, Tibor. 1986. *Köztéri Szobraink.* Budapest: Gondolat Kiadó.

Williams, Raymond. 1961. *The Long Revolution.* New York: Columbia University Press.

———. 1977. *Marxism and Literature.* Oxford: Oxford University Press.

Wittner, Mária. 1994. "'Lelkiismeret-furdalásom Van, Hogy Életben Maradtam.'" In *Pesti Utca: Válogatás Fegyveres Felkelők Visszaemlékezéseiből,* ed. Györgyi Bindorffer and Pál Gyenes, 15–29. Budapest: Századvég Kiadó.

Wogan-Browne, Jocelyn. 1994. "Chaste Bodies: Frames and Experiences." In *Framing Medieval Bodies,* ed. Sarah Kay and Miri Rubin, 24–42. Manchester: Manchester University Press.

Wood, Nancy. 1991. "The Holocaust: Historical Memories and Contemporary Identities." *Media, Culture, and Society* 13 (3): 357–79.

Yampolsky, Mikhail. 1995. "In the Shadow of Monuments: Notes on Iconoclasm and Time." Trans. John Kachur. In *Soviet Hieroglyphics: Visual*

Culture in Late Twentieth Century Russia, ed. Nancy Condee, 93–112. Bloomington: Indiana University Press.

Zelinsky, W. 1975. "Unearthly Delights: Cemetery Names and the Map of the Changing American Afterworld," in *Geographies of the Mind: Essays in Historical Geosophy in Honor of John Kirtland Wright,* ed. David Lowenthal and M. Bowden, 171–95. New York: Oxford University Press.

INDEX

Italic typeface indicates pages with photographs

ISBN 1-58544-405-7